DATE			

OBAMA'S GUANTÁNAMO

Obama's Guantánamo

Stories from an Enduring Prison

Edited by

Jonathan Hafetz

NEW YORK UNIVERSITY PRESS

New York

NEW YORK UNIVERSITY PRESS
New York
www.nyupress.org

References to Internet websites (URLs) were accurate at the time of writing. Neither the author nor New York University Press is responsible for URLs that may have expired or changed since the manuscript was prepared.

Library of Congress Cataloging-in-Publication Data
Names: Hafetz, Jonathan, editor.
Title: Obama's Guantánamo : stories from an enduring prison / edited by Jonathan Hafetz.
Description: New York ; London : New York University Press, 2016. |
Includes bibliographical references and index.
Identifiers: LCCN 2016001626 | ISBN 9781479852802 (cl : alk. paper) |
ISBN 1-4798-5280-5 (cl : alk. paper)
Subjects: LCSH: Prisoners of war—Legal status, laws, etc.—Cuba—Guantánamo Bay Naval
Base. | Guantánamo Bay Detention Camp. | Detention of persons—Cuba—Guantánamo
Bay Naval Base. | Military courts—Cuba—Guantánamo Bay Naval Base. | Obama, Barack. |
Prisoners of war—Legal status, laws, etc.—United States. | Detention of persons—
United States. | Military courts—United States. | LCGFT: Essays.
Classification: LCC KZ6495 .O23 2016 | DDC 344.7303/548—dc23
LC record available at http://lccn.loc.gov/2016001626

New York University Press books are printed on acid-free paper, and their binding materials are chosen for strength and durability. We strive to use environmentally responsible suppliers and materials to the greatest extent possible in publishing our books.

Manufactured in the United States of America

10 9 8 7 6 5 4 3 2 1

Also available as an ebook

CONTENTS

Introduction

JONATHAN HAFETZ

A preceding volume, *The Guantánamo Lawyers: Inside a Prison outside the Law,* was completed in early 2009, a time of considerable excitement and hope. President Barack Obama, who was just beginning his first term, had ordered the closure of the U.S. detention center at Guantánamo Bay and declared that the United States must respect both its Constitution and international law even when defending its security against terrorist threats. To be sure, difficult questions lingered, including what would happen to the remaining prisoners once the U.S. closed Guantánamo and whether U.S. officials would be held accountable for the past mistreatment of detainees. But at least it seemed that the Guantánamo Bay prison, the overarching symbol of lawlessness and abuse in America's global war on terror, would be shut and this notorious chapter in American history would come to an end.

Predictions of Guantánamo's demise would soon prove premature. Within months, it became clear that Obama would not meet his original pledge of closing the prison within his first year in office. Now, deep into Obama's second term, it seems unlikely that Guantánamo will be closed at any time in the foreseeable future. When Obama took office, 242 prisoners remained at Guantánamo. Today, that number is 107. The drop has been slow, uneven, and arbitrary. Approximately half of those who remain have long been cleared for release by the Obama administration. But most of those cleared detainees are from Yemen, whose security conditions have dissuaded the U.S. from transferring prisoners there. Meanwhile, the legal and political obstacles to closure have become more entrenched. In many respects, the prospect of Guantánamo's closure seems as remote now as when the first prisoners were brought there in January 2002. The 9/11 attacks have grown more distant, but Guantánamo remains ever present.

How did we get here? *The Guantánamo Lawyers* described the Bush administration's creation of a prison beyond the law. *Obama's Guantánamo: Stories from an Enduring Prison*, recounts the Obama administration's failure to close it. Like its predecessor, *Obama's Guantánamo* consists of accounts from lawyers who have not only represented Guantánamo detainees, but also served as those detainees' principal connection to the outside world. The lawyers poignantly describe their clients' plights and deepening sense of despair. In many respects, the landscape has become increasingly difficult to navigate. Lawyers and their clients face a relentlessly hostile legislative branch, a judiciary that has become less receptive to their claims, and an administration that refuses to expend the political capital necessary to close the prison.

The seeds of failure were sown from the beginning of Obama's presidency. After ordering Guantánamo's closure, Obama created a task force to study what to do with the remaining prisoners rather than immediately taking action. In 2015, Obama himself would recognize this as a mistake, acknowledging that he should have closed Guantánamo on his first day in office. As opposition grew during his first year, Obama proved weak and indecisive. Two critical missteps stand out. First, in the spring of 2009, Obama abandoned his plan to resettle detainees in the United States, a move that, if taken, would have transformed the political landscape around Guantánamo. The first detainees slated for resettlement in the U.S. were ideal candidates: a handful of Uyghurs, a minority group from northwestern China, who by all accounts posed no threat to the U.S. and never should have been detained in the first place. The Uyghurs could not be returned to China because of the risk of persecution there, thus making their resettlement in another country essential. But Obama caved at the first sign of resistance, fearful that he would be painted as soft on terrorism. Abandoning the plan to bring the Uyghurs to the United States not only revealed that Obama lacked resolve on Guantánamo, but also discouraged other countries, in Europe and elsewhere, from doing more to resettle detainees. Because the U.S. was unwilling to help clean up its own mess, other nations felt less compelled to come to its rescue.

The second critical mistake was maintaining the legal architecture supporting Guantánamo. In a May 2009 speech at the National Archives, Obama indicated that he would seek to prop up military commissions, the discredited tribunals established by President Bush to try terrorism suspects of largely made-up war crimes in violation of domestic and international standards of justice. Rather than scrap military commissions, Obama tried to reform a system that was beyond repair, breathing new life into Guantánamo. Obama also adopted the Bush administration's position that the president had the authority to continue detaining individuals indefinitely without trial under the Authorization for Use of Military Force (AUMF) on the theory the U.S. was engaged in a global armed conflict against Al Qaeda and associated terrorist organizations and those individuals at one time were part of or had supported those groups. Without that authority, the legal basis for Guantánamo would have collapsed; with it, Obama could maintain that detentions at Guantánamo were lawful as long as the war continued, however undesirable as a matter of policy.

As Obama wavered, the backlash against closing Guantánamo grew fiercer and the politics more toxic. By the end of 2009, Congress began restricting Obama's ability to move prisoners from Guantánamo. Initially, Congress barred bringing detainees to the United States, not merely for release, but also for continued detention or prosecution. It then limited Obama's ability to send detainees to other countries by imposing unprecedented restrictions on the commander-in-chief's authority to transfer wartime prisoners. Although Obama protested, he always acquiesced. Obama, moreover, failed to use aggressively the limited authority Congress had left him to transfer prisoners. Between early 2011 and mid-2013, the transfer of prisoners from Guantánamo came to a virtual halt. In January 2013, the administration shut down the one office dedicated exclusively to closing the prison. As the chasm grew between Obama's postinaugural promise and the reality of the prison's continued existence, it became difficult to remember that the presidential candidates from both parties had previously supported shutting the prison. Closing Guantánamo had gone from a bipartisan issue to the new third rail of American politics.

In the past, the Supreme Court had intervened to protect the rights of Guantánamo detainees. During the Bush administration, the Court issued landmark rulings affirming the right of Guantánamo detainees to habeas corpus and mandating basic protections against mistreatment for all detainees in accordance with the Geneva Conventions. In the first days of the Obama administration, district judges scrutinized the government's often thin claims for detention and granted relief in the overwhelming majority of cases they heard. But the U.S. Court of Appeals for the D.C. Circuit, which exercises jurisdiction over all Guantánamo detainee appeals and which has long been hostile to detainee claims, reversed this trend. It interpreted broadly the president's detention authority and created procedural and evidentiary hurdles that made it exceedingly difficult for detainees to prevail. This time, the Supreme Court declined to interfere, seemingly content to watch as the D.C. Circuit deprived the Court's own prior rulings of any real impact on the ground.

Ultimately, it was the Guantánamo prisoners themselves who ensured that they would not be forgotten. In February 2013, detainees began a mass hunger strike that galvanized international attention and catapulted Guantánamo back into the news. Forced to respond, Obama seemed pained by his failure to close the prison. He promised more action, and the pace of transfers started to pick up. But progress remains slow and the obstacles substantial. Even reports of the prison's staggering costs—estimated at around $3 million per prisoner annually—have not generated momentum for closure. Most likely, the administration's latest push will prove too little, too late.

Obama's Guantánamo describes the failure to close America's enduring offshore detention center and the costs of that failure for those still imprisoned there. The lawyers and advocates who have worked to defend Guantánamo detainees and hold the U.S. government to its legal and moral obligations supply the book's chapters. In some instances, lawyers overcame obstacles and achieved success. But more often, they struggled in the face of adversity. Together, their stories provide a picture of Guantánamo during the Obama administration, as the promise of closing America's prison outside the law was replaced by the reality of the forever prison, hope supplanted by despair. The book aims not only to inform readers about conditions at Guantánamo today, but also to provide a historical record so that future generations understand how America abandoned its ideals and then abandoned its attempt to restore them. If *The Guantánamo Lawyers* described the loss of the rule of law, *Obama's Guantánamo* describes the failure to repair it. Absent a dramatic last-minute turnaround, that failure will be Obama's legacy.

The book opens with Sabin Willett's "Twelve Years After," which details how the Obama administration abandoned its plan to bring a small group of Uyghur detainees to the United States at the beginning of Obama's first term. As "Twelve Years After" explains, by ceding ground at this critical early stage, Obama encouraged the political backlash and fearmongering that would dominate the rest of his administration and doom his efforts to close Guantánamo.

Chapters 2 and 3 examine this backlash in greater depth. In "The Wrong Person: How Barack Obama Abandoned Habeas Corpus," Gary A. Isaac laments the transformation of Barack Obama from a presidential candidate whose defense of constitutional rights earned him the overwhelming support of Guantánamo lawyers across the country, to a president whose sacrifice of those rights produced widespread disappointment. As Mr. Isaac explains, Obama's initial moves of ordering Guantánamo's closure and banning torture would mark the highpoint of a presidency that would, in time, look increasingly like his predecessor's on many national security issues.

In "President Obama's Failure to Transfer Detainees from Guantánamo," J. Wells Dixon examines the collapse of Obama's proposal to close Guantánamo through the experiences of his client Djamel Ameziane. Mr. Dixon describes how Mr. Ameziane eventually obtained his release from Guantánamo after a years-long battle in which the U.S. government sought to return him to the one place Mr. Ameziane did not want to be sent: his native Algeria, where he feared persecution.

Chapter 4, Mark Fleming's "The *Boumediene* Case after the Supreme Court," revisits an important district court case decided in late 2008, after the Supreme Court had recognized the constitutional right of Guantánamo detainees to habeas corpus. In that case, the district judge ruled in favor of five of Mr. Fleming's six clients, thus paving the way for their eventual release. In time, however, such forceful decisions by district court judges would become the exception, as appellate court rulings required judicial deference to the government and made it difficult for detainees to prevail.

The next five chapters examine various aspects of indefinite detention at Guantánamo. In chapter 5, "Too Dangerous to Release: Debunking the Claim," Pardiss Kebriaei describes the plight of a Yemeni citizen, Ghaleb Al-Bihani, whom the Obama administration initially slated for legal limbo, classifying him as someone who could not be prosecuted, but who was nonetheless too dangerous to release. In 2014, Mr. Al-Bihani appeared before the Periodic Review Board (PRB), established by President Obama to determine whether law-of-war prisoners, such as Mr. Al-Bihani, should continue to be detained as a matter of military necessity. Although the PRB ruled in Mr. Al Bihani's favor, he still remains at Guantánamo.

In "Mental Illness before Guantánamo," Shayana Kadidal describes the fate of a detainee who, it appears, remained at Guantánamo not because the U.S. suspected him of terrorist activities, but rather because of a mental illness that the U.S. was unable or unwilling to address. Mr.

Kadidal and his colleagues fought to prevent their client's repatriation to Libya, where he faced almost certain death in one of Muammar Gaddafi's jails. As a result of their advocacy, the client was sent instead to Albania, where Mr. Kadidal and his colleagues helped him obtain treatment for his mental illness, before the client eventually returned to Libya after Gaddafi's fall.

In the next chapter, "You Love the Law Too Much," Martha Rayner tells the story of her client Sanad al-Kazimi, who endured torture for nearly two years in various U.S.-run secret prisons before he was brought to Guantánamo, where he continues to be held today. Ms. Rayner describes how Mr. al-Kazimi's experiences reinforce a painful but powerful lesson: that the law, despite its promise, remains largely meaningless for many prisoners at Guantánamo.

Chapters 8 and 9 address hunger strikes at Guantánamo. In "First, Do No Harm," Alka Pradhan describes how the brutal force-feeding of her client Abu Wa'el Dhiab was intended not to keep him alive, but rather to make him suffer as a punishment for engaging in this form of resistance to his indefinite imprisonment. Ms. Pradhan recounts how she and other members of Mr. Dhiab's legal team mounted a challenge to his force-feeding, which resulted in an important district court ruling—presently on appeal—ordering the release of the video recordings of the force-feeding.

Omar Farah's "Nourishing Resistance: Tariq Ba Odah's Eight-Year Hunger Strike at Guantánamo Bay" shares the plight of his client, who has been on hunger strike since 2007. As Mr. Farah explains, a hunger strike has become the one meaningful act of resistance for men like Tariq Ba Odah, who suffer from the failure by the U.S. government to remedy endless detention at Guantánamo. In fact, Tariq Ba Odah was cleared for release by the government five years ago. But because Mr. Odah is from Yemen, where the government fears returning detainees because of security concerns, and because the government has failed to find another country to transfer him to, he remains at Guantánamo.

In chapter 10, "The 'Taliban Five' and the Prisoner Exchange," Frank Goldsmith describes the high-profile transfer of his client Khairullah

Khairkhwa (and four other Afghan detainees from Guantánamo) to the custody of the government of Qatar in exchange for the release by the Taliban of U.S. Army Sergeant Bowe Bergdahl. The Bergdahl–Taliban prisoner exchange prompted a fierce protest by conservative politicians and pundits. But, as Mr. Goldsmith explains, the exchange was consistent with longstanding U.S. wartime practice. And the facts about Mr. Goldsmith's client—a moderate member of the former Taliban government who could help facilitate peace in Afghanistan—were grossly distorted amid the fear and irrationality that dominates public discourse around Guantánamo.

The next three chapters examine military commissions, the controversial tribunals established at Guantánamo to try individuals for war crimes. In "Hamdan: The Legal Challenge to Military Commissions," Joseph McMillan describes the legal odyssey of his client Salim Hamdan. Mr. Hamdan was at the center of two important cases: first, the initial challenge to the military commissions created by President Bush after 9/11, which led to the Supreme Court's landmark 2006 decision in *Hamdan v. Rumsfeld* invalidating the commissions for lack of congressional authority; and second, a subsequent challenge to the first trial conducted before the new military commissions created under the Military Commissions Act of 2006, enacted by Congress four months after the Court's *Hamdan* decision. Mr. McMillan argues that the commissions are still plagued by various flaws, including trying individuals for offenses that do not violate the laws of war—an argument that, in Mr. Hamdan's case, the federal courts ultimately vindicated after a long legal battle.

"A Tale of Two Detainees," by David Frakt, describes two other military commission cases, those of Mohamed Jawad and Ali Hamza al Bahlul. Mr. Frakt describes the misguided attempt to prosecute Mr. Jawad, who was a child at the time of his arrest and who had been repeatedly tortured, for allegedly throwing a grenade at a military vehicle. Not only did the U.S. fail to support its allegation with evidence, but also the allegation itself did not establish a war crime under any accepted meaning of the term. "A Tale of Two Detainees" further conveys the disappointment in President Obama for reviving the discredited military commissions, rather than terminating them.

Chapter 13, "More Kafka than Kafka," details the military commissions' flaws and absurdities. Jason Wright, an army officer and criminal defense lawyer, was assigned to represent Khalid Shaikh Mohammad, the alleged mastermind of the 9/11 attacks, as well as another detainee. In "More Kafka than Kafka," Major Wright describes how, until he was eventually forced to resign from the U.S. Army, the commissions sought to prevent him from fulfilling his duty of zealously representing his clients, whether by attempting to classify instances of U.S. torture so they could not be discussed publicly or by spying on attorney-client communications and seizing attorney-client materials.

In the final chapter, "Storytelling #Guantanamo," Aliya Hana Hussain describes her work outside the courtroom on behalf of Guantánamo detainees. Ms. Hussain, an advocate at the Center for Constitutional Rights, explains how she uses social media to build support and sympathy for Guantánamo detainees and to help prevent them from vanishing from the public eye. Despite all the impediments advocates face, "Storytelling #Guantanamo" ends on a note of hope, as Ms. Hussain describes a watercolor painting depicting glimmering sunlight amid a storm at sea that was left to her by one Guantánamo detainee who finally gained his freedom and is now slowly rebuilding his life.

As the stories recounted in this volume and the prior one show, a diverse array of advocates from various backgrounds rose up to fight for civil liberties and human rights when they were most seriously threatened. Yet nothing can ever erase the stain of Guantánamo, whose continued existence is a living reminder of lawlessness and abuse. Despite President Obama's intention to close Guantánamo, his lasting legacy is likely to be the normalization deep into the future of what should have been condemned and marginalized as a temporary deviation from America's Constitution and ideals.

December 2015

1

Twelve Years After

SABIN WILLETT

The Flat Tire

One spring morning in 2009, my partner Susan Baker Manning and I walked out of the offices of the Department of Homeland Security in Washington, D.C., grinning ear to ear. We'd cut the deal. Two Uyghur clients would be freed from Guantánamo and brought to northern Virginia—perhaps within days. More than seven years had passed since the first interrogator told these men that they were innocent and would soon be freed. We'd been hard at their legal cases for more than four years. The cases had taken us to Guantánamo and the trial court, to Congress and the D.C. Circuit, to Albania and Sweden. At last, these two men had the end in sight. Ablikim and Salahidin would be freed. We were almost giddy.

It was a cold, sunny morning, and quiet outside the Nebraska Avenue complex. We knew things would not be quiet for long. A press fracas would erupt when our clients arrived in Northern Virginia. We'd have to prepare the men for sound trucks, shouted questions, microphones thrust at them. But over four years we had learned something about the press. If our clients could weather the initial flurry, the press's attention would pass to other things. And as the excitement faded, perhaps the mythology of the Guantánamo "terrorist" would begin to fade with it.

We crossed the street to where Susan's Austin Mini Cooper was parked, and found the right rear tire was flat.

The president's bold pledge to close Guantánamo would soon be as flat as the tire. The deal we'd struck would collapse, and not just for

Ablikim and Salahidin, the two Uyghur clients whom a senior officer of the department had just committed to bring to the United States. In a broader way, our deal would take the air out of the whole program for closing Guantánamo—out of Executive Order 13492 (which ordered the prison's closure two days after Obama's inauguration), out of the hopes of hundreds of men. Our deal would end up double locking the gates of the iconic prison, rather than opening them.

Of all the inmates, it was the Uyghurs who made Guantánamo the forever prison. Of all the prisoners, it was the indisputably innocent ones—the ones everyone agreed did not belong there—who inspired our country to make Guantánamo a monument and its inmates perpetual exhibits. The law of Guantánamo is the law of unintended consequences.

The Uyghurs

The Uyghurs are a Turkic people. They come from a region of Asia known to them as "East Turkestan," and to the Chinese as Xinjiang, and practice a less conservative Islam than is common on the Arabian peninsula. Between Han and Uyghur people there has always been tension. In the last century, Uyghurs staged several uprisings against Chinese rule, and twice (in 1933 and 1944) briefly gained their independence. The First East Turkestan Republic, a short-lived attempt at independence, fell in 1934. A second East Turkestan Republic, a Soviet puppet state, existed from 1944 until Mao Tse Tung seized power in 1949.

Enforced limits on religious worship and child rearing are a staple in the region, and in early 1997, mass imprisonment of Uyghur dissidents sparked demonstrations in the city of Ghulja. On February 5, 1997, after two days of protests calling for independence, marchers were crushed by the army. Official reports put the death toll at nine, while dissident reports estimated the number killed at more than 100. According to Uyghur sources, more than 1,000 people were arrested on charges of "splittism," "conducting fundamental religious activity," and "counter-revolutionary activities." Amnesty International documented as many as

190 executions carried out in the years immediately following the Ghulja demonstrations.

Before 9/11, the U.S. represented a beacon of hope to the Uyghurs, a place where religious freedom was secure. The World Uyghur Congress sometimes met here. Two Uyghurs who later would serve as our law firm's translators, Nury Turkel and Rushan Abbas, had reached the U.S. as students and remained as refugees.

Other Uyghurs were fleeing the country in different directions. In the late 1990s and early 2000s, many young Uyghur men fled across the Chinese border into Pakistan, and then made their way across the border to Afghanistan, whose ruling Taliban regime welcomed any Muslim refugee. Many came across the border to Jalalabad. In the mountains nearby a Uyghur village was established. Here many of our future clients came together to "learn to pray," as they would describe it. This meant, quite literally, learning Arabic and the required forms of worship in the Qur'an.

They were in this village when the towers fell on 9/11, and there in October 2001, when the U.S. bombing campaign began.

The bombing killed a number of men outright. Others fled to nearby caves. In the morning they awoke to a moonscape. With winter coming on, they began a journey on foot across the mountains to Pakistan, where they arrived sometime in December. By this time the U.S. had flooded the region with pamphlets promising bounties for the capture of terrorists fleeing the Tora Bora mountains. In December 2001, 16 Uyghur prisoners were delivered to the Americans and taken to Bagram Airfield Military Base in Afghanistan.

It was a hard winter. The detention cages at Bagram were cold and filthy, and the interrogations brutal and unsophisticated. There were no Uyghur translators. But some of the group spoke enough Arabic to be understood, and over those first months, interrogators came to understand that these men were not the enemy.

"You are fish flopping in the wrong net," one interrogator told our future client Adel Abdul-Hakim.

The military did not know what to do with the clients. In classic form, some unknown officer decided to make them someone else's problem. So in May and June 2002, they were flown to Guantánamo Bay, Cuba.

Guantánamo

The first Uyghur prisoner, seized from a hospital in Northern Afghanistan, arrived at Guantánamo in January 2002. Most of the other Uyghurs came from the village near Jalalabad, and arrived several months later. Twenty-three Uyghur men would ultimately arrive at the base.

During the next decade, Guantánamo would become a fencing ground for lawyers. In the beginning, prisoners had no legal rights and all status review was discretionary. Early habeas corpus challenges, brought by the Center for Constitutional Rights for other prisoners in February, 2002, were quickly dismissed, and the dismissal affirmed by the court of appeals. So for two years there was no interference from the courts. In those early days, every one of the 23 Uyghurs was told—repeatedly—by U.S. interrogators that his detention was a mistake, an error, and that the government was working to remedy it. Because U.S. law prohibits sending a person to a country where it is likely he will be tortured, and because country reports prepared annually by the U.S. State Department made plain that in China separatists faced torture, the men could not be sent home. There is some evidence that, very early in their captivity, the government made half-hearted efforts to settle them elsewhere. But it was a confusing time: the Afghanistan war was underway and the Iraq invasion was about to begin. For any host nation, offering refuge to the Uyghurs meant damaging relations abroad with China, while resettling "Guantánamo terrorists" risked political attack at home. Long before we met them, our clients had been branded with the indelible taint of Guantánamo.

Still, the Uyghurs' early on-base relationship with U.S. interrogators was good. They volunteered their personal histories, believing that the U.S. would help them find a safe harbor, a refuge from Chinese communism. The interrogators told them that the U.S. was "looking for a country" to resettle them. They merely had to be patient.

But something else was brewing in Washington, an episode in U.S.-China relations of which a small but remarkable chapter would play out at the base.

In the summer of 2002, the Bush administration sought UN Security Council support for a war resolution against Saddam Hussein's Iraq. In order to procure, at minimum, China's agreement not to veto a resolution, the U.S. government agreed to various concessions to the Chinese. Many related to Taiwan, but a few touched on Uyghur matters. In September, the U.S. agreed to designate a new group, the "East Turkestan Islamic Front," on the State Department's list of foreign terrorist organizations. It also agreed to grant to Chinese interrogators permission to come to Guantánamo and interrogate the Uyghurs. Although our clients were seized long before this designation, and although Congress never authorized war against "ETIM," in years to come we would often contend with the allegation that our clients' imprisonment at Guantánamo was justified by their "membership" in ETIM.

Guantánamo is, largely, a classified facility. I first visited in 2005, and was not permitted to meet clients there before undergoing an FBI background check. Finding translators was difficult because they too were required to be U.S. citizens. (The number of U.S. citizens willing to work as translators and fluent in Uyghur is limited.) Yet agents of the Chinese government were welcomed at Guantánamo in the fall of 2002 to interrogate the Uyghurs and given complete access to classified information that our clients had earlier volunteered to interrogators.

In 2003, the UN did not support the Iraq invasion and the Uyghurs were not delivered to China. But the 2002 interrogations had searing consequences for the Uyghur prisoners and for lawyers who would arrive years after. Prior to the arrival of the Chinese, our clients believed America was attempting to resettle them and candidly discussed details concerning their families and backgrounds. When they learned that this information was turned over to the Chinese, they lost faith in Americans, a loss of faith the lawyers would struggle for years to overcome.

By mid-2003, the government had largely lost interest in our clients. They were interrogated less often. They were living in Camp Four, the lowest-security camp. It was a Spartan existence, but peaceful. The men slept in a small dormitory and, within the fenced compound, could go in and out of doors at will. They generally ate outdoors at a shaded picnic table. They practiced their faith together, praying five times daily.

From early 2002 through mid-summer 2004, lower courts had consistently dismissed habeas challenges brought on behalf of detainees and denied lawyers even client visits, reasoning that there was no habeas jurisdiction over the Guantánamo naval base and so there was no reason for lawyers to have access. But late in June 2004, the Supreme Court issued its decision in *Rasul v. Bush*, which held that Guantánamo detainees enjoy the privilege of habeas corpus. In the fall, the first lawyers began visiting the base, and late that year, or early the following year, Abu Bakker Qasim, a historian of the struggles of the Uyghur people, dictated a letter, which another detainee wrote out in English. The letter, which bears an "unclassified" stamp and a fax legend of "Feb. 8, 2005," lives in a frame on my office wall today. It requested legal assistance. Abu Bakker, his friend Adel Abdul-Hakim, and others signed it. The letter reached our firm late in February.

I knew little of habeas corpus or military law, and nothing of Uyghurs when I received this letter. Like most Americans, I assumed that Guantánamo Bay was a sort of POW camp where, as our government had put it, the "worst of the worst" were held. So I attended a post-*Rasul* conference and learned from military lawyers on the panel that the government contended that the base was a place beyond law. The government defended against claims that torture was practiced there by asserting that the courts had no jurisdiction over anything that happened at Guantánamo—a defense I didn't find wholly reassuring. We decided to get involved.

We had never met the men and could not speak with them by phone, but our firm decided to take on Abu Bakker and Adel's case. We filed a habeas petition for them in March 2005. It took more than three months to meet them, though. Susan and I, and then other members of our team, had to go through FBI background checks and then wait for the government to grant our request for a meeting. We met the men in mid-July 2005 in interrogation cells at Camp Echo, one of the camps at Guantánamo Bay.

The government had been surprised by the *Rasul* decision. *Rasul* meant lawyers would come to the base, and it meant that courts would begin to receive information about who the detainees actually were. So in late summer 2004, the government hastily implemented Combatant Status Review Tribunals (CSRTs), panels staffed entirely by military officers, whose avowed object was to determine whether a given detainee was properly designated as an "enemy combatant." The strategic purpose of these tribunals was to head off judicial review. The government would argue that courts should defer to the CSRTs, much as courts defer to administrative agencies.

The tribunals were roundly criticized for failing to provide a modicum of due process—and those failings later would be confirmed by the Supreme Court. But in the meantime, the blizzard of legal thrust and parry that would characterize the next years had already begun. Each challenge from lawyers would be met with a new system of "status review": CSRTs in Guantánamo trailers, administrative review boards, habeas corpus hearings in district courtrooms in Washington, and briefly, Detainee Treatment Act cases in the Court of Appeals.*

No one in the government could say, "Well, it's a foreign war in a strange land, fought, in the beginning, from the air—not surprising that the military made a few mistakes. Let's put them right." With the bar assaulting the whole concept of Guantánamo root and branch, and the

---

*Editor's note: The Detainee Treatment Act of 2005 provided a short-lived substitute for habeas corpus review in the U.S. Court of Appeals for the D.C. Circuit, which the Supreme Court found inadequate in its 2008 ruling in *Boumediene v. Bush*.

Bush administration battling back, no mistake could be admitted. So detainees who had been cleared for release years before were put back through review tribunals—and many, having previously been cleared, were now designated as "enemy combatants" in order to stave off judicial review.

What happened to the Uyghur detainees in this regard was passing strange. Some panels determined that Uyghur detainees were not "enemy combatants." The Pentagon's response? Put them through a second panel. In some cases the "mulligan" cleared the prisoner again, and in some cases the panel got the message and discovered that the prisoner was in fact an enemy. Detainees who emerged from the Kafkaesque gauntlet were labeled persons "*no longer*" enemy combatants—because mistakes were never made.

One can imagine how the men felt about this. All of them had been told, years before, they were innocent and the government was "trying to find a country for them." Now they would be put through tribunals? And if the tribunals cleared them, put through a second round of tribunals?

"Siz Gunasiz!"

On Bastille Day 2005, I walked into that first hut with high anxiety. I had never met the men, never seen any military file about them. I had no idea whom I would meet. We had not even been able to secure a Uyghur translator, and spent much of our first meeting in an elaborate game of charades, attempting to work through our Arabic-language translator.

But I learned from Abu Bakker that he and Adel had just emerged from this strange time warp. Years after being reassured that they would be resettled, they were sent back for "status review." Abu Bakker told us about his own CSRT review. They had given him a paper, he said. The paper read, "Siz gunasiz." We were struggling with translation that first day, and so we went through this part again, slowly. He'd been through the CSRT—in the trailer, with the three military officers? Yes—and then another one. (Another one? Did he mean a second day? No, he meant another one, a second tribunal. Susan and I looked at each other, not quite comprehending.) At the end they gave him a piece of paper? Yes—he had it in his cell. And it said what?

"*Siz Gunasiz!*" ("You're Innocent!")

(Confronted with the bureaucratic doublespeak of the form—"the detainee is no longer designated as an enemy combatant"—our clients had asked an MP what the English meant. It means you're innocent, he said.)

The same, we learned, had happened to Adel.

On our return from Guantánamo, we filed emergency motions in federal court, and District Judge James Robertson summoned the parties to a hearing. All through that fall he demanded to know what the government was doing about our clients' situation. But just before Christmas, he issued his ruling, dismissing the case because, he concluded, the court could not order the release of the men in the U.S. and it could not order release anywhere else. As Virgil says, there is a heartbreak at the heart of things.

We filed an expedited appeal. In May 2006, on the eve of argument, the government mooted the appeal by sending Abu Bakker, Adel, and three other Uyghurs, all of whom had been cleared by a CSRT, to Tirana, Albania. Four of them live there still. In 2007, Adel was able to claim asylum in Sweden, where his sister was granted refuge some years before. He has since remarried and has a child. Abu Bakker remains in Tirana.

Habeas Corpus: Book Report or Remedy?

In those first meetings with the clients, we had learned something interesting—many companions of Abu Bakker and Adel, having been cleared by one CSRT, had been put through a second, which declared them to be enemy combatants. So we filed petitions for them as well.

But the government resisted, arguing that we did not have the correct permission from the clients to do so. Almost a year of wrangling ensued before we could meet many of our new clients, including Khalil, Abdullah, and Ablikim, for the first time in 2006.

Our work for them was interrupted by the Detainee Treatment Act, which went into effect that year and briefly stood as a bar to habeas review until the Supreme Court pronounced it constitutionally inadequate in *Boumediene v. Bush*, issued in June 2008. The subsequent legal proceedings were complex, but later in 2008, the Uyghurs had all "won" habeas corpus review in the district court. Early in 2009, in a split decision that stands today, the U.S. Court of Appeals for the D.C. Circuit—the federal appeals court in Washington, D.C., where all detainee cases go to die—ruled in *Kiyemba v. Obama* that their win meant precisely nothing. A judge could not order that they be freed. Freedom meant releasing the detainee in the United States (since a U.S. court can order no sovereign but our own to receive a prisoner), and such a release order ran into the political branches' exclusive control over immigration, the appeals court reasoned. So the Uyghurs enjoyed the privilege of habeas corpus, were entitled to court review, and prevailed in that review. And after they prevailed they were entitled to be sent back to the same cells. The third branch's power to "check the executive" was this: it had the power to require the executive to report, once every quarter or so, that it was continuing to try to arrange a release, on its own terms and timing, to a place of its own choosing.

Kiyemba remains law. It is what the Great Writ of habeas corpus means in America today.

Politics

The Uyghurs passed the gauntlet—the CSRTs, habeas corpus hearings, even the late-lamented Detainee Treatment Act. They passed every review except *Kiyemba*'s. Though written in elegant prose, with nods toward the Constitution, *Kiyemba* dressed in rouge and lipstick the more primal xenophobia that informed a review that our clients could never pass: the review of the mob.

Early in the Obama presidency, we engaged with the president's advisors, and negotiated a deal to bring two Uyghurs to Virginia. It was a sensible idea from each side's perspective. The men would reach a free country, where they might at last begin to rebuild their lives. The government would, without risk to its citizens, advertise to the world that it was participating in the process of closing down the prison. This would make it politically easier for allies to take other detainees.

But in May 2009, news of the planned Uyghur release leaked. Our clients had been in Guantánamo for seven years. The district court determined that none of them was an enemy belligerent or posed a danger to the United States. Even the D. C. Circuit had previously ruled for one of them in an earlier case. It wasn't just that these people were not our enemies; they were religious refugees from Communist China, people who long had held us in the highest esteem, as a nation that venerated freedom of worship. The proposition that these people were our enemy was not simply false. It was not simply disproved by the executive branch itself. It was an embarrassment.

But that did not matter, because they came from Guantánamo. And so Rep. Frank Wolf went to the House floor to denounce the release of "terrorists" into his district in Virginia. John Thune did the same in the Senate. Others took up the hue and cry, all of them either factually ignorant or politically strategic, all of their political denunciations counterfactual, jejune, idiotic.

From the White House came a ringing silence.

From the president's political impotence an idea was born. If the right wing could embarrass the president over Uyghur releases—if the White House would let itself be pushed around here, why not make the closure of the base a battle cry. Why not keep the detainees there *forever*?

The inflection point came one day in May. The president of the United States spoke at the National Archives about charting a course to protect the nation from enemies in ways that did not betray our founding principles. That same day a right-wing civilian gave a luncheon talk at the conservative American Enterprise Institute. And the media presented the speeches as equivalent. The headline in the next morning's *Washington Post* was typical: "Obama and Cheney Deliver Dueling Speeches on National Security." That former Vice President Cheney—the architect of the disastrous Iraq invasion and of a national torture policy—could be set up as a strategic equivalent to the White House told us much about the press and the country at large. Americans were ready to be frightened, but unready to stand up for constitutional principles.

A quaint provision of the first article of our Constitution bans bills of attainder. An "attainder" was a punishment meted out to a specific person or identifiable group by a legislative body. The fear was that legislators, responding to the passions of the moment, could be dangerous, while the hope was that a nonelective judiciary would ignore passions to determine whether punishments were consistent with due process of law. Our founders were wise to proscribe bills of attainder, knowing that letting legislatures punish specific individuals brings out the *demos* in democracy, swiftly amending the translation of "*demos-kratia*" from "people power" to "mob rule." Mobs do not care very much about due process. But because of the aborted Uyghur releases, Congress began engaging in bill-of-attainder-like behavior, making it harder for the president actually to release human beings from Guantánamo by passing a series of increasingly onerous transfer restrictions. Mining for votes, Congress passed laws whose aim and effect was to imprison a specific set of men, already held for years, at Guantánamo.

This was all because President Obama planned to bring Ablikim and Salahidin to Virginia and then, when confronted, flinched.

Bermuda

Ablikim and Salahidin were fortunate—they were transferred before the congressional restrictions were implemented. They were sent by the United States to freedom in Bermuda, where they have lived peacefully for six years, have married, have children, hold jobs, and pay rent. On the way to mosque, they toot their scooter horns at passersby. The passersby toot back. If you visit the Princess Hotel in Hamilton, admire the palm trees on the back lawn. Abdullah, another Uyghur who reached Bermuda, is a contractor who helped plant them. These men have broken bread with, among other people, my children.

But they were too dangerous for the Congress of the United States.

I learned from Daniel Klaidman's *Kill or Capture*, an account of the early Obama presidency's attempt to grapple with the so-called War on Terror, that about the time our four clients were photographed arriving in Bermuda, a fierce debate was raging over whether to try Khalid Shaikh Mohammad, the alleged mastermind of 9/11, in a U.S. criminal court. According to a contemporary account, Attorney General Eric Holder met with family members of victims of the 9/11 atrocities, one of whom had come to the meeting with a newspaper showing our clients' joyful arrival in Bermuda. The family member pronounced himself sickened by the account. The attorney general quietly pointed out that the men had nothing to do with the murder of his loved one. It didn't matter. They were from Guantánamo, weren't they?

* * *

Bermuda was a small and improbable miracle, a ray of sunshine in a long storm. While the administration's resolve to bring our clients to Virginia was collapsing, Greg Craig, White House general counsel, called me to suggest a transfer to Bermuda. At first I thought he was joking. But Bermudian premier Dr. Ewart Brown was willing to try to help the Obama administration, and now the White House strapped in. Greg stressed that this had to be handled quickly and discreetly. It didn't need to be said that the slightest publicity would lead to Britain's intercession, and probably that of our own Congress.

It was then that we managed to claw back a point we had argued for and lost in the Virginia deal. Ablikim and Salahidin had been chosen for purely legal reasons, based on Ablikim's status in one of the lead cases.

But I knew that neither was an ideal candidate for the baptism by press fire that awaited. Neither was fluent in English and Ablikim, who had suffered greatly in Camp Six, which was modeled on a high-security U.S. prison, was simply unable to smile for the cameras and play the necessary ambassador's role. So I had urged the U.S. to bring in at least four of our clients, adding irrepressible Abdullah and gentle Khalil. Both are extremely intelligent, and were conversant in English. Both "got it." And both could help their brothers navigate a brave new world.

Two only, the U.S. had said. But when we came onto Bermuda, Col. David Burch, the foreign minister, got it as well. Four would be better than two. He agreed, and that is why Abdullah and Khalil made it to Bermuda.

As lawyers we felt a little at sea: how would we learn of our clients' habeas corpus rights, or any other rights in Bermuda? Citizenship appeared to depend on Bermudian or UK birth, and while Bermuda controlled its "guest worker" policy, there were limits on the ability of guest workers to stay, and no path to citizenship. We telephoned one of the major law firms in Bermuda, which we knew mainly from large commercial deals. "We have a client," we said, "who needs to better understand the guest worker law." We supposed they thought we meant a corporation.

We also quickly arranged a call with the clients in Guantánamo (there wasn't time for a visit), and laid out for them what we could about Bermuda. I had worried that, to them, Bermuda would sound like just another tiny island, far removed from friends, family, or any Muslim community. But as we described its climate and economy, Abdullah interrupted. "Sabin, how much time do we have for this call?" When I told him, he said, "Then stop talking! I don't want to run out of time and I want it clearly understood that I accept this deal!"

In the space of a couple of weeks the entire deal was negotiated. The day came. We flew to Bermuda, and in Hamilton met with Greg Craig and Dan Fried of the State Department, and then sat down with their Bermudian counterparts at Cabinet House on Front Street. Susan and I watched as the two governments exchanged their "diplomatic notes," that is, their understanding of their deal. At one point Dan asked whether the government would agree to interview our clients once a week, to "keep an eye on them." Col. Burch said, "Ambassador Fried, this is Bermuda. There's nobody here I need to meet with once a week."

That night we boarded a private plane and flew to the base. We arrived about 3:30 in the morning and found that our clients had been brought by bus onto the tarmac. Our translator, Rushan Abbas, and I boarded the bus. There the four men were, in ill-fitting street clothes, surrounded by two dozen Marines. They stepped down from the bus and crossed to the plane, where their ID bracelets were snipped off and a Marine photographed their departure. Then we boarded.

We landed about 6:30 a.m. on June 10 in Hamilton and taxied to the end of the runway. I sent an email to my lawyer colleagues in the United States: "Four X Joy as the Eagle Lands in Bermuda." Outside, I looked nervously for press, but there were none. The story had not leaked. It soon would, and more press fracases awaited, but for the moment, there was peace. White roofs, pastel-colored houses, gardens, blue water. Our clients' eyes were wide.

* * *

Very few of the men in Guantánamo were ever, on any remote construction of the word, terrorists. Some of those who remain were, or may have been, fighters who joined up with the wrong side in an Afghan civil war that ended more than a decade ago. But it doesn't matter. The public and Congress make no distinction.

Were we always a timorous people, who ran from our Constitution at the first sign of trouble? Guantánamo was a galvanizing concept, at first, a national disgrace, a blot on the flag. We elected a president in part on the promise of shuttering it. But freedom as a bumper sticker is easier than the real freedom of real human beings. The latter was too much for us. The fearmongering of politicians was too much for us. If a delusional Nigerian tries to blow up a plane, keep the men in Guantánamo. If a murderous band of brigands forms in the Levant, more than a decade after 9/11, and starts beheading journalists, keep the men in Guantánamo. And if you're running for office, and want cheers from a crowd in New Hampshire or a pundit on Fox News, call all the Guantánamo detainees terrorists, although the government never did, and vow never to release them, even though many have long been cleared for release.

I often think of the haunting last sentence of George Orwell's *1984*. Like Winston Smith, the hero of the novel, America transitioned from her fear and disgust over the iconic prison. Like him, she awakened to a revelation: she loves Guantánamo.

2

The Wrong Person

How Barack Obama Abandoned Habeas Corpus

GARY A. ISAAC

Since I became involved in the Guantánamo litigation in 2003, I've written or read dozens of court filings, heard myriad speeches, and participated in countless discussions about habeas corpus. But perhaps the most stirring explanation of habeas corpus that I've ever heard came during a "town hall" campaign rally in Michigan in September 2008. Calling habeas corpus "the foundation of Anglo-American law," candidate for president Barack Obama told the audience that the principle "says very simply: If the government grabs you, then you have the right to at least ask, 'Why was I grabbed?' And say, 'Maybe you've got the wrong person.'" And, Obama explained,

> The reason you have that safeguard is because we don't always catch the right person. We may think this is Mohammed the terrorist, it might be Mohammed the cab driver. You might think it's Barack the bomb thrower, but it's Barack the guy running for president. So the reason that you have this principle is not to be soft on terrorism, it's because that's who we are. That's what we're protecting. Don't mock the Constitution. Don't make fun of it. Don't suggest that it's un-American to abide by what the Founding Fathers set up. It's worked pretty well for over two hundred years.

I remember thinking at the time that Obama's remarks were extraordinary. He was, after all, speaking in Michigan, one of the states hardest hit by the ongoing economic meltdown, and yet he chose that occasion, and that venue, to highlight the issue of habeas corpus rights for Guantánamo detainees. And at a time when Fox News and others were questioning his patriotism, his religion, and even his citizenship, Obama used his own foreign-sounding name to highlight that some of the detainees at Guantánamo might not be the "right" people—"you might think it's Barack the bomb thrower, but it's Barack the guy running for president."

But while I found Obama's defense of habeas corpus electrifying, I can't say that I was surprised by it, because he had been showing leadership on the issue for several years. In 2006, I and several of the other "habeas lawyers" had worked closely with Senator Obama in opposing legislation designed to strip the courts of jurisdiction to hear the detainees' habeas cases. Although we ultimately lost the battle in Congress, Senator Obama's strong support made a powerful impression on many of us.[1] And in 2007, I was struck by how Obama often seemed to go out of his way during the early Democratic presidential candidates' debates to talk about the importance of habeas corpus to the rule of law. As the struggle over the detainees' status unfolded, the lawyers involved in the litigation had come to recognize that this was a political as much as a legal fight, and we'd become adept at organizing and Capitol Hill advocacy.[2] We knew as well that the executive branch, i.e., President Bush, had created the mess at Guantánamo, and however the habeas litigation turned out in the courts, the president elected in 2008 could clean it up. Senator Obama's embrace of habeas corpus led me to conclude that he was far and away the best choice on this issue, and that our well-organized band of habeas counsel—which by now had grown to several hundred lawyers around the country—should do whatever it could to help elect him the next president.

So in January 2008, with Obama and Hillary Clinton running neck and neck for the Democratic nomination, I drafted an open letter, on behalf of "Habeas Lawyers for Obama," stating that we believed that Barack Obama felt "in his bones" the need to "restore the rule of law, demonstrate our commitment to human rights, and repair our reputation in the world community." We released the letter on the eve of the critical Super Tuesday slate of primaries, and I ultimately enlisted 130 lawyers from around the country who were involved in the detainee litigation—with a focus on the battleground states—to sign onto and circulate it. The letter was the subject of stories in the *Miami Herald*, *Boston Globe*, and *Wall Street Journal*, and garnered extensive attention on the internet. Over the next several months, I forwarded the letter to thousands of lawyers in the key states.

The Bush administration had treated the lawyers representing the detainees at Guantánamo with undisguised hostility—in one notorious episode, its deputy assistant secretary of defense for detainee affairs, Cully Stimson, had been forced to resign after questioning the habeas lawyers' patriotism and suggesting that the prominent law firms working on the Guantánamo litigation pro bono should be fired by their large corporate clients. The Obama campaign, on the other hand, enlisted civil liberties and human rights lawyers to help develop the campaign's positions on the very issues that many of us had been litigating with the Bush administration for years. During the spring of 2008, I was in regular contact with the campaign's staff concerning Guantánamo-related issues, and when the Supreme Court issued its *Boumediene* decision that June—holding that the detainees at Guantánamo had a constitutional right to challenge their detention via habeas corpus and that legislation passed by Congress in 2006 to strip the courts of jurisdiction over the detainees' habeas cases was unconstitutional—I helped draft the public statement that Obama issued in response.

For several days following the decision, whether *Boumediene* had been rightly decided—and whether the detainees should have the right to challenge their detention in our courts—was one of the main points of debate between Obama and John McCain, the Republican nominee for president. McCain denounced *Boumediene* as "one of the worst decisions in the history of this country." Obama, on the other hand, hailed

Boumediene as "a rejection of the Bush Administration's attempt to create a legal black hole at Guantánamo" and "an important step toward reestablishing our credibility as a nation committed to the rule of law, and rejecting a false choice between fighting terrorism and respecting habeas corpus."

I decided that the best way for me to assist the campaign was to recruit lawyers who could serve in battleground states on Election Day to provide "voter protection," that is, to make sure that no one who came out to vote was denied the opportunity to do so. I started an organizing committee in Chicago that ultimately recruited over 2,500 Illinois lawyers to volunteer on Election Day, and also used the national networks that we had built up during the habeas corpus fight to recruit lawyers from across the country. So when I read Senator Obama's defense of habeas corpus at the town hall in Michigan that September, I immediately blasted out an e-mail to my "Habeas Lawyers for Obama" list with a simple message: "WE'VE GOT TO ELECT THIS MAN!"

During the next several months, hundreds of habeas lawyers threw themselves into the Obama campaign—raising money, knocking on doors, and volunteering to do voter protection. I'm not suggesting that the habeas lawyers were unique—millions of other Americans were doing the same things. But I can attest to the fact that many of the lawyers working on Guantánamo and other "rule of law" issues felt, as I did, an almost evangelical zeal to help elect Obama.

Although I was going to my office every day and was still ostensibly employed by my law firm, the reality is that from mid-August through Election Day I spent every day, all day, making calls and sending e-mails to line up more lawyers, and then went home to continue doing that late into the night. I worked directly with the campaign's "voter protection coordinators" in all the battleground states, endeavoring to ensure that they had all the lawyers they needed come Election Day. A couple of my close friends—also lawyers and also pivotal participants in our Chicago organizing committee—and I spent the last weekend of the campaign in Indianapolis, helping prepare for Election Day there. We spent Election Day in the campaign's "boiler room" helping oversee voter protection throughout Indiana, and Barack Obama became the first Democratic presidential candidate since Lyndon Johnson in 1964 to carry the state.

As soon as the election was over, the focus of our habeas lawyers group shifted to working with the incoming administration. Although many of the habeas lawyers were disappointed, after Election Day, that Obama's transition team did not include anyone from our ranks, we were encouraged that it did include a number of lawyers with whom we had personal or professional connections. And in the months that followed the election, I was able to use my own contacts to arrange a series of meetings with the transition team, one for representatives of the habeas counsel group, another for lawyers representing detainees in military commission proceedings, and a third for nongovernmental organizations working on Guantánamo and other "rule of law" issues.* The meetings seemed to represent a good start toward opening lines of communication and developing working relationships with those in the administration who would be responsible for detainee issues.

During the habeas lawyers' meeting with the transition team, we addressed a range of issues related to the detainees, but two stood out. First, we emphasized the flimsiness of the evidence against many of the detainees at Guantánamo and that in virtually all of the cases that had been adjudicated up to that point, the courts had rejected the government's evidence and found no basis for detention. And second, we emphasized that if the Obama administration was serious about closing Guantánamo, it should act swiftly to resettle at least a few of the detainees in the United States. Because many of the detainees, such as the Chinese Uyghurs, could not be returned to their home countries due to fear of persecution, to close Guantánamo, the new administration would

---

*Editor's note: Habeas corpus proceedings challenged the indefinite detention of prisoners without charge in federal court; military commissions involved the prosecution of a limited number of prisoners for war crimes before military tribunals.

need to resettle many detainees in third countries, and it would be difficult to prevail on *other* countries to take in detainees if the U.S. was not willing to do the same.* We also argued that bringing a few of the detainees who had won their habeas cases to live in the U.S. would be the best way to forestall attempts to derail President Obama's Guantánamo plans by demonizing all the detainees as "the worst of the worst." And, we told the transition representatives, the ideal candidates for resettlement in the U.S. were the Uyghur detainees, who had already been cleared of wrongdoing by the Bush administration, who could not return to China, and whose opposition to the Chinese government had gained them the support of some Republican members of Congress. Indeed, although the Bush administration's appeal of the decision was still pending, in October 2008, in *Kiyemba v. Bush*, a federal district court in Washington, D.C., had granted habeas to 17 of the Uyghur detainees and ordered that they be brought to his courtroom for a hearing to determine appropriate conditions under which they would be released in the United States.

Following the meeting, a number of us continued to communicate informally with the transition representatives, and although they made no commitments, they seemed interested in cooperating with us to work through many of the detainee issues. Indeed, at the transition team's request, we put together a comprehensive calendar of upcoming litigation deadlines so that the administration would have advance notice of controversial legal questions on which it would be required to take a public position in court.

From day one, the new Obama administration faced a host of critical issues, and so it seemed all the more remarkable that President Obama's first official act was to address not the economy or health care, but Guantánamo. In a moment of high drama, and surrounded by a phalanx of retired military brass, President Obama signed a series of executive orders acknowledging that "[t]he individuals currently detained at Guantánamo have the constitutional privilege of the writ of habeas

*Editor's note: The plight of the Uyghurs is discussed in Sabin Willett's "Twelve Years After," chapter 1 in this volume.

corpus," providing that the executive branch would undertake "a prompt and thorough review" of whether the "continued detention" of the men at Guantánamo "is in the national security and foreign policy interests of the United States and in the interests of justice," and ordering that "[t]he detention facilities at Guantánamo . . . shall be closed as soon as practicable, and no later than 1 year from the date of this order." President Obama issued a separate executive order banning the use of so-called "enhanced interrogation techniques," i.e., torture.

What we did not know, and could not foresee, was that at least as far as Guantánamo was concerned, those executive orders would represent the high-water mark of the Obama presidency. As it turned out, the first year of his administration was noteworthy not for the closure of Guantánamo, but for a series of unilateral actions that were starkly at odds with Barack Obama's rhetorical defense of habeas corpus and that doomed his much-heralded directive to close Guantánamo:

- *The Obama administration caved on its plan to resettle two of the Uyghur detainees in the United States.* In its first months, the Obama administration had reached an agreement with habeas counsel for the Uyghur detainees to resettle two of their clients in the Washington, D.C., area, where there was an existing Uyghur American community ready to help the detainees with jobs, housing, and other support. But in mid-2009, only a few days before the Uyghurs' scheduled arrival, word of the plan was leaked, and in the face of opposition by some members of Congress, the Obama administration walked away from the agreement.

- *The Obama administration not only abandoned its plans to voluntarily resettle two of the Uyghurs in the United States, but also argued, as the Bush administration had done, that the courts have no authority to order the president to release detainees here, even if there was no basis to continue to detain them and they presented no security risk.* In the waning days of the Bush administration, the district court hearing the Uyghur detainees' habeas cases ruled in their favor and ordered their release in the United States. The Bush administration immediately appealed, and in February 2009, just

after President Obama assumed office, the U.S. Court of Appeals for the
D.C. Circuit issued its decision, ruling that the courts had no authority to
order the president to release detainees into the United States. The decision
gutted the detainees' habeas corpus rights, for habeas is meaningless if the
court reviewing the lawfulness of a prisoner's imprisonment has no authority to order release. The detainees quickly sought review in the Supreme
Court, but in May 2009, the Obama administration filed a brief opposing
review and urged the Supreme Court to let the Court of Appeals' ruling
stand. The administration then effectively avoided review, and persuaded
the Supreme Court to dismiss the case as moot, by arranging for the Uyghur petitioners to be released in Palau (a tiny island nation in the Pacific
Ocean) instead.

- *President Obama chose to sign legislation barring transfer of detainees from
  Guantánamo to the U.S. and restricting transfer of the detainees elsewhere.*
  In June 2009, Congress passed a supplemental appropriations bill that
  barred the use of funds to release any of the Guantánamo detainees in the
  United States or, as a practical matter, even to transfer them to the U.S. for
  detention or prosecution. The legislation also restricted the use of funds
  to transfer the detainees to other countries. At the time, the Democrats
  overwhelmingly controlled both houses of Congress, so passage of the
  legislation cannot be laid at the door of obstructionist Republicans. That
  the legislation was passed at all by a Democratic Congress reflects a failure
  of leadership on the part of President Obama. The legislation was seen as a
  repudiation of his detainee policies, and would make it impossible for him
  to make good on the executive order to close Guantánamo. Obama could
  have vetoed the legislation and used the "bully pulpit" of the presidency to
  explain why the restrictions were unacceptable. But he did neither. Obama
  chose to sign the bill. Indeed, over the course of his presidency, Obama
  would repeatedly sign such legislation.

- *President Obama continued the Bush administration's indefinite detention
  of individuals without charge.* President Obama's executive order had
  banned the use of torture going forward, but the only "evidence" against

many of the detainees was tainted by torture or coercion. Because such evidence is considered inherently unreliable and would be inadmissible, it could not be used as the basis for criminal prosecution in our regular courts. But in May 2009, President Obama announced that his administration would simply detain indefinitely, without charge, those at Guantánamo "who cannot be prosecuted for past crimes, in some cases because evidence may be tainted, but who nonetheless pose a threat to the security of the United States." The Obama administration came to describe this category of detainees as "impossible to try but too dangerous to release." If the "rule of law" means anything, however, it is that the law must be applied consistently and may not be ignored or manipulated to achieve a particular result. Candidate Obama had campaigned on a pledge to restore the rule of law. Adopting a policy to detain individuals *without charge* precisely because there is no lawfully obtained and admissible evidence with which to *charge* them is the antithesis of the rule of law.

- *President Obama rejected calls to prosecute, or at least appoint an independent inquiry to investigate, the torture of detainees during the Bush administration.* When queried about the possible appointment of a special prosecutor to investigate the use of torture during the Bush administration, president-elect Obama stated that it was his "belief that we need to look forward as opposed to looking backwards." And in April 2009, when President Obama approved the release of the so-called "torture memos" issued during the Bush administration, he "assure[d] those who carried out their duties relying in good faith upon legal advice from the Department of Justice that they will not be subject to prosecution," stating that "nothing will be gained by spending our time and energy laying blame for the past." Again, a bedrock principle of our system of justice is that no person is above the law and that the criminal laws apply equally to all. High-ranking members of the Bush administration may or may not have violated the law in authorizing the use of torture. But President Obama's policy of "looking forward"—of ignoring possible crimes by high-ranking officials because it was politically expedient to do so—is anathema to the rule of law.

- *The Obama administration broadly invoked the "state secrets" doctrine to forestall litigation seeking redress for torture.* Candidate Obama had decried the Bush administration's practice of "extraordinary rendition"—transferring detainees for interrogation to countries whose authoritarian regimes were known to engage in torture—as the "outsourcing of torture." Candidate Obama had also promised to restore transparency to government, and criticized the Bush administration's broad invocation of the "state secrets" doctrine to obtain dismissal of litigation challenging government actions on the ground that the very subject of the litigation was a "state secret." But in 2009, in *Mohammed v. Jeppesen Dataplan, Inc.*, a case brought by foreign nationals who claimed they were victims of extraordinary rendition and torture at secret detention facilities in other countries, the Obama administration, like the Bush administration, argued that the case should be dismissed under the "state secrets" doctrine. The Obama administration likewise invoked the "state secrets" doctrine in 2009 to seek dismissal of litigation challenging the NSA's warrantless surveillance program.

- *The Obama administration argued that U.S. courts do not have jurisdiction to hear habeas corpus petitions brought by detainees held at Bagram Airfield Military Base in Afghanistan.* When President Obama took office, his administration also had to address pending habeas corpus litigation brought on behalf of detainees held by the United States at Bagram Airfield Military Base. Citing the executive orders issued by President Obama, the district court in the Bagram litigation asked whether the new administration intended to change the government's position that the court had no jurisdiction to hear the Bagram detainees' habeas cases. In February 2009, the Obama administration responded: "Having considered the matter, the government adheres to its previously articulated position." Two months later, the district court rejected that position, explaining that "these petitioners are virtually identical to the detainees in *Boumediene*—they are non-citizens who were (as alleged here) apprehended in foreign lands

far from the United States and brought to yet another country for detention. And as in *Boumediene*, these petitioners have been determined to
be 'enemy combatants,' a status they contest." The Obama administration
appealed, arguing, as the Bush administration had done, that the detainees
at Bagram had no right to challenge their detention in U.S. courts. In June
2008, candidate Obama had praised the Supreme Court's *Boumediene* decision as "a rejection of the Bush Administration's attempt to create a legal
black hole at Guantánamo." Now, the Obama administration was attempting to legitimate just such a "legal black hole" at Bagram.*

* * *

There were so many things that I admired about the Obama campaign
in 2008—the way it encouraged and empowered ordinary people to participate in the political process; the way it refused to cede states (like
Indiana) or ideas (like patriotism) to the Republicans; and the way it
seemed always to be proactive in defining the issues that it would talk
about. But President Obama has often seemed the antithesis of candidate Obama—indecisive, in retreat, unwilling to speak up for basic
principles, and utterly *reactive*. Even worse, his administration has
become a proponent of policies directly antithetical to those he staked
out during the campaign. In writing this piece, it was painful to confront
the juxtaposition between candidate Obama's personal and powerful
defense of habeas corpus—by saying that it is necessary to make sure
you have the right person, because you might think you have "Barack
the bomb thrower, but it's Barack the guy running for president"—and
his abandonment of those principles once he occupied the White House.

The president's apologists have argued—and no doubt will continue
to argue long after he has left office—that Obama did the best he could
in the face of unprecedented opposition from the Republicans in Congress. But as the timeline of his first year in office shows, whatever opposition he might have faced in *other* policy areas, with respect to many

*Editor's note: In 2010, the U.S. Court of Appeals for the D.C. Circuit ruled that Bagram detainees
had no right to habeas corpus and could not challenge their detention in U.S. courts.

fundamental "rule of law" issues, the fault for Obama's failure to bring about change lies not in his stars, but in Obama himself.

NOTES

1 Two years later, in *Boumediene v. Bush*, the Supreme Court held the jurisdictional provision unconstitutional.

2 I discuss this period in greater detail in *The Guantánamo Lawyers: Inside a Prison outside the Law* (New York: New York University Press, 2009), 200–218.

3

President Obama's Failure to Transfer Detainees from Guantánamo

J. WELLS DIXON

Introduction

In 2007, the Center for Constitutional Rights (CCR) committed to represent and free Algerian citizen Djamel Ameziane from the horrors of Guantánamo Bay. It was clear from our first meeting with him, in a tiny windowless room in Camp 6, which the detainees refer to as a "tomb above the ground," that he was not a terrorist or terrorist sympathizer. It was an essential fact that the Bush administration would later concede to us and to the federal court in 2008, together with a promise to transfer him expeditiously. The Obama administration cleared Ameziane for release again through an interagency review process in 2009, and reiterated that he would be released as soon as possible. It used this promise successfully to convince the court, over our objections, to stay his habeas case and forestall a ruling on the legality of his detention. But it was also a truth that the government struggled successfully to keep secret from the public until 2012, more than three years into President Obama's first term in office, and more than two years after his deadline to close Guantánamo, as Ameziane continued to languish in prison with his case suspended indefinitely and no practical ability to challenge his detention. For despite the president's purported desire to shutter the prison, he inexplicably fought CCR all the way to the U.S. Supreme Court to prevent Ameziane from simply saying to the world, "I am cleared for release," and using that one piece of information to advocate for his transfer to a country other than Algeria, where the government wanted to send him but where he feared persecution.

It was in this context, without meaningful access to the court and without the ability to answer the one question that nearly every foreign diplomat wanted to know—i.e., was Ameziane approved for transfer—that CCR undertook an extensive campaign to find a new home for our client. It was an effort spanning seven years and involving Ameziane's attorneys and other advocates in multiple countries, as well as his family members, several international human rights organizations, and government officials from countries as far afield as Algeria, Canada, Chile, and most of the European Union member states. It was a process that did not end as Ameziane had hoped, but one that exposed a series of costly missteps and lost opportunities by President Obama to repatriate and resettle detainees, and ultimately to close Guantánamo.

The Perfect Resettlement Candidate

In a strategically coordinated effort led in large part by Ameziane's London-based barristers Sophie Weller and Jennifer Oscroft, together with his Canadian attorney Andrew Brouwer and his Latin America–focused counsel Francisco Quintana and Charles Abbott, my CCR colleagues and I canvassed the world for several years looking for a country to resettle Ameziane. We needed to find somewhere other than the United States or Algeria, where he feared persecution—a fear based on his ethnic Berber minority status and reinforced by repeated threats from his interrogators to send him home to face torture—to offer him refuge so that he could rebuild his life after Guantánamo. We were supported in this effort by many human rights advocates and organizations including Reprieve, Human Rights Watch, the Canadian Council for Refugees, and the Anglican Diocese of Montreal, to name a few, and we were very successful—or so it would seem until the bitter end. Ameziane was an easy sell for third-country resettlement, and there were few foreign officials who could not be convinced, cajoled, charmed, or otherwise persuaded through relentless efforts to inquire with the U.S. government about his possible resettlement, which was all we could do given that we lacked the authority or ability actually to negotiate a detainee transfer on behalf of the United States.

Ameziane's story was one to which many people could relate. It was the classic refugee flight from violence and instability in search of a better life. It was the journey of Odysseus, ten years adrift from the chaos of war and searching for home, an ideal, although unlike the Greek hero Ameziane was not a warrior. He was born into a large, close-knit Berber family that originates from the mountainous Kabylie region of Algeria. He was raised and educated in Algiers, and worked as a hydraulics technician after graduating from college. As documented in numerous news stories, including a series in the *Toronto Star* by Canadian journalist Michelle Shephard, and a series in *Profil* magazine by Austrian journalists Gunther Muller and Martin Staudinger, Ameziane was forced to flee Algeria in the early 1990s to avoid a civil war that resulted in more than 100,000 casualties. He traveled to Vienna, Austria, where he obtained a work permit and sold newspapers near the opera house, and where he later washed dishes and ultimately became the head chef at Al Caminetto, a well-known Italian restaurant that still serves outstanding pasta dishes in Vienna's First District. But following the election of a new government in 1995, Ameziane was unable to renew his work permit and remain in Austria.

Fearing continuing turmoil in Algeria, he traveled to Canada and immediately sought political asylum upon arrival at the Toronto airport. He then settled into life in Canada, working and living in Montreal, while his asylum application was considered. In 2000, however, his application was denied and he was forced once again to uproot his life and leave the country he had made his home for five years. Displaced, still fearful of being returned to Algeria, and, perceiving that he had few options after eight years of being denied refuge time and again, he fled to Afghanistan a few months before the September 11 attacks. After the U.S. invasion and the start of the war, he fled Afghanistan with thousands of other refugees, crossing the border into Pakistan. He was rounded up by a local tribe that turned him over to Pakistani authorities, who then sold him to U.S. forces, reportedly for a bounty of $5,000.

Ameziane was sent to the U.S. airbase in Kandahar, Afghanistan, and eventually to Guantánamo. He arrived in February 2002, and was initially held in the open-air cages of Camp X-Ray, notorious for their resemblance to dog kennels. There he was threatened by his captors with rendition to Algeria to face torture, an interrogation tactic that continued throughout most of his time in the prison. He was a casualty of a war in which he had no part and wanted no part.

In February 2005, shortly after CCR won the case *Rasul v. Bush* in the U.S. Supreme Court, which established the right of Guantánamo detainees to challenge their detention in federal court, Ameziane filed a habeas case challenging his indefinite detention. But by the time that CCR took over his representation, the question of whether he was lawfully detained had become less important than where he would be sent when he was released. As the government explained to the court in a sealed filing in 2008, Ameziane's detention was "no longer at issue" and "the only issue truly remaining [wa]s the country to which [he] should be sent." The government admitted that there were no longer any "military rationales" for his continued detention, and promised that "steps [were] [being] taken to arrange for the end of such custody." The government wanted to force him to return to his home country, however, where he feared persecution, and it wanted to do so in secret. Indeed, the Bush administration tried to force him back to Algeria in 2008, but the transfer was blocked by the court due in part to Ameziane's persecution fears. None of this was revealed publicly until 2012, however, when the U.S. Court of Appeals for the D.C. Circuit unsealed the legal documents. CCR needed to find another country to safely resettle Ameziane or he would remain at Guantánamo indefinitely.

A Promising Start to Guantánamo Closure

At the time President Obama entered the White House in 2009, Ameziane was one of several dozen men remaining at the prison who needed to be resettled in other countries due to credible fears of torture and persecution in their home countries. Most of these men were from Central Asia (notably Uyghurs and Uzbeks) and North Africa (notably Algerians, Libyans, and Tunisians), as well as several Syrians, a handful of Palestinians, and an assortment of others. Whereas the Bush administration had sometimes forcibly repatriated detainees to their home countries with seeming indifference to (if not because of) their poor human rights records, President Obama's election offered these men hope—hope that they would be granted refuge so that they could begin the slow process of restarting their lives in peace after years of indefinite detention and abuse at Guantánamo. Although the Obama administration started off well in terms of transfers, including resettlements, the hopes of these men—including Algerians like Ameziane, who would ultimately be callously returned to the one place they did not want to be sent—were soon dashed.

By the time President Obama was elected in 2008, both Democratic and Republican leadership in Washington recognized that the closure of Guantánamo was a moral imperative and necessary to safeguard the national security and foreign policy interests of the United States. President Obama had campaigned for office in part on a promise to close Guantánamo. As he explained early in his first term in office at a speech at the National Archives in Washington, "instead of serving as a tool to counter terrorism, Guantánamo became a symbol that helped Al Qaeda recruit terrorists to its cause. Indeed, the existence of Guantánamo likely created more terrorists around the world than it ever detained." President George W. Bush, the architect of indefinite detention at Guantánamo, had also come to recognize the need to close the prison by the end of his presidency, as had Republican Senator John McCain, who, while campaigning against then Senator Obama for the White House in 2008, stated that he "strongly" favored closing the prison because it was a negative "symbol" of U.S. torture and abuse of prisoners that served as a recruiting tool for terrorists.

It therefore came as no surprise that President Obama started out strongly on Guantánamo, issuing a series of executive orders on his second day in office that prohibited torture, established an interagency task force to review each detainee remaining at Guantánamo, and mandated closure of the prison within one year. CCR was highly critical of the one-year time frame, believing that the prison could be closed in a matter of months. Indeed, in retrospect it could have been closed sooner had the president not lacked the political fortitude and leadership necessary to accomplish this important goal. But there is little dispute that he started out in the right direction on Guantánamo closure issues in the first few months of his administration, and achieved some successes during his first two years in office.

Among the series of orders that President Obama signed on his second day in office was Executive Order 13492, which mandated a baseline review of each detainee remaining at Guantánamo, many of whom, like Ameziane, had already been approved for transfer by the Bush administration. The baseline review was conducted by a new interagency task force comprised of every U.S. military, intelligence, and law enforcement agency with a stake in Guantánamo, including the CIA, FBI, Defense Department, Justice Department, and Homeland Security Department. The task force reviewed each detainee's case over the course of a year and determined whether that person should be approved for transfer, held in continued "law of war detention," or prosecuted. Each decision had to be unanimous.

According to the final report of the Guantanamo Review Task Force, issued January 22, 2010, exactly one year after President Obama's executive order creating the task force was signed, 240 detainees were subject to the review. The task force unanimously approved 126 men for release, including Ameziane; referred 44 men for prosecution in federal court or before military commissions; and designated 48 men for continued indefinite detention under the laws of war. An additional 30 detainees from Yemen were slated for "conditional" detention, meaning they could be released when the security situation in their home country improved. In order for a detainee to be eligible for resettlement specifically, he had to be either (a) cleared for transfer by the task force, which meant that the task force had concluded unanimously that the individual did not pose an unmitigated risk of future harm to the U.S. or its allies, or (b) ordered released by a U.S. court on the ground that he was not part of the Taliban or Al Qaeda or associated groups engaged in hostilities against the U.S. or its allies. In either case, there had to be a determination that the individual posed no future threat to the U.S. or the resettlement country.

By the time the task force issued its report, 44 of the 126 men approved for transfer had already been transferred from Guantánamo to countries other than the United States, including a number of men who were resettled in third countries due to fears of persecution and other concerns. Notable among them was Algerian citizen Lakhdar Boumediene, lead petitioner in the 2008 Supreme Court case *Boumediene v. Bush*, which held that the right of Guantánamo detainees to challenge their detention through habeas corpus was rooted in the U.S. Constitution and thus could not be eliminated by Congress. Boumediene himself was resettled in France in May 2009, in a move that French president Nicholas Sarkozy reportedly intended to curry favor with President Obama and upstage other European allies that had thus far refused to accept within their borders anyone from Guantánamo. Among those who had not yet been resettled in Europe were a small number of Uyghurs captured by mistake, who could not be returned safely to China, and whom the Bush administration had also refused to allow into the United States despite their exoneration by a federal court.* France's acceptance of Boumediene was also a move that would quickly set the stage for a Europe-wide effort to resettle detainees and help President Obama close the prison.

Another 23 men were transferred over the course of the next year. All told, between January 22, 2009, and January 22, 2011, the Obama administration transferred 67 detainees to 24 different countries, including 40 detainees resettled in third countries. The countries that accepted detainees for resettlement included for the most part European Union

---

*Editor's note: The plight of the Uyghurs is discussed in Sabin Willett's "Twelve Years After," chapter 1 in this volume.

member states such as France, Spain, Portugal, Germany, Ireland, Italy, Belgium, Sweden, Hungary, Latvia, Slovakia, and the United Kingdom. In addition, several small island nations graciously offered refuge to detained men, including Cape Verde, which accepted a Syrian refugee, and Bermuda and Palau, which each accepted several of the Uyghurs whom both the Bush administration and, by that point, the Obama administration refused to shelter. Albania and Switzerland likewise agreed to resettle Uyghurs.

Unfortunately, the Obama administration did not do everything that it reasonably could to transfer detainees from Guantánamo. As CCR and its allies witnessed during our efforts to find safe refuge for Ameziane and other Algerians who feared persecution in their home country, several viable resettlement opportunities were squandered by the United States during the 2009–2011 period. Notably, in January 2010, CCR and its allies approached Luxembourg about the possibility of resettling Ameziane and another Algerian prisoner, Ahmed Belbacha. Those discussions continued for several months to the point where Luxembourg expressed a strong interest in resettling Ameziane. Notwithstanding our inability to say publicly that Ameziane was approved for transfer, as that information was still sealed at the time, Luxembourg was keen to offer him safe refuge because of a combination of unique factors, including Ameziane's ability to speak French, English, and some German, the three official languages of Luxembourg, as well as his higher education, his lengthy employment history, his lack of a criminal record, and the fact that he was single with no dependents. But as press reports from that time period recount, the U.S. government rebuffed Luxembourg's inquiries about resettling Algerians—a fate that would also befall the Algerian detainees with other possible resettlement countries.

As Ambassador Daniel Fried, special envoy for the closure of the Guantánamo Bay detention facility at the U.S. State Department, explained in a then-sealed declaration to the federal court in support of the Obama administration's bid to keep Ameziane's clearance for transfer secret, the U.S. government was purportedly concerned that there were a limited number of opportunities to resettle detainees in Europe. It did not want to use up a potential slot for a detainee like Ameziane, whom the government was content to forcibly return to Algeria despite his persecution fears. This scarcity rationale would eventually give way where the potential resettlement country, Luxembourg in this case, expressed an interest in resettling only a particular detainee such as Ameziane. More likely at issue, at least with respect to the Algerians, was a second concern expressed in Ambassador Fried's declaration: the U.S. government did not want to cause "friction" with "important bilateral and strategic relationship" partners even if it might be unsafe to return detainees to those countries. Thus, in one sense, reading between the lines, the U.S. government plainly appeared to be more concerned about upsetting its relations with authoritarian regimes like Algeria than it was about maximizing its opportunities to safely transfer detainees from Guantánamo and close the prison.

It was a phenomenon that would play out publicly over the course of the next several years, particularly with the forced return of several Algerians to Algeria despite their viable opportunities for safe resettlement elsewhere. In July 2010, for example, President Obama forcibly sent home Algerian detainee Abdul Aziz Naji, despite his pending request for political asylum in Switzerland and fears of persecution at home—fears that were subsequently realized when he was jailed in a sham trial at which no evidence was presented against him by the prosecution. It was a transfer that the *New York Times* editorial board called "an act of cruelty that seems to defy explanation." Another Algerian, Farhi Saeed bin Mohammed, was similarly forcibly returned to his home country in January 2011, although he has fared better than Naji. And eventually, in what the *New York Times* editorial board called a "perverse move," Ameziane and fellow Algerian detainee Belkacem Bensayah were forcibly repatriated to Algeria in December 2013, notwithstanding the opportunity to resettle Ameziane in Luxembourg and Bensayah's desire to rejoin his family in Europe, with whom he feared he would never be reunited.

President Obama Loses the Initiative on Guantánamo Closure

President Obama's failure to take advantage of viable opportunities to resettle these men was simply one of his many missteps and lost opportunities to close Guantánamo. It was part of an unfortunate pattern that began early in his administration and has continued in recent years.

The president began to lose the initiative on Guantánamo issues by mid-2009, due to a series of errant political calculations and a lack of willingness to do what was necessary to close the prison, which the president nonetheless continued to claim was in the national security interest of the United States. In his May 2009 speech at the National Archives, President Obama reaffirmed his promise to close the prison, but embraced the concepts of military commissions and indefinite detention despite earlier campaign promises to dismantle these vestiges of the prior administration's lawlessness. Around the same time, President Obama lost his nerve and abandoned plans to resettle some of the Uyghur prisoners in the United States when word leaked to Congress and sparked a political backlash. It was a loss that Ambassador Fried reportedly warned would make it more difficult to transfer detainees to other potential host countries, which routinely asked—and still to this day ask—why they should resettle anyone the United States itself is unwilling to accept.

As the year continued, President Obama's resolve to close Guantánamo continued to weaken. On Christmas Day 2009, Nigerian citizen Umar Farouk Abdulmutallab attempted to crash a Detroit-bound airliner with a bomb hidden in his underwear. On January 5, 2010, in response to a political backlash caused by reports that Abdulmutallab had been trained in Yemen, President Obama imposed a moratorium on all transfers from Guantánamo to that country. Although the moratorium was partially lifted in July 2010 to allow the repatriation of Yemeni detainee Mohammed Odaini, pursuant to a court order of release, at the time of this writing no other Yemeni citizen has been released from

Guantánamo to Yemen since the ban was imposed, and there is no indication that will change in the near future.

In addition, on January 5, 2010, the U.S. Court of Appeals for the D.C. Circuit issued a decision in the case *Al-Bihani v. Obama*, which was the first appellate ruling to address the merits of a Guantánamo detainee's challenge to the legality of his detention. The decision substantially altered and strengthened the government's detention authority by concluding, among other things, that international law was not binding in U.S. courts and that detainees could be held indefinitely on the thinnest of evidence that they were part of Al Qaeda, the Taliban, or "associated forces" engaged in hostilities against the United States. The ruling was soon followed by other court of appeals decisions that, if not overtly hostile to detainee claims, collectively had the effect of authorizing the government to hold detainees indefinitely, potentially for life, based on little more than its own say-so that they were terrorists at some point in the past. The president thus had little incentive by the end of 2010 to work expeditiously to transfer detainees and fulfill his promise to close the prison. Instead, while his administration continued as vigorously as the prior administration had to fight detainee cases in the courts, the president largely turned his back on Guantánamo and the men who had reportedly cheered his name on the night he was elected president.

The Forgotten Years: 2011–2013

By early 2011, President Obama had all but abandoned efforts to close Guantánamo. Farhi Saeed bin Mohammed was forcibly repatriated to Algeria on January 7, 2011, and would essentially become the last detainee the administration voluntarily transferred out of the prison until 2013.

As the president surrendered the field on Guantánamo, his political opponents in Congress saw an opportunity to take the initiative and undermine his promise to close the prison in order to gain partisan advantage. On the same day that Mohammed was forcibly returned to Algeria, Congress stepped in to fill the void and enacted—with President Obama's acquiescence and ultimate signature—the 2011 National Defense Authorization Act (NDAA). The NDAA contained a requirement that, absent very limited circumstances such as a court order of release, the administration had to issue written certifications prior to transferring detainees from Guantánamo. The certification requirements were practically, if not by design, impossible to satisfy because they effectively required the secretary of defense to guarantee personally in writing that no detainee who was transferred would ever do anything in the future that was contrary to the interests of the United States or its allies. The restrictions were extended for a year with passage of the 2012 NDAA on December 31, 2011, albeit with a new provision that allowed the administration to waive certain objectionable parts of the certification requirements. The certification and waiver provisions were further extended by the 2013 NDAA on January 3, 2013. But not until mid-2013 did the administration attempt either to certify or waive certification for any detainee transfer—and even then, it did so only for transfers to Algeria, Sudan, and Saudi Arabia, authoritarian regimes that were willing to do the administration's bidding and impose harsh restrictions on former detainees.

Rather, for most of the 2011–2013 period, the president was content to issue meaningless signing statements criticizing the transfer restrictions and to blame Congress for his failure to close the prison. He disingenuously claimed that Congress had barred all transfers, which was not what it had done (although it had surely attempted to interfere with the president's ability to transfer detainees held in military custody for the first time in U.S. history by making the transfer process as burdensome as possible). It was not until enactment of the 2014 NDAA on December 26, 2013, that Congress finally did away with the certification requirements for transfer, replacing them with requirements that the administration consider certain factors, make certain risk determinations, and provide notice to Congress before transferring detainees. As would become clear, however, not even that favorable change in the law would be enough to restart transfers in a meaningful way.

Faced with the president's unwillingness to expend the political capital needed to address the plight of the detainees and transfer men his administration did not want to continue to detain, congressional obstruction of even the minimal efforts by the White House to close the prison, and the D.C. Circuit's overt hostility to detainee legal challenges, CCR continued throughout 2011–2013 to develop opportunities to resettle detainees such as Ameziane. Yet following the failure to resettle him in Luxembourg and a series of other missed opportunities by the administration to reduce the prison population substantially, many European allies—even France, which had led resettlement efforts during the early years of the Obama administration—appeared to give up hope that President Obama would finally close Guantánamo and to turn away from the prospect of resettling additional detainees. Europe, it seemed, was finished with trying to help a U.S. president who did not appear to take full advantage of its assistance and no longer appeared invested in closing Guantánamo.

As a consequence, and because there remained more than a dozen detainees who needed resettlement, CCR expanded its efforts to generate resettlement opportunities in Latin America. CCR appealed directly to several countries in Central and South America, as well as the Caribbean, to consider taking in Ameziane and other detainees, including in particular Brazil, Chile, Costa Rica, and Uruguay. We also appealed to various member states of the Organization of American States through the Inter-American Commission on Human Rights, which in March 2012 accepted jurisdiction over a human rights petition and request for precautionary measures filed by Ameziane in 2008, seeking to avoid forced repatriation to Algeria. We did so in part because we believed then, as now, that Latin American countries would be receptive to resettling detainees as a profound humanitarian gesture, especially in light of some of their own histories with indefinite military detention and abuse, and as an expression of their close partnerships and strong alliances with the United States and President Obama personally. As in Europe, we were successful in generating interest among various Latin American countries in resettling detainees. But also as in Europe, the Obama administration continued to rebuff resettlement opportunities that we generated and appeared uninterested in transferring anyone from Guantánamo. At the time of writing, the only detainees who have been transferred to Latin America are two Uyghurs resettled in El Salvador in April 2012, finally fulfilling a 2008 court order to release them, and six men from Syria, Tunisia, and Palestine, who were resettled in Uruguay in December 2014.

In the two years that followed Farhi Saeed bin Mohammed's transfer to Algeria in January 2011, only four detainees would leave the prison alive: the two Uyghurs who were sent to El Salvador and two detainees who had pled guilty before military commissions and were sent home to Sudan and Canada after completing their sentences. Three other men died in prison during the same period, including Yemeni detainee Adnan Farhan Abdul Latif, who had been approved for transfer four times by the Bush and Obama administrations. Neither administration was willing to send him home despite his clearance, ostensibly because his home country was too unstable, and each administration continued to oppose his court challenges to the legality of his detention. President Obama, in particular, relentlessly pursued an appeal of a district court ruling granting Latif's habeas petition and ordering his release, even though the president had cleared him for release. Although he had acquiesced to a similar habeas ruling and sent Mohammed Odaini home to Yemen in 2010, President Obama knew by now that the D.C. Circuit would reverse virtually any ruling in favor of a detainee. Indeed, that is precisely what happened when Latif's release order was overturned by the D.C. Circuit, and the Supreme Court denied further review in 2012. Latif reportedly killed himself in despair at this turn of events; how he died remains unknown, but there is no dispute that Guantánamo and President Obama's refusal to transfer him killed him.

The Fleeting Resumption of Transfers

Adnan Latif's death was a natural and entirely predictable reaction to the president's failure to transfer detainees, most of whom his own administration had unanimously cleared for release years earlier, and reflected the human tragedy that continued to unfold as a consequence throughout the president's first term in office. Adding to the growing despair of the men who remained trapped in indefinite detention, most with the bittersweet knowledge that no one really thought they were terrorists or should continue to be detained, the Obama administration shut down Ambassador Fried's office at the State Department in January 2013. The irony of shutting down the one office dedicated solely to closing the prison was not lost on the detainees. The detainees were also acutely aware when the newly reelected president failed to mention Guantánamo in his January 2013 inauguration speech or in his State of the Union address to Congress in February 2013. Again, the results were plainly foreseeable.

February 2013 saw the beginning of a mass hunger strike by the men detained at Guantánamo. Sparked by detainee claims that authorities at the prison had mishandled copies of the Koran, the detainees' anger, frustration, and disappointment at the president's failure to close the prison caused them such despair that they began to starve themselves— some, eventually, to the brink of death. They saw no other way out of Guantánamo. As Marine Corps General John Kelly, commander of the U.S. Southern Command that oversees Guantánamo, testified before the House Armed Services Committee on March 20, 2013, the fundamental cause of the hunger strike was that the detainees "had great optimism that Guantánamo would be closed," and "were devastated when the president backed off . . . of closing the facility." In response to the strike, which soon began to spiral out of control, the military cracked down and imposed severe restrictions on conditions of confinement, including nearly round-the-clock, single-cell isolation and highly offensive genital searches of any detainee coming or going from the cell blocks, including to receive telephone calls from his attorney. Thus, by April 2012, the hunger strike exploded to the point where well more than a hundred detainees—two thirds of the population—were starving themselves, and dozens were being force-fed in violation of international medical ethical standards.

Faced with an avalanche of public criticism and the prospect that additional detainees would die as Adnan Latif had months earlier, President Obama was forced to return his attention to Guantánamo. In a May 2013 speech at the National Defense University, the president acknowledged that the prison had "become a symbol around the world for an America that flouts the rule of law." He restated his commitment to closing Guantánamo, but once again tried to blame Congress for his failure: "I have tried to close GTMO. I transferred 67 detainees to other countries before Congress imposed restrictions to effectively prevent us from . . . transferring detainees. . . . These restrictions make no sense." He was promptly challenged by audience member Medea Benjamin, co-founder of CODEPINK, a social justice organization that had long advocated for closing Guantánamo. In a move that prompted both surprise and applause from the CCR conference room in which we watched the president's televised address, she heckled him and demanded that he use his existing power to transfer detainees from the prison. To anyone who saw the reaction on his face, it was obvious that President Obama knew that his attempt to blame Congress for failing to close the prison was unconvincing and inadequate.

The president concluded his address on Guantánamo by appointing new envoys from the Departments of Defense and State to close the prison. He also lifted the 2010 moratorium on transfers to Yemen, promising to review them (again) on a case-by-case basis, and committed to transfer cleared detainees to other countries "to the greatest extent possible." Speaking to himself, perhaps more than to the audience, he said:

[H]istory will cast a harsh judgment on this aspect of our fight against terrorism and those of us who fail to end it. Imagine a future—10 years from now or 20 years from now when the United States of America is still holding people who have been charged with no crime on a piece of land that is not part of our country. Look at the current situation, where we are force feeding detainees who are being held on a hunger strike. I'm willing to cut the young lady who interrupted me some slack because it's worth being passionate about. Is this who we are? Is that something our Founders foresaw? Is that the America we want to leave our children? Our sense of justice is stronger than that.

And then nothing happened. It was not until that summer that the president appointed Clifford Sloan and Paul Lewis as special envoys at the State and Defense Departments, respectively, and renewed efforts to transfer detainees began. But those transfers did not all go as expected or hoped. Beginning in the late summer of 2013, two detainees were returned voluntarily to Algeria; they had feared persecution but apparently decided they would rather take their chances with the security services at home than remain in Guantánamo. That transfer was followed in December by the transfer of Ameziane and Bensayah to Algeria, which they vigorously opposed for fear of persecution and despite their other resettlement opportunities. The move caused tremendous controversy and criticism, including strong statements by several international human rights officials when the men disappeared for a time into secret detention. Two other detainees were transferred to Sudan, including one who had pled guilty in a military commission and completed his sentence, and one who was so gravely ill that he could not care for himself. In addition, two detainees were sent to Saudi Arabia, and the last three remaining Uyghurs who had won their court cases in 2008 were resettled in Slovakia. Eleven men in total were transferred in 2013, all of them between August and December.

In the first several months of 2014, six more detainees were released. These men included Algerian Ahmed Belbacha, who had once sought resettlement in Luxembourg with Ameziane. Although he had once feared repatriation due to an in absentia conviction hanging over his head in Algeria, which had been imposed as retribution for publicly expressing a fear of return, he apparently decided in March 2014 that he, too, would rather take his chances at home than remain in prison. Two months later, in what is perhaps the most controversial transfer ever from Guantánamo, five "senior Taliban officials" were resettled in Qatar as part of a prisoner exchange for the return of a U.S. soldier held by the Taliban. In the months that followed, however, despite public statements by Messrs. Sloan and Lewis that they were continuing to make progress toward transferring additional detainees and closing the prison, no one left.*

It was not until seven men were released in November 2014 that transfers resumed in earnest. They included one Kuwaiti who was sent home, three Yemenis resettled in the Republic of Georgia, and a Yemeni and a Tunisian who were resettled in Slovakia. The four resettled Yemenis were the first Yemeni men to leave Guantánamo alive since 2010. Fifteen men were also released in December 2014, including the six men resettled in Uruguay, four Afghanis who were sent home, and three Yemenis and two Tunisians who were resettled in Kazakhstan. The transfer momentum continued into January 2015 with the resettlement of five more Yemenis, four in Oman and one in Estonia.

At the time of writing, however, the secretary of defense has indicated publicly that he has not signed any additional transfer authorizations, and new transfers are not expected in the near future given his announced departure from the Pentagon. Clifford Sloan, the Guantánamo envoy at the State Department, also resigned effective January 1, 2015, to return to his private law practice, and at the time of writing his successor has not been named. As a consequence, notwithstanding the president's repeated promises to close Guantánamo, including a mention during his State of the Union address to Congress in January 2015, there is presently great concern that transfer momentum could be lost as it was in 2010 and 2013, and that there may not be enough time left to

*Editor's note: This transfer is discussed in Frank Goldsmith's "The 'Taliban Five' and the Prisoner Exchange," chapter 10 in this volume.

regain the initiative and close the prison before President Obama leaves office in January 2017.

The Consequences of Failing to Close Guantánamo

With Guantánamo now in its 14th year in operation, the consequences of President Obama's continued failure to close the prison are increasingly grim, especially for the Yemeni men who comprise the clear majority of the remaining detainee population. The men are growing older, and many now suffer from serious medical conditions that remain untreated at the prison; predictably, indications of a new hunger strike are beginning to emerge. But despite the recent increase in transfers and a clear effort by the administration to resettle a modest number of Yemeni men, there do not appear to be many cleared detainees who can expect realistically to be transferred in the near future absent substantial intervention and direction from the White House to the Defense and State Departments to continue the transfer momentum and close the prison.

At the time of writing, there are 122 men who remain indefinitely detained at Guantánamo. Among the current population, 54 men are approved for transfer. Another 35 are slated for continued "law of war detention." There are seven men facing military commission charges, and three who have been convicted or are awaiting sentencing before commissions. The remaining 23 men were referred for prosecution in 2010 by the task force, but are unlikely to be prosecuted, due mainly to the fact that not a single military commission conviction to date has been finally upheld on appeal. Rather, military commission convictions continue to be undone by appeals court rulings.

It is also notable that all of the 122 remaining men are Muslim, and nearly two thirds are from Yemen, including all but a small handful of the cleared men. Indeed, by looking at the raw statistics and considering that no Yemeni detainee has been transferred to Yemen since Mohammed Odaini went home in July 2010, and only a small number of Yemenis have been resettled recently, it is entirely correct and appropriate to conclude that Guantánamo is no longer just a prison for Muslim men, but increasingly a prison for Muslim men *from Yemen*. Like Latif, it is clear that most of these men continue to be detained not because they are terrorists or terrorist sympathizers, but because the administration believes that Yemen is too unstable to accept all of its citizens held in Guantánamo. But even if that were true as a general matter, which is debatable, it hardly explains why not one Yemeni has been sent home since 2010 or why these men have not been resettled in greater numbers over the last several years. To answer President Obama's own question, at present we are a country that indefinitely detainees Muslim men at Guantánamo *based on or because of their Yemeni citizenship*, and this could be the country that he will leave our children.

President Obama's current record on Guantánamo is poor, and there is little basis for optimism, even by comparison to what he inherited from President Bush. At the time of writing, a total of 780 men have been held at the prison since it opened on January 11, 2002. A total of 658 men have since been transferred out, including nine men who died there. The Bush administration transferred 539 men, including five who died, and the Obama administration has transferred 119 men, including four who died and the 44 men transferred since August 2013. Although the two administrations have presided over Guantánamo for close to the same amount of time, the disparity in transfers is staggering by any measure. At least in terms of making progress toward the closure of Guantánamo, President Obama has a long way to go to catch up to President Bush. President Obama has surely had to deal with unprecedented obstacles, including a Congress intent on frustrating his efforts to close the prison for partisan political reasons and a secretary of defense who has been slow to the point of insubordination in signing the necessary paperwork to effectuate transfers, but the president himself has failed to do everything that he reasonably could have done to transfer detainees. CCR will continue its efforts to help him close the prison by traveling the world and generating opportunities to resettle detainees, including Yemenis, but it is imperative that the president take full advantage of these opportunities and transfer men now. Whether President Obama will continue to engage and take concrete steps toward closing the prison remains unknown. What is known is that he is running out of time before the end of his presidency to fulfill his promise to close Guantánamo. If President Obama falters now in his efforts to close the prison, it will surely be as much a part of his legacy as it is of President Bush's.

* * *

As is often the situation with Guantánamo, CCR knew Ameziane would be transferred back to Algeria before it happened, but could not say anything about it. Ameziane also knew in advance, and he did not take the news well. In the last weeks before his transfer, he was in bad shape. Although he had endured Guantánamo remarkably well, and, shockingly, for many years seemed relatively unfazed by everything that had happened to him since he was captured and turned over to U.S. forces in 2002, he had not been well for the last few years. He had participated in the hunger strike over the spring and summer of 2013, during which he lost about 60 pounds and suffered other serious physical ailments. Although he rebounded briefly that August, he never really recovered to the point he was at when CCR first started meeting with him in 2007. He had finally lost all hope, it seemed, and when he learned that he would be transferred to Algeria—the one place in the world he did not want to go—he was devastated.

Thankfully, after a very rough start, he has endured and is doing reasonably well in Algeria. President Obama callously discarded him, confiscating his life savings that he had earned in Canada many years before and leaving him utterly destitute, with little but the prison uniform on his back. But, to their credit, the Algerian authorities so far have not caused him any problems. Ameziane also continues to have the support of CCR and our many allies who advocated for his safe resettlement and spoke out publicly and privately to ensure that he was not mistreated when ultimately sent back to Algeria. He will also forever be grateful to Luxembourg for considering him for resettlement. But nothing can

diminish his great disappointment in the United States, which has continued to demonstrate that it does not care whether it ruins the lives
of the men it has detained at Guantánamo. After years of imprisonment
and abuse at Guantánamo, Ameziane deserved better from the United
States. It was not to be, but perhaps in retrospect Ameziane was lucky to
be one of the few men released from Guantánamo by President Obama.

4

The *Boumediene* Case after the Supreme Court

MARK FLEMING

The Supreme Court's June 2008 decision in *Boumediene v. Bush*, now taught in law school classes across the country, was a landmark constitutional ruling that made it possible for all Guantánamo prisoners to ask a federal judge to hold a habeas corpus proceeding to evaluate the basis for their detention and, if it proved insufficient, to order their release. But the Court gave no guidance on what procedures and standards should be used in such a proceeding, leaving such matters to "the expertise and competence of the District Court to address in the first instance."

In July 2008, in the weeks after the Supreme Court's decision, the district judge to whom the *Boumediene* case was assigned—Judge Richard J. Leon of the U.S. District Court for the District of Columbia—informed us that, consistent with the Supreme Court's directive, he planned to hold hearings in all of his Guantánamo-related cases before the close of 2008. He also said he would start with the *Boumediene* case itself, which had been returned to him from the Supreme Court.

Boumediene promised to be one of the most complex of the Guantánamo habeas cases, not least because it involved six prisoners—six Algerian-born men who had relocated to Bosnia and were living there with their wives and children at the time of the September 11 attacks. All six (Lakhdar Boumediene, Mustafa Ait Idir, Hadj Boudella, Mohamed Nechla, Saber Lahmar, and Belkacem Bensayah) were clients of my law firm, WilmerHale, and we had successfully represented them in the Supreme Court. The government's claim against our clients was that they were part of a Bosnia-based terrorist group that had plotted to attack the U.S. Embassy in Sarajevo shortly after September 11.

We knew from the outset that the government would work as hard as it could to try to convince Judge Leon that our clients were "enemy combatants." This was not only because it was going to be the first Guantánamo case to proceed to the merits, but also because President George W. Bush himself had stated his certainty on the matter. Shortly after our clients arrived at Guantánamo, President Bush mentioned our clients in the first State of the Union address after September 11: "Our soldiers, working with the Bosnian government, seized terrorists who were plotting to bomb our embassy."

Judge Leon set an aggressive schedule for the parties' preparation. The government was ordered to file its "return"—the grounds on which it claimed authority to hold our clients at Guantánamo—on August 22, 2008, and we were required to file our "traverse" (response) on October 17, with a hearing to begin on November 6. The government's return was over 680 pages long, including 130 exhibits. The government also submitted an "*in camera, ex parte* supplemental narrative and supporting materials"—information the government believed Judge Leon could rely on to uphold our clients' detention without even showing it to us and permitting us to respond.

In September 2008, we worked furiously on preparing our traverse. We gathered together documentary evidence from our clients' lives in Bosnia; declarations from their families, employers, and friends; and other information designed to rebut the government's accusations. Much of the government's case was based on raw, unfinished intelligence reports. With Judge Leon's permission, we arranged for three well-respected, highly credentialed intelligence specialists to review the government's classified evidence and provide expert reports explaining how a trained intelligence professional would interpret them, and what inferences could (and could not) be drawn from that evidence. We also obtained declarations from senior Bosnian officials, who attested that our clients' arrest in Bosnia was not due to any actual suspicion of wrongdoing, but because U.S. officials had threatened the Bosnian government with abandonment of the Bosnian peace process unless our clients were taken into custody.

At the same time, we were making frequent submissions to Judge Leon regarding the framework of the habeas hearing, on which no court had previously opined. We presented detailed briefing and oral argument regarding the appropriate legal standard for finding someone detainable under the laws of war. We sought discovery from the government into the basis for the various assertions it made in its filings. (Most of these requests were denied.) And we argued that Judge Leon should not open the government's "black box" of information that it wanted the court to review without ever allowing us to see it.

On October 17, 2008, we submitted a traverse, setting forth our response to the government's allegations against our clients. It was over 1,600 pages long, including 120 pages of classified legal and factual briefing, 18 expert declarations, several fact declarations, and numerous documentary exhibits obtained through our investigation. We then started to prepare for the habeas hearing, which was scheduled to begin in a few weeks' time.

Interestingly, as the case was prepared, the government dropped the accusation that our clients had plotted to bomb the U.S. Embassy in Sarajevo. Despite that claim's inclusion in the State of the Union address, the government made no effort to prove it. Instead, the government focused on accusing our clients of intending to travel to Afghanistan to fight against U.S. and coalition forces.

On November 6, 2008—two days after Barack Obama won the presidential election—the habeas hearing in *Boumediene v. Bush* began with unclassified opening statements. Judge Leon had ordered that the unclassified openings be relayed by a secure telephone connection to Guantánamo, where our clients had been assembled in two rooms to hear the statements and receive a version translated into Arabic. Although Judge Leon was clear that he wanted our clients to receive a simultaneous translation, technical errors by officials at Guantánamo prevented our clients from hearing the original or translated opening statements live. After Judge Leon expressed his extreme displeasure, the government arranged to have the recorded openings translated and presented to our clients the following day.

The courtroom was cleared after the unclassified opening statements, and the hearing then proceeded in an entirely closed courtroom. The parties first presented classified opening statements to Judge Leon, and then proceeded to go through the government's allegations one by one. The government offered no live witnesses, and the only witnesses Judge Leon allowed us to present were our clients. Mustafa Ait Idir and Hadj Boudella testified by videolink from Guantánamo and were subject to cross-examination by a government lawyer in Washington.

On November 11, 2008, after the government had argued its entire case, Judge Leon announced that the government was "not clearly in a zone" where it had proven the lawfulness of any of our clients' detention. Over our objection, he invited the government to put on a "rebuttal" case, and the government promptly took advantage, submitting 20 new documents, most of which we had never seen before and (as Judge Leon later confirmed) "focused primarily on evidence relating to Mr. Bensayah." We urged that we needed more time to investigate and respond to the government's new documents; Judge Leon ruled that "a day and a half" was enough. We asked for further discovery regarding the new material; Judge Leon ruled that "[d]iscovery is over." We attempted to file what further evidence we could locate in time as a response to the "rebuttal" case; Judge Leon excluded it, stating that we had no right to "surrebuttal." Judge Leon's rulings did not bode well for Mr. Bensayah.

The case closed on November 14 with classified closing arguments. Judge Leon directed the parties to return on November 20, when he promised to render his decision. Then, in a courteous and uncommon gesture, Judge Leon descended from the bench and shook hands with all counsel, thanking both sides for a well-presented case.

On November 20—barely four months after the Supreme Court's decision in *Boumediene*—we gathered in the ceremonial courtroom in

Washington's federal courthouse. The house was packed, not just with our legal team and other detainee counsel, but also with numerous attorneys from the Departments of Justice and Defense, as well as other government entities. Judge Leon took the bench and delivered his opinion, in which he ruled that he was granting the writ of habeas corpus to five of our six clients.

Judge Leon noted that the government's assertion that our clients "had a plan to travel to Afghanistan to engage U.S. and allied forces" relied exclusively on information in a "classified document from an unnamed source." Judge Leon ruled that the government had failed to provide him with "enough information to adequately evaluate the credibility and reliability of this source's information." He noted that while the source's information "was undoubtedly sufficient for the intelligence purposes for which it was prepared, it is *not* sufficient for the purposes for which a habeas court must now evaluate it"—whether to uphold our clients' continued indefinite imprisonment.

However, Judge Leon denied relief as to Mr. Bensayah, ruling that the government had provided "credible and reliable evidence linking Mr. Bensayah to al-Qaida and, more specifically, to a senior al-Qaida facilitator." He also concluded that Mr. Bensayah intended to "facilitat[e] the travel of others to join the fight," which he believed qualified as "support" for Al Qaeda, which in turn justified detention under the legal standard he had adopted.

Judge Leon then took an extraordinary step. He turned to the government lawyers in the courtroom, who represented the president who had appointed him to the bench, and urged them not to appeal:

> The Court appreciates fully that the government has a right to appeal its decision as to these five detainees whose petitions I have granted. I have a right, too, to appeal to the senior-most leadership at the Department of Justice, Department of Defense, and the CIA and other intelligence agencies. My appeal to them is to strongly urge them to take a hard look at the evidence, both presented and lacking, as to these five detainees. Seven

years of waiting for our legal system to give them an answer to a question so important, in my judgment, is more than plenty.

The government took Judge Leon's advice and did not appeal. By the end of 2008, three of our clients (Messrs. Ait Idir, Boudella, and Nechla) had been reunited with their families in Bosnia, and by the end of 2009—following intricate diplomatic talks—Messrs. Boumediene and Lahmar were accepted for resettlement by the government of France.

We appealed Judge Leon's decision regarding Mr. Bensayah to the U.S. Court of Appeals for the D.C. Circuit. Our appeal raised several issues, some of them particular to the case against Mr. Bensayah. We argued that the government's raw intelligence reports failed to show that he "intended" to facilitate anyone's travel, much less to do so for Al Qaeda's benefit. We also argued that, even if Mr. Bensayah "intended" to facilitate the travel of others to Afghanistan, that would not make him a detainable "enemy combatant," particularly where there was no evidence that any others actually planned to travel.

We also appealed regarding issues that had the potential to affect other cases, such as the impropriety of allowing the government to ambush the prisoner with "rebuttal" evidence to which no response was permitted; the low standard of proof ("preponderance of the evidence," which is typically used in garden-variety civil cases, not matters involving individual liberty) that Judge Leon had ruled sufficed to justify Mr. Bensayah's detention; and the government's claim of authority to detain anyone who "supported" Al Qaeda, even if unintentionally or in a way completely unrelated to combat. This last issue—defining the limits of the government's power to detain—apparently created a sharp division in the new Obama administration. According to a report later published in the *New York Times*, State Department attorneys contended that mere "support" for an enemy force, the standard adopted by Judge Leon, was insufficient to justify detention at Guantánamo; rather, a prisoner would have to be either "part of" Al Qaeda or directly participating in hostilities on its side. The Defense Department, by contrast, argued for a more flexible definition.

The government's reassessment of its detention authority produced a surprising filing two days before oral argument in Mr. Bensayah's appeal, when the government filed a letter with the court announcing that it would not defend the "support" standard that it had argued to Judge Leon and on which he had relied. Instead, the government argued that Mr. Bensayah's activities should allow the court to infer, using a flexible, fact-specific approach, that he was effectively "part of" Al Qaeda. However, the government made clear that it was "*not* arguing in this case that [the D.C. Circuit] should affirm on the independent ground that the support Bensayah provided to al Qaida rendered him detainable even if he was not functionally part of the organization."

Another surprising event occurred when we unexpectedly received disclosure of significant exculpatory evidence from the government. By sheer coincidence, two of the government attorneys who had litigated Mr. Bensayah's case were later assigned to the case of a different Guantánamo prisoner. In preparing a filing in that case, they came across additional evidence that undermined the government's case against Mr. Bensayah. Acting out of commendable professionalism, they chose to disclose the evidence to us, rather than simply remain silent (in which case we might never have learned of it). We informed the D.C. Circuit of this development, arguing that Guantánamo prisoners should not have to rely on the chance reassignment of government lawyers in order to find out that the government possesses important evidence undermining its position.

I argued Mr. Bensayah's appeal—which by then had been renamed *Bensayah v. Obama*—on September 24, 2009. The courtroom was closed in order to permit discussion of classified evidence, and no public transcript or recording has ever been made available.

On June 28, 2010, the D.C. Circuit issued its decision, reversing Judge Leon's denial of habeas corpus and remanding for further proceedings.

By that time, other panels of the D.C. Circuit had issued decisions in cases that were argued later than Mr. Bensayah's. Those other decisions were all favorable to the government and adverse to Guantánamo prisoners—including upholding the "preponderance" standard of proof and the lawfulness of the Obama administration's slightly modified, but still broad, detention standard. These rulings limited the ability of district judges to rule in favor of detainees, as Judge Leon had done for five of our clients. In Mr. Bensayah's case, the D.C. Circuit also rejected all of our challenges to the conduct of the hearing, including our requests for further discovery and our objections to the government's "rebuttal" case.

However, the D.C. Circuit ruled that, even taking all of the government's evidence on its face, the government had failed to provide sufficient evidence showing that Mr. Bensayah was part of Al Qaeda. "The Government presented no direct evidence of actual communication between Bensayah and any al Qaeda member," and the record did not support the government's allegations that anyone was supposedly planning to travel to Afghanistan with Mr. Bensayah's help. Although the court decided to allow the government a further bite at the apple, it was clear that the government could not rely on its existing evidence "in the absence of additional corroborative evidence not already considered."

Rather than move into a further hearing, we then began efforts to negotiate a diplomatic solution to the case. We engaged in many discussions with the U.S. and foreign governments to procure Mr. Bensayah's resettlement. On December 5, 2013, the U.S. government returned him to Algeria. On February 1, 2014, Judge Leon dismissed Mr. Bensayah's case as moot in light of his release.

Our clients then embarked on the long, difficult road of rebuilding their lives after several years of unjustified, unnecessary detention at our government's hands. *Boumediene v. Bush*, a case that lasted nearly ten years and involved two appeals, a Supreme Court case, and a groundbreaking district court hearing, was finally over.

5

"Too Dangerous to Release"

Debunking the Claim

PARDISS KEBRIAEI

Now, finally, there remains the question of detainees at
Guantánamo who cannot be prosecuted yet who pose a clear
danger to the American people. And I have to be honest
here—this is the toughest single issue that we will face. . . .
Examples of that threat include people who've received extensive explosives training at al Qaeda training camps, or
commanded Taliban troops in battle, or expressed their allegiance to Osama bin Laden, or otherwise made it clear that
they want to kill Americans. These are people who, in effect,
remain at war with the United States.
—Barack Obama, National Archives speech, May 21, 2009

We paused for a baklava break from work and passed the box of Middle Eastern sweets around our small circle, each taking a syrupy pastry.
Ghaleb, we should be having salad, you know. I bit into my dessert and
eyed the nearly empty box, scolding us both for not being more mind-
ful of his diabetes. Ghaleb pointed to my crowded paper plate, elbowing
my colleague for backup. *You're the one who just took two of the biggest
pieces!* They cackled and high-fived in agreement. I rolled my eyes and
took another bite, shielding my second generous helping from scrutiny
with my free hand.

It was an afternoon in April 2014. We were in one of the huts-turned–
legal meeting rooms in the U.S. military prison camp in Guantánamo

Bay, Cuba, letting off steam after a long day of preparation as the AC
churned listlessly. In a few days, my client Ghaleb Al-Bihani, who had
been held in Guantánamo since 2002 without charge—indeed, whom
the government had determined it could not charge yet deemed "too
dangerous to release"—would be appearing before the Obama administration's new Periodic Review Board. While the government believed it
had the legal authority to hold Ghaleb without charge indefinitely, the
board was tasked with determining if his imprisonment was militarily
necessary after 12 years. The review board would decide whether Ghaleb
posed a "continuing significant threat" to the United States and should
remain detained or could be approved for release.

Ghaleb's designation as unchargeable yet potentially forever unre-
leasable came after the Obama administration took office in 2009 and
conducted a fresh examination of all 242 detainees remaining in Guantánamo at the time. Of that population, the administration approved
just over a majority—126—for transfer; referred a minority—44—for
prosecution (although the number to be prosecuted is about half that
today); and placed the rest—48—in a netherworld between charge and
release. For this last category, the administration concluded that its evidence was either insufficient for prosecution or tainted and unreliable,
or that charges weren't available for the alleged conduct, owing in part
to the fact that these detainees had not participated in specific terrorist
plots. For years, the makeup of this group was secret: it was not until
2013, when the government was compelled by a Freedom of Information
Act lawsuit, that it disclosed the identities of the four dozen men it had
officially designated for indefinite detention.

While the government's reasons for these designations remain secret,
the public allegations against Ghaleb mainly concern his role as a cook
in a group allied with the Taliban in its fight against the Northern Alliance in Afghanistan in 2001. Ghaleb had traveled to Afghanistan that
summer, before the United States came into the picture. After the U.S.
bombing campaign began in October, the group of about 150 men surrendered to the Northern Alliance and subsequently disbanded. That

conduct was ostensibly enough not only for the U.S. government, but also for the courts to justify Ghaleb's perpetual imprisonment. As the district court stated in denying his habeas corpus petition in 2008, "helping to prepare the meals" of the unit's fighting forces was "more than sufficient" to justify a potential life sentence.

For a long time, it was not clear whether or when the administration intended to revisit the status of men it was holding in this particular limbo—"forever detainees," as some called them. In March 2011, President Obama issued an executive order establishing the Periodic Review Board to reevaluate—every three years—these detainees to determine if their detentions were still necessary, ordering initial reviews of the whole group within one year from the date of the order. But by then, Guantánamo's closure no longer held the same priority for the administration. Congress had just passed new restrictions on detainee transfers, bringing to a grinding halt the administration's steady stream of releases in 2009 and 2010, and thwarting its plans to close the prison. The U.S. Court of Appeals for the D.C. Circuit was in the process of overturning virtually every habeas win by detainees in the district court, taking any pressure from the judiciary off the administration. And whether because of fear, fatigue, or apathy in light of other domestic crises, the public largely supported, or tolerated, Guantánamo's status quo. Faced with significant opposition and little incentive to continue the work of resolving the fate of detainees, the administration rationalized its failure to muster the will to press forward by blaming Congress, and turned its attention elsewhere. The promised board reviews, along with every other administration effort to close Guantánamo, went on hold.

When I first met Ghaleb in mid-2011, neither one of us knew quite what to do. Not many fellow attorneys and advocates did. In contrast to the flurry of activity in years past, my visits to the base during that period were quiet, with usually only one or two other legal teams visiting at the same time, if that. My meetings with Ghaleb were similarly muted and followed a predictable script. He would report to me on his diabetes and latest ailments. I would make requests for medical care that would get denied. He would ask me if there was any news on transfers. I would explain about the battle between Congress and the president. He would tell me that it was pointless to go back to the courts. I would review the legal options and agree that they were limited. He would tell me about his fear of dying in Guantánamo. I would struggle with how to make his torment visible and visceral to everyone not in the room with us.

It was not until two years later, in 2013, when detainees' own quiet desperation finally began to turn the tide. In February of that year, the majority of prisoners went on a hunger strike, which grew into the largest and longest protest in the history of the prison camp. At a White House news conference on April 30, against the backdrop of over 100 men on strike and dozens being forcibly fed with tubes, President Obama was pressed to address the crisis: "I'm going to go back at this. . . . The idea that we would still maintain forever a group of individuals who have not been tried—that is contrary to who we are, it is contrary to our interests, and it needs to stop."*

In September 2013, over 11 years into his imprisonment without charge or any clear end, Ghaleb finally received notice of his periodic board review.

The review was far from a panacea, but it was also a step closer to release. Still, there were reasons to be wary of the process. There was no real opportunity to rebut the government's information, because detainees weren't allowed to see more than a short unclassified summary. There was no impartial decision-maker, because the board was made up of government officials with vested interests in the outcome. There was no accountability for the final decision, because the board's deliberations and reasoning were secret, except for a one- or two-paragraph summary of its decision. And at the end of the day, a determination approving a man for transfer was unenforceable, requiring only the government's best efforts—and we'd seen how well that had gone before. Dozens of men who had been cleared in 2009 were still languishing in Guantá-

*Editor's note: This incident is also discussed in J. Wells Dixon's "President Obama's Failure to Transfer Detainees from Guantánamo," chapter 3 in this volume.

namo alongside Ghaleb. He had a decision to make about whether to participate, and whether to have me help him. It was a dilemma that detainees and their lawyers had faced many times before—whether to be part of an inherently unfair process because it was a chance at release.

He asked me what I thought he should do. We were among the first up, so there was little experience to draw from. I gave him my cynical view. He took the chance. I have hope, he said.

We had a good team, which included two members of the military who were appointed, per the rules, as Ghaleb's primary advocates; my Yemeni colleague, who was Ghaleb's same age and countryman, who often wondered aloud about the arbitrariness of his good fortune and opportunity, and different trajectory; and our trusted interpreter. We spent months preparing—longer than most other teams had. In the days leading up to the hearing, we sat as Ghaleb's audience as he practiced reading the statement he had written for his review. He asked for public speaking tips. Ghaleb, try to look up at the board when you say that you were brought to Guantánamo when you were 22 and you are now 34 years old. Try not to rush when you say that you have struggled on a daily basis because of your health, and feel desperate. Try to show what you feel when you say that you want to become a father, that you pray for the day when you can hold your baby in your hands, that you want to give your children a better life than you had. We pumped our fists when he was done. We wanted to believe that this would all mean something.

The day of the hearing, we crowded around Ghaleb on one side of a conference table in a nondescript room in Guantánamo, looking at a video monitor where the board would appear from Washington, D.C. Preselected press and other public observers were watching from another video feed, though we couldn't see them. And our witnesses were connected from yet another link, though they couldn't see us. There were a few false starts with the video, but then we began. The military representative and I made our opening statements, and then it was Ghaleb's turn. He gripped his statement in his hands and looked up.

I am still learning English, so I would like to present my statement in Arabic.

My name is Ghaleb Nasser Al-Bihani and my ISN is 128.

I was brought to Guantánamo when I was 22 and I am now 34 years old. . . .

The board issued its decision the following month, in May. One of Ghaleb's military representatives and I called Ghaleb to give him the news. We were jumpy. *Ghaleb, are you sitting down?* Of course he was sitting down. He was shackled to the floor. *The board made its decision. They approved you for transfer. Ghaleb?*

Today, more than a year later, Ghaleb's elation over the phone has long since faded. His status has changed. His reality hasn't. While the Obama administration has picked up the pace of transferring detainees approved for release, Ghaleb remains unclear about when his turn will come. He wonders if the current momentum will fade—again—before it does. The Periodic Review Board's work has also been inexplicably slow, with only nine men reviewed in its first year of operation—seven of whom were approved for transfer—and dozens more in line. Ghaleb and his fellow detainees recently began their 14th year of imprisonment without charge. That untenable situation that needs to stop still continues.

6

Mental Illness before Guantánamo

SHAYANA KADIDAL

"The petitioner[1] admitted that he was at Tora Bora, Afghanistan in December of 2001," announced the government's executive summary of its account of why our client should be detained. "Tora Bora became Usama bin Laden's headquarters in November of 2001. The battle for Tora Bora lasted for two months," it added, helpfully. Surprisingly, this accusation was buried way down in paragraph 34 of 35, but as it turned out, it was the hardest of the assortment of disconnected allegations against him to deal with.

Most were incredibly stupid: that he fought with Afghan forces during the post-Soviet conflict in 1994 (this was supposed to be a bad thing, just two years after the U.S. had sent Stinger missiles to various parties fighting the Russians?), that he was seen at some flophouse by some other detainee who was tortured when he made the claims, etc., etc.

So this Tora Bora thing was the main remaining accusation against him. We had to get rid of it.

* * *

There was a single source document for this accusation. It was an interrogation report of a conversation with our client in the summer of 2002. He had been arrested in front of his wife and infant child in a house in Lahore, the most sedate of Pakistan's large cities, a stone's throw from India and far from the wild western part of the country. From there he was taken to the detention and interrogation facility the U.S. had set up at Bagram Airfield Military Base in Afghanistan. The place was notorious for brutal interrogations; it was not long since 9/11, and the interrogators were largely young military kids out of their depth. Everyone there recalled being asked, "Where is Osama bin Laden?" even if they had been detained a world away from the last known whereabouts of the Al Qaeda leader in the mountains of Tora Bora.

The interrogation report of our client had just one line of substance. Our client had fled the fighting in Afghanistan after the U.S. invasion, and the report said that in doing so he "WANTED TO GO TO PAKISTAN, AND [HIS FRIEND] TOOK A TAXI WITH THE DETAINEE TO BORA, AF, AND THEN ON TO PESHAWAR." *Bora, Afghanistan.* It might as well have had an exclamation point for emphasis, though that might have been redundant given that the whole document was in capital letters.

It was a rather spectacular allegation given what followed immediately after: "detainee has displayed severely nervous behavior, and tenses his hands and feet so his fingers and toes stick straight in the air. . . . Detainee claims he is possessed by the devil and it enters him through a mark on his leg. The devil enters him and 'mixes things up.' . . . Detainee is kept awake at night because Allah and the devil are fighting in his head." Voices in the head, somatic delusions . . . an odd person to be kept in the trusted circle around UBL at Tora Bora, for sure. In reading all of this, I always picture a probably twentysomething interrogator disinclined to take any behavior at face value—but here's what the interrogator wrote, after noting our client's behaviors were consistent around both guards on the cell blocks and interrogators: "If the detainee is acting, he has been very convincing since he arrived at the facility. Recommendations: Detainee should be psychologically evaluated."

That was a good recommendation. It seems to have never really been acted upon in the eight years he was held at GTMO.

* * *

Another (normally) good recommendation: talk to your client about what the real story might be.

Yet we never managed to have a conversation with him about the substance of any of the allegations the government made, no matter how outlandish. He would suddenly be rendered completely out of it the second the conversations turned to the details of the government's claims, but that was at some level entirely typical for detainees for a variety of reasons—most often, anxiety at answering the same questions they'd been asked during early, brutal interrogations at Bagram, Kandahar, or Guantánamo. But this client started tapping his head *every time* we talked about the past, and soon after the tapping started, invariably he was unable to speak or function. Was it just anxiety, a block that we'd eventually get through together? Conscious avoidance that just appeared exactly the same as mental illness? (And why was I more skeptical than the skeptic who interviewed him in Bagram?) Or was he trying to shut down another voice in his head?

I met with him in a little meeting shed at Guantánamo in May 2009, telling him that we'd have to talk in some detail about all of this on the next visit. In mid-April I went down to Guantánamo again, and he wouldn't come out to meet me. For a whole week. So I had no choice but to look for clues in the sterile record back stateside.

First off, it didn't seem to make sense that anyone could take a taxi to Tora Bora, located high up in the White Mountains, a relatively impassable part of the border between Afghanistan and Pakistan, certainly way out of the way if you were heading to Peshawar. And there were references to a "Bara" (with two As, and no O) elsewhere in the early interrogation notes. So we looked for any Bara we could find. Maps were no help at first. But if our guy had taken a taxi from Jalalabad to Pakistan, the Khyber Pass was almost the only plausible route; it had been open to nonofficial traffic at various times even in the months directly after 9/11. And a straight line from Jalalabad over the pass led to Peshawar, the final destination of that cab ride. Could the Bara I was looking for be somewhere along that line? After weeks of looking, a clue—references in an old tourist book to a "Fort Bara"—led me to look on 19th-century maps. And then finally, on Google Books, there it was: Ft. Bara, built out by the

British on what was then the western frontier of Imperial India. Now it was a suburb,[2] long ago swallowed by the metastatic city of Peshawar, a place flush with refugees and migrants since the dictatorship of Zia ul Haq and perhaps long before then as well.

So he did indeed take a taxi from Jalalabad to Bara and then into Peshawar. But in the round of bin Laden bingo being played in all those early interrogations, "Bara" became "[Tora] Bora."

In an opening scene of the Terry Gilliam/Tom Stoppard movie *Brazil*, there is a moment when a fly happens into the mechanism of a manual typewriter, causing the name of a suspected terrorist ("Tuttle") to type out on a form as "Buttle." A hapless cobbler, Archibald Buttle, is then detained by a party of storm troopers who raid his home, carving a hole in his ceiling, rappelling down through it, and whisking him away from his easy chair in front of the disbelieving eyes of his wife and children. In our case, the typo came after the fact, only taking on significance as the authorities tried to justify holding him for eight years. And the police, Pakistanis, probably didn't drop out of a hole in the ceiling. But they did take him away in front of his wife and infant daughter. More on them later.

* * *

Unlike poor Buttle, who died in the interrogation chair, our client hadn't been as horribly abused as the typical prisoner held at Bagram or Guantánamo. Even according to his own accounts he hadn't been mistreated. They hadn't even really seemed that interested in interrogating him much in his early days at GTMO, when just about everybody else we represented had been the subject of intense scrutiny. What did *they* believe his story was?

Apparently, after a brief window of observation by military medical teams, they decided that he wasn't a hardened Muslim extremist terrorist, but actually fell into the other generic category of Guantánamo detainees that officialdom recognized: opiate addict. Now, thinking that someone who seems out of it, hears voices in his head, has tics that occa-

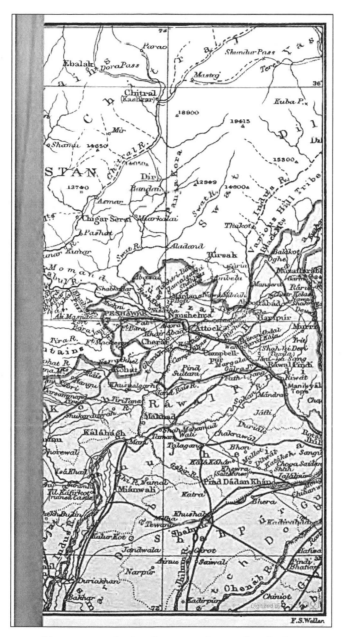

The century-old map on which I first saw the mythical place name "Bara."
Source: John Murray, *A Handbook for Travelers in India, Burma and Ceylon*
(4th ed., Calcutta, 1901)

sionally resemble shaking, etc., is a withdrawing heroin or opium addict might be excusable for a few days. But it's odd to attribute this behavior to opiate withdrawal when it goes on for months and years, as it did for our client, because (as anyone who's seen *Trainspotting* can tell you) opiate withdrawal symptoms last a few days at most. (Seventy-two hours is about the average.) Our client certainly wasn't getting a fresh supply at GTMO. Yet this initial medical diagnosis—so obviously wrong—lasted forever, in classic military style. "Once an enemy combatant, forever an enemy combatant"; label someone a druggie on day one and there's no need to bother treating them for, say, psychosis.

But the military's definitive conclusion[3] was reassuring in one sense. The government seemed generally incapable of believing that the prisoners it had purchased from various proxies—Afghan warlords, corrupt Pakistani police, hungry villagers—had innocent reasons for being in the region. But if they labeled someone a druggie, that was sort of a signal that they believed your guy wasn't a fundamentalist. They thought he wasn't a proper Muslim? Couldn't be a bad thing.

* * *

As it turned out they were wrong about his religious belief too. He'd grown up in Libya, in a large family—one of ten siblings. He'd been drafted into the military at 19, but right around that age (the classic time frame for psychotic breaks) he'd started to develop his symptoms. They got worse and then Gaddafi started a war with Chad. He fled the country, fell in with a bunch of exiles, and ended up shuttling for a decade between western Pakistan and Afghanistan.

Other than the folks at GTMO who decided he was a junkie (and did nothing in response), he had never had any exposure to Western psychiatry, never received any medication.

He had exposure to me. But despite my best intentions as an undergrad pre-med, I was not a psychiatrist. I did, however, have a phone card that let you connect to the mainland from Guantánamo for 20 cents a minute on a government-monitored line, and so I used the time freed up

MENTAL ILLNESS BEFORE GUANTÁNAMO | 81

by our client's unwillingness to come out and meet in April 2009 to find and consult with a wonderful Arabic-speaking psychiatrist at the medical school of the University of California, San Francisco. Talking to him, the pieces started to connect: in much of the Arab world, either there is no physical access to Western psychiatry or common people lack the financial ability to take advantage of whatever resources are available locally. So upon the onset of psychosis, concerned parents take their children to the only help accessible to them: faith healers. The diagnosis is typically couched in religious terms: the young man "has the Djinn," or, in other words, is possessed by a devilish spirit. And the consultations invariably result in a simple, low-cost prescription: "pray more." Who wouldn't follow that advice? So our client became far more devout than his brothers and sisters, something that was eventually marked with all the outward signs—he grew a beard, read Koran to himself when the outside world became overwhelming, and so forth.

The contrast with his siblings, all mostly secular, was striking enough that he himself had noted it. Plenty of men I've met at GTMO are from highly secular families, relative to their larger community; for several, they stood out because in their adolescence they either had a psychotic break (the typical age of onset being roughly 18 to 24) or they lost their mother during that vulnerable period. And either the illness drove them to religion, or, seemingly, they embraced it in the void left by the absent parent.

Perhaps this pattern, where the onset of mental illness leads to increased religiosity, will change as time passes and pharmaceuticals become more widely available and cheaper. But there are obviously a lot of forms of resistance to the very concept of mental illness that may continue to draw people from every culture to understand its symptoms in other terms. Ironically, one of the few reliable tools for confirming a diagnosis of psychosis is to treat the patient with the drugs that that form of psychosis usually responds to and see if things change. The magical effect of psychotropic drugs has convinced many a parent that their child's uncanny symptoms were in fact physiological in origin.

* * *

At Guantánamo, the ritual you go through when a client won't come out and meet you is pretty routine. You take the ferry from the empty side of the base, where pesky human rights lawyers are warehoused overnight, to the windward side of the base, where some 11,000 troops and the prisoners are kept. (The vast majority of those troops have nothing to do with detainee operations.) You spend an hour and a half entering the camps, and along the way the military escorts inform you the client has refused his meeting. You write a short note on half of one side of paper and have your translator render it into Arabic. A military lawyer takes the note back to the cell and returns telling you either that it worked, or that the client still refuses (or sometimes, more troublingly, that the client refused to read the note or have it read to him). Unlike in regular prisons, even with mentally ill patients one isn't allowed to enter the cell block and walk up to the front of your client's cell and confirm his understanding of what's happening or at least have a chance to observe his physical and psychological condition briefly in person. (Nor has there been any success to date in getting the courts to order outside doctors into the prison to treat mentally ill clients; again, administering drugs is sometimes the quickest way to confirm a diagnosis of psychosis.)

Instead, you head back on the ferry to the hotel. Oddly, for five days straight during that April 2009 trip when our client wouldn't come out to talk, I noticed a small bump on my elbow gradually swell up to the point where it was clear something was wrong. Spending the day musing over the lack of proper mental health care for Guantánamo prisoners made me not want to try my own luck with the health clinic there. In retrospect, like many decisions to avoid medical intervention, this was a bad choice: eventually the bump got to be the size of a ping pong ball and was surgically cut out of my arm; only now, five years later, is the scar finally starting to disappear. But for the first two months afterward I was on Cipro, sick, trekking almost daily to a well-hidden Defense

Department office in dystopian Crystal City, Virginia, to work on our classified court filings on behalf of this client.

This place—the "Secure Facility"—feels more isolated to me than being down at the empty side of Guantánamo. Like meeting rooms (and cell blocks, I am told) at GTMO, it is frigid and devoid of natural sunlight, and, ironically, I generally subsist while working there on meals from the local Afghan Kebab House. The Facility occupies one corner of a commercial office building, and, as far as I could tell, there was only one thermostat on each floor of the building, located in another office that didn't have its shades drawn all day (to prevent leaks by telescope, surely). I'm guessing that the comfortable air conditioning in the adjacent offices was rendered freezing in the Facility by the absence of the heat of the sun. I spent most of the next two months there, drafting papers from morning to night. The day we filed the 290th page of classified briefing in the case, I opened my email on my BlackBerry and saw that that morning the government had notified us that our client had been cleared for transfer out of Guantánamo.

* * *

This was not the first time in the history of the legal profession that a huge mound of paper was consumed in vain. Nor was it the first time our client was cleared. In 2007, the Bush administration had also cleared him, but to be released to Libya, where he was certain he would be tortured as a beard-wearing, presumptive Islamic militant extremist who'd surely been in Afghanistan just biding the decades whilst plotting to overthrow Gaddafi. Whether he was or wasn't mentally ill when he absconded from military service during that long-ago war with Chad wasn't going to matter one bit.

In the spring and summer of 2007, we had tried to get the courts to intervene on an emergency basis to stop him being sent to what we felt certain would be a horrible death in Gaddafi's jails. We ended up filing legal requests all the way up to the Supreme Court. All of the paperwork was in vain; none of the courts wanted to touch the issue. So for all CCR's work on his case, the thing that saved his life was a photograph.

When the bombing in Afghanistan started in late 2001, as the U.S. prepared the way for its allies to take the country back from the Taliban, our client had crossed the border separately from his wife and infant child. His wife was an Afghan and, of course, a woman; with an infant child in tow, she would invariably have an easier time getting across the border than an able-bodied, recognizably foreign man would. They all made it across and were reunited in Lahore, far from any conflict, and lived in a house with some other exiles until Pakistani police showed up to arrest him. (More Guantánamo prisoners were arrested in Pakistan than in Afghanistan, helping Musharraf rack up millions of dollars in bounty payments.) After that, she returned with their daughter to live with her family in their village in rural Afghanistan.

The Afghan Human Rights Organization (AHRO) somehow tracked her down there during our client's asylum crisis in 2007. His wife and child made the long trip to AHRO's offices in Kabul, from where they emailed us a photograph of a sad-eyed little girl, recognizably our client's child, holding up a small wrinkled photograph of her father. Next to her sat her mother, eyes downcast to the floor but with her veil pulled back to show her face.

The next day we had a brief phone call to ask permission to use the photo in public advocacy to stop our client from being sent back to Libya. We presumed it would be a difficult discussion, but it was not. His wife agreed. With Human Rights Watch working behind the scenes to make it happen, the *Washington Post* ran a story about the situation, featuring the photo, and before two weeks had passed, word got to us that the State Department would block our client's repatriation.

That phone call was almost the last we ever heard from her. Our client was eventually released to Albania and granted refugee status there in 2010. Afterward, we spent years trying to connect the two of them, but as quickly as his wife was found in 2007, she managed to not be found after he was out. Perhaps she was fearful that custody of her daugh-

Our client's wife and daughter, holding a crumpled photo of her father. (As it worked out, this photo might be the last he ever saw of them.) Source: CCR/ AHRO

ter would become an issue. One condition of almost all releases from Guantánamo, even to places where men have been taken as refugees from their countries of birth, is that they not be allowed to travel freely internationally, and there seemed to be no chance that they would ever be reunited in Afghanistan.

* * *

I never had any idea what that marriage might have been like for her. They didn't speak the same language. He frequently expressed that she was a nice woman and he wished he could have done more for her. But surely his illness was a mutual burden.

Nor did we (despite *our* sacred relationship, attorney and client) ever have the slightest connection. Most of the time it was like he was trapped in a box in his head, even after he got out of Guantánamo. After he was sent to Albania, he spent most of his time outside his room playing football with the wary Kosovar refugee kids in the refugee center where he was held for his first few months of freedom. Later he got an apartment (paid for by the state), and, eventually, two kittens.

Albania was a miserable place for him. As an underdeveloped former Eastern bloc country, social services there were far less well funded than elsewhere in Western Europe where other Guantánamo refugees had been sent—a fact of which those sent to Albania were all aware, thanks to the Internet (high-speed connections being one of the few luxury perks those ex-detainees had). In the refugee center in Albania the detainees experienced cold (natural cold—not the cold from the air conditioners at GTMO, which were always on high for the layered-up guards) for the first time in decades, with only the thin prison smocks from Guantánamo that they still wore to protect them. The refugee authorities gave them propane burner heaters, but they had to ration out the canisters, so the three men would sit in a circle between their three heaters, sharing this as they had shared everything in the prison for years.

None of the clothes they were offered by the authorities fit. We flew there to be there with them during their first week. After a day, we bought them clothes, although Albania, like Williamsburg, Brooklyn, is a land of tight-fitting jeans, and these were all big men who were used to things fitting loosely. We promised to send back more from the land of XXL, the United States, but they were skeptical. Finally, I snuck in a DSLR camera to take pictures of them—without flash, as that would have given us away—to send to their parents, who hadn't seen them in years. (This was before the International Committee of the Red Cross routinely started being allowed to take and send home glossies from Guantánamo.) I took over a hundred pictures of our client's two companions. But he did not want any pictures of himself made, thinking he didn't look well. He was right about that.

Another thing not routinely available in Albania was quality mental health care. Though we had tried to impress on the State Department that our man should be resettled in a country with modern psychiatric care—Finland was one place high on our wish list—they claimed the burden of taking care of him was too daunting for the countries that were actually capable of doing it to want to take him. Albania was pliant, willing to take anyone rejected by the rest of Europe, but unable to care for them. In Albania, most working locals didn't have adequate health care. And as to psychiatry, as one local psychiatrist who'd worked with Yugoslav civil war refugees put it, it was mostly "Soviet style": if you were labeled as "mentally ill," you'd end up hospitalized and put on Haldol or some other overwhelmingly powerful drug, turned into a zombie and forgotten. The middle ground between that and neurosis was not an acknowledged category. So even seeking local treatment seemed fraught with danger (putting to one side that the local language was impenetrable—exceptionally hard to learn by reputation, the sole surviving offshoot from ancient Illyrian on the modern-language family tree).

At great effort, our Arabic-speaking psychiatrist and a fellow native-speaker colleague from Montreal both volunteered to treat him, traveling from North America to Tirana on their own time. A year after his release, they found him severely depressed but improved to the point that they wondered whether their initial suspicions of psychosis were correct. That was encouraging news, though later we started to believe they had caught him during a good month. We had hoped to get him more advanced care than what was on offer in Albania—most likely involving medication as well as talk therapy, which he sometimes found useful and sometimes found absurd. But eventually Gaddafi was overthrown, and he went home to his family in Libya, where his story began.

NOTES

1 I have chosen not to identify our client by name here given the personal nature of some of parts of his story. He gave us proxy to use his story in our advocacy efforts on behalf of the men still at Guantánamo, and, for her part, many years earlier his wife did as well.

2 To make sure it would continue to be acknowledged as a real place, I immediately did what every college student would do—I created a Wikipedia page for it: "Bara, FATA," available at http://en.wikipedia.org/wiki/Bara,_FATA.

3 It's worth noting that, depending on what the military was trying to rationalize at the moment, the government occasionally did acknowledge his mental illness. So, in trying to justify his continued detention, his Combatant Status Review Tribunal noted, "Detainee was previously treated for psychosis but now is in good health" (!), and from there somehow concluded, "Detainee's psychological issues allow him to be easily influenced by extremist groups, who may utilize him for his talents, and who may possibly recruit him to act as a martyr, should he be released; therefore, it is imperative detainee be retained in the custody of the U.S. Government or the Libyan Government." His documents from the Administrative Review Board, set up under President Bush to determine whether Guantánamo detainees should continue to be held, likewise refer to a "schizotypal personality disorder."

7

You Love the Law Too Much

MARTHA RAYNER

Despite freezing temperatures, I was warm and happy out in New York City's snowy Central Park celebrating Barack Obama's first inauguration with my eight-year-old daughter, whom I permitted to skip school on this historic occasion. Within days, Obama signed a presidential order directing his administration to close GTMO within one year. I did not expect an immediate parade of planes ferrying my clients and the other prisoners of GTMO to their home countries, but Obama stood for hope and change, and all indicators were that GTMO, and the indefinite imprisonment without trial that it stood for, would soon end.

A week later, I was sweating in one of the squalid shacklike structures of Camp Echo, Guantánamo Bay, Cuba, where attorney-client meetings take place, visiting one of my clients, Sanad al-Kazimi, a husband and father of four from Aden, Yemen. He was abducted by some arm of some government in the United Arab Emirates in January 2003 and subjected to brutal torture, including secret detention, confinement in a dark cell the size of a grave, prolonged shackling, and nudity with cold air blasting, beatings, and sexual abuse and molestation. Men tied his hands and legs together and hooked him up to a mechanical lift device that hoisted him in the air and dropped him into a pool of freezing water.

His imprisonment had no legal contours. He was not arrested, he was not charged with a crime nor provided any review or opportunity to be heard. He was not captured by soldiers on a battlefield and registered with the International Committee of the Red Cross, an independent organization that monitors treatment of war detainees. He was disappeared.

Then, without notice or explanation, Mr. al-Kazimi was moved to another prison in the UAE, where he remained for almost six months with no access to the outside world. Then, just as suddenly and jarringly, he was secretly relocated to a CIA-run site in Afghanistan dubbed the "Dark Prison" by prisoners who emerged to describe the imposition of 24/7 complete darkness.

There, Mr. al-Kazimi was subjected to physical and psychological torture that is difficult for him to talk about to this day. His head was shaved, and he was hooded and locked in a small cell. There was no light, only utter darkness. The guards, dressed in all black including black ski masks that revealed only their eyes, brandished large flashlights. They suspended him from the ceiling by his arms for hours at a time, causing his legs to swell painfully. As he hung naked, guards, both male and female, took photos of his dangling body. The hangings usually took place before interrogations so, unable to walk, he was dragged along the floor to interrogation rooms. There, his head was bagged, causing disorientation, and he was forced to face interrogators kneeling in a position of subjugation.

The CIA used sensory manipulation to damage Mr. al-Kazimi's mind. Deprivation was imposed through darkness and isolation, then alternated with overload through bombardment of deafening music for long periods. Mr. al-Kazimi tried to kill himself on three separate occasions by hitting his head against the wall of his cell. Each time, his U.S. captors intervened and injected him with drugs that put him out.

Four months in the Dark Prison was followed by another relocation, accompanied by all the uncertainty and dread of what was to come. Next was military imprisonment at the United States' Bagram Airfield Military Base in Afghanistan.

This move was designed to transform what was unquestionably illegal detention under unlawful conditions by the CIA into military imprisonment that had a veneer of legality. He was assigned an internment number and met with the International Committee of the Red Cross. The conditions of detention remained harsh—he was at times chained to a wall of his cell and subjected to long periods of loud music. He was continually threatened by soldiers with dogs, sticks, and rifles.

Unlike secret detention, however, the abuse may not have been directly connected to interrogation. It appears the opposite was true: the military brought in interrogators, literally called a "clean team," tasked to obtain inculpatory statements in a manner designed to avoid admissibility objections in a court of law. The goal was to take "fresh" statements intended, like a miracle stain remover, to clean up the filth, dirt, and toxic taint of torture.

The U.S. military colluded in torture by attempting to erase what the CIA had done. The "clean team," a Department of Defense–invented entity called the Criminal Investigation Task Force (CITF), composed of armed services investigators, sought to create a cordial atmosphere by offering food and drink and projecting ease and comfort, efforts designed to permit investigators to later testify in court (as they did) that the statements obtained were voluntarily given and not coerced. The clean team turned a blind eye to what had been done to Mr. al-Kazimi before he surfaced from secret detention, just as they turned a blind eye to his treatment at Bagram. The CITF interrogators engaged in the pretense that all that came before, all that was imposed on Mr. al-Kazimi outside the walls of the interrogation room, did not matter. The U.S. military assiduously avoided having to contend with the fact that the CIA engaged in conduct that violated domestic and international law and, what should have been of most concern to the military, the laws governing the conduct of war, all of which without exception prohibit torture.

Mr. al-Kazimi languished for four months in the harsh conditions of Bagram and then, once again, he was, for a fourth time, trussed like an animal, diapered, blind folded with blackout goggles, made deaf with earmuffs, wrapped in tape, and strapped to a stretcher—packaged for shipment—to where, he knew not.

The chaos of Bagram was replaced by the eerily austere and sterile cells of GTMO. The black box of the Dark Prison was replaced by a cell of white walls, bright lighting, and sparkling cleanliness. The lights never dimmed. GTMO imposed a regime of 24 hours lighting and the extreme social, cognitive, and intellectual isolation that comes with solitary confinement. In addition, GTMO imposed a complete blackout on current events—the few letters Mr. al-Kazimi received from his family were heavily censored. After almost two years of secret captivity, torture, movement from one prison to another, manipulation by a procession of shadowy interrogators, and ceaseless uncertainty, my client was suffering from severe post-traumatic stress disorder.

The GTMO regime of isolation from family and other prisoners— from any sense of what was happening in the outside world—pressed upon my client relentlessly. It left him with little opportunity for meaningful engagement with thoughts other than the painful memories of torture. These memories and the constant hum of uncertainty dominated his existence, exacerbated his PTSD, and led him to relive the terror of secret detention over and over. His pleas for help, emotional distress, and reports of torture were ignored by military medical personnel. No one wanted to know what had been done to him.

I knew none of this when I first met Mr. al-Kazimi a little less than two years later, in the summer of 2006. I did know that Mr. al-Kazimi had somehow sent word to another prisoner, Binyam Mohammed, a British national who would be released from GTMO in 2009, that he sought help. That message was conveyed to Mohammed's lawyer, Clive Stafford Smith, who then conveyed it to the Center for Constitutional Rights (CCR). It was the lawyers of CCR—a talented and intrepid group, out in front challenging the legality of indefinite detention at GTMO— who filed a court case challenging the legality of imprisonment on behalf of over a hundred men, including Sanad al-Kazimi.

I also knew that just a month before I met my client, three prisoners, including a man from my client's home country of Yemen, died at GTMO on the same day. The military immediately deemed the deaths suicides, though a Marine sergeant would later come forward with information that cast doubt on this claim. My client mentioned the "suicides" during this first meeting, but I did not fully appreciate how this news must have impacted him since, at the time, I was unaware of his own history of seeking death rather than enduring another day in the Dark Prison. In the ensuing years, four men did commit suicide, each representing a human being who gave up on life locked in solitary, or under continual forcible feeding, or just worn out from the pressure of indefinite imprisonment.

My client had many questions at this first meeting, many of which, unlike most client questions I encounter in my work in the U.S., I could not answer. Some I could not answer because the rules governing my communications with Mr. al-Kazimi prohibit me from discussing many topics, but most because there were no answers. My client requested the most reasonable sort of information: who would decide his fate, how it would be decided, when it would be decided. He wanted resolution— some sense of certainty or at least a path to knowing what was to become of him.

He also wanted to know why he remained at GTMO when so many others had been released. In 2006, almost 500 men were imprisoned at GTMO, but almost 300 others had already been released. My client often mentioned a Moroccan named Tabarak, who was known throughout GTMO as Osama bin Laden's chief bodyguard and confidant and, as investigative reporting would later reveal, one of the prison's most valuable intelligence assets at the time. His repatriation to Morocco in 2004 defied explanation.

The short, deeply unsatisfying answer to my client's questions was that release was solely at the discretion of the Bush administration. What did that mean? Releases such as Tabarak's, and there were others, demonstrated that the route to release was utterly opaque, murky, and unpredictable. Although my client's imprisonment was no longer secret and he now had a lawyer, he remained at the mercy of discretion that was exercised in secret and had no fixed contours or standards.

Having been at the receiving end of the unbridled power of the Bush administration during his forced journey through secret sites and torture, my client craved the defining features of the "rule of law"—accountability, transparency, certainty, and reasonable predictability. From the very first time I met Mr. al-Kazimi he sought a trial—he wanted that which the U.S. proudly touts as one of its defining features. Surprisingly, despite all the U.S. had done to him, he still believed the U.S. could deliver justice and treat him fairly. His expectation that U.S. law would put an end to the frightening uncertainty of his imprisonment would, in time, be dashed despite his efforts to rally again and again after "the law" failed to resolve his future.

The first chink in the rule of law came early on when I and my client had to navigate the rules imposed on our communications and my client knew a portion of those rules designed to protect the confidentiality of our exchanges would simply not be followed. My client was particularly perplexed, then incredulous, and ultimately very rankled by the U.S. government's control over my notes taken during our attorney-client meetings. On the one hand, I informed him that everything he told me was protected from disclosure by rules that protected the confidentiality of attorney-client communications. On the other hand, the notes I took during our meetings would be given over to U.S. officials for review.

This incongruous practice arose out of the government's position that every word my client utters is presumed to be classified information. This is the same reason a lengthy and intrusive government security clearance is a prerequisite to meeting a client locked up at GTMO. I cannot disclose my notes to colleagues and students (without security clearance), my client's family, or the media, or even store my notes in my office unless I submit my client's thoughts, words, and communications to Justice Department officials who then read the contents to determine a classification designation. Almost all of my notes are deemed unclassified. But to obtain that designation and eventually get those notes to my New York office, where I and my students can work with them, I must give over my notes to officials at GTMO, who then courier the notes to officials in Washington, who then review and determine classification levels.

My client understands the contorted logistics of the procedure and is aware there is a court order that restricts the use of the contents by the reviewing government officials, but that is of little comfort to him. When I first explained the process, he raised his hands in an expression of incredulousness while leaning back in one of those white plastic chairs ubiquitous in the backyards of Americans while he looked at the ceiling of cheap Styrofoam tiles. Since the U.S. had kidnapped him, secretly imprisoned him, and tortured him—all in violation of universal standards of law and decency—he found the notion that a court order would limit the use of my notes frankly amusing. His amusement turned sour when I expressed tepid faith that I expected the reviewing officials would abide by the order, not yet knowing my client's experience of being at the receiving end of U.S. lawlessness. Eventually, I came around to his view; I have no doubt that intelligence agencies monitor attorney notes for much more than determining classification levels.

This is not based solely on my client's experience of rampant unlawfulness by the U.S. government nor on paranoid conspiracy theories on my part. There have been numerous incidents of intelligence agencies operating at GTMO outside the standard operating procedures of the military, who run the day-to-day operation of the base and prison. In the ongoing military commission proceedings at GTMO, in which five men known as the "9/11 defendants" are charged with war crimes, an unnamed agency, presumably the CIA, cut off public access to court proceedings unbeknownst to the presiding military judge, and mysterious listening devices were installed in attorney-client meeting areas that military commission staff were unaware of and could not explain. The FBI has investigated military commission defense teams, including questioning defense team members and keeping that fact secret from other members of the defense team. And the CIA destroyed videotapes documenting its use of torture, despite a court order prohibiting such destruction. My client may or may not have known of these facts—we never discussed them, but he knew U.S. intelligence agencies would swat away a court order, like a fly, if it was in their interest to do so. My client knew very well that the law's prohibitions do not necessarily dictate the reality on the ground at GTMO.

The next crack in the rule of law broke through when my client came to learn that the law may exist, but he could not rely on its stability. From the moment the first habeas corpus cases were filed challenging the legality of imprisonment without trial, which was a month after the first shipment of men were brought to GTMO in January 2002 and caged in outdoor pens, the Bush administration fought to prevent any judicial review of the president's power to imprison men seized all over the world in the wake of 9/11. This delayed the court cases a long two and a half years, until the Supreme Court first determined in June 2004 that federal law bequeathed courts the power to review the legality of detention at GTMO. Mr. al-Kazimi's case was filed in the wake of this ruling, but Congress then passed legislation, the Detainee Treatment Act of 2005, snatching this judicial power away. Although the Supreme Court found the legislation did not apply retroactively and thus preserved Mr. al-Kazimi's pending habeas case, the ease with which "the law" could be changed taught my client that it is fragile and vulnerable to politics.

Congress and President Bush underscored that teaching when, just months later, they again created "law"—the Military Commissions Act of 2006—that took away the last reserve of judicial power to meaningfully review the legality of my client's imprisonment. Again, the rule of law was rendered frighteningly tenuous as my client witnessed the law vanish.

It was not until the summer of 2008, over five years after my client was grabbed by shadowy figures in the UAE and eventually shipped to GTMO, and not long before Obama would win his first presidential election, that the Supreme Court declared, as a matter of constitutional law, that the men at GTMO could not be deprived of the right to challenge the legality of their detention in a U.S. court through use of the writ of habeas corpus. The power of courts to question, review, and check presidential power was restored by that decision, *Boumediene v. Bush*. But my client was unimpressed; my explanation that this time Congress and the president could not change the law—the Constitution—did little to assure him that this time he could rely on the stability of the "rule of law."[1]

And, in fact, tangible results from this historic "win" were far from immediate. Courts had power, but there would be much more litigation to determine how that power could be exercised. A series of "threshold issues," as they came to be called—from the scope of discovery to evidentiary issues to the burden of proof and who should bear it—had to be sorted out. But the Supreme Court's support for judicial review and the election of Barack Obama several months later created buoyant momentum. As I flew into GTMO in January 2009 to meet with my client, I was under the spell of Central Park snow, Beyoncé's ballad to the Obamas, and Michelle Obama's perfect inauguration outfits—I was optimistic my client's suffering would end.

I had not seen my client in almost four months. When I entered the dark shed from the glaring Caribbean sun, I was blinded. I knew my client would be sitting in a chair behind a table with one foot chained to an eyehook on the floor, but initially I could make out only the color of his clothes, which are often orange, as was true at this visit. The color of the prison-issued med-student smocks and pants signal each prisoner's compliance rating by the guard staff. White is most compliant, tan is medium, and orange, my client's color, apparently informs the guard force that this "detainee"—as my client is called—is not "compliant."

As I fumbled to adjust the scarf I wear to cover my head out of deference to my client's culture and religion, and extended greetings, my eyes adjusted and I saw my client's aging face; he was unusually silent. By this time I had been meeting with him for three years. I and my students prepare an agenda for each meeting based on issues that arose in previous meetings, relevant news, and litigation updates, but inevitably, the meetings are often driven by the many indignities, large and small, that accompany the deprivation of liberty.

This is all the more so at GTMO. In U.S. prisons, the vast majority of inmates have definite release dates—they are doing time. Not at GTMO.

Each day of imprisonment does not bring my client one day closer to release. Under the law, my client is not being punished. The purpose of his imprisonment is not retribution or rehabilitation or deterrence. The legal fiction that operates at GTMO contends that my client is not imprisoned to be punished for past conduct. It is preventive detention. Personnel at GTMO never refer to my clients as prisoners; they and all the men locked up there are always called detainees. At GTMO, each day locked up is another day of pounding uncertainty.

Uncertainty, and the lack of information that comes with it, is debilitating and exacerbates the already great stresses of imprisonment. The language and cultural differences between my client and the guard staff, composed of U.S. soldiers, is vast. There are no visits or care packages from family and friends. There are no commissary accounts providing access to comfort items. There are none of the work opportunities that are common in U.S. prisons. At that time, there were no educational programs—a meager few exist now. And there are no phones on the prison blocks from which calls to the outside world can be made. For many years, the prisoners had no access to current events and everyday information about their home countries; information was painstakingly controlled as part of a concerted effort to instill helplessness and soften the men for interrogation. GTMO does so much more than "detain"— the loss of liberty goes wide and deep.

The International Committee of the Red Cross did eventually negotiate an agreement with the U.S. military to permit phone calls with family members. The opportunities were sporadic and unpredictable at first and calls are monitored by U.S. officials, but for Mr. al-Kazimi, the opportunity to talk with family is precious. When my client broke his silence, I learned he was grieving the loss of an opportunity for this treasured communication. Guard staff told him he "refused" his family call, which was not true. Who knows what happened. A guard's oversight. A miscommunication. Purposeful harassment. Outright punishment. Inquiries and complaints by lawyers are met with ever so polite references to SOPs—standard operating procedures—that are said to govern every aspect of GTMO. But SOPs are "elastic," as my client always tells me— procedures change continually and irrationally, and exceptions abound. The operation of GTMO is obscure and cloaked in great secrecy, which greatly contributes to my client's sense of insecurity, imbalance, and dislocation.

It was secrecy—the lack of transparency engaged in by the Bush administration and its continuation by the Obama administration—that ultimately dismantled the rule of law for my client. Since my last visit, I had sent Mr. al-Kazimi the "unclassified" version of the U.S. government's claimed basis for deeming him "detainable." Yet, after three years of litigation to obtain this information, over 90% of its almost 180 pages were redacted—page after page of blackness. My lawyerly letter accompanying the document acknowledged that the government's secrecy undermined the fairness of the habeas process, but this did not ease how jarring and frightening it was for my client to receive the emptiness of this long-awaited document. The sliver of substantive content he could access was overwhelmed by the vast expanse of hidden content. What the government labeled a "disclosure"—inferring the shedding of light— was just the opposite—they were Dark Pages. That I was permitted to read most of the contents, but could not share what I learned, further strained my ability to communicate with my client and added to his isolation. He asked me why everything was not in the open so he could defend himself.

The pain of the mysteriously missed family call and the severe disorientation caused by receipt of the government's secret document was compounded by the release of another Yemeni prisoner, Salim Hamdan, since I had last met with my client. Hamdan was sent home because he had benefit of trial, conviction, punishment, completion of his sentence, and release.*[2] When I expressed disappointment that not even one of the many Yemenis cleared for transfer by the Bush administration had been repatriated with Hamdan, Mr. al-Kazimi responded with cutting sarcasm

*Editor's note: Hamdan's case is discussed in Joseph McMillan's "*Hamdan*: The Legal Challenge to Military Comissions," chapter 11 in this volume.

that there simply must not have been enough seats on the plane. His witty retort did not mask how deeply troubled he was by the inequity and irrationality of repatriating Hamdan but not the other Yemenis who had done nothing or were so insignificant they were of no interest to prosecutors.

He returned to this subject again and again during our meeting. The issue of who went home and why is a source of great pain for the Yemenis at GTMO. There is no doubt that decisions about repatriation have been foremost determined by politics and nationality. The Brits and the Europeans went home first—their countries advocating for their return from positions of power. The Saudis went back in droves—their rich country sending jumbo jets to hurry them home. The Australian, David Hicks, had the support of his country's president, who personally advocated for his release, which came about through secret negotiations and a plea deal through the military commission system. I was startled to learn that Hicks's family was allowed to travel to GTMO and visit with him before he was released. No family member had before or since been provided such a basic feature of incarceration. Then there is Tabarak, the Moroccan repatriated in 2004. But the Yemenis remain, despite the fact that scores of them have been approved for release by both the Bush and Obama administrations for many years. The uncertainty of indefinite imprisonment coupled with the arbitrariness of who goes home is a source of constant pain for my client.

In the midst of all this turmoil, I needed to turn the conversation to litigation business—the painful process of asking a client to remember, and remember in detail, events he has tried desperately to forget. Over the years, my client would sporadically tell me pieces of information about his imprisonment before he landed at GTMO. His recollections were fragmented and incoherent at times. The lawyer in me wanted clarity, chronology, and details, but recounting trauma can cause retraumatization—actual experience of pain. This is especially risky for my client, who remains at the mercy of the same country that inflicted the trauma.

But during this January meeting, perhaps because my client gave in to my optimism and my claim that it mattered, he began to recount details of the Dark Prison. His harrowing description of torture caused him to curl inward as he spoke. What I could see of his face revealed agony and tears. A student who accompanied me on this visit cried. We were interrupted by guards warning us the meeting would end in ten minutes. We ignored them and my client continued. But soon the guards came back and announced the morning meeting was over and ordered us to leave. I should have opposed the order and requested to speak with the OIC—officer in charge. Though I have built up a fair amount of thick skin from years of meeting with clients in jails and prisons, often at the lowest points in their lives, witnessing emotional suffering and taking in the histories of broken lives and injustice, this session with Mr. al-Kazimi brought me near my breaking point. I was drained, weak, and my usual impulse to protest fizzled; I packed up and left.

It is conduct I will always regret. I left my client alone in a dark, nasty cell suffering due to all the pain I had called upon him to summon up. He had no book, not even his Koran for comfort or diversion. His stability was already precarious. His efforts to push back the ugly memories of torture, to find some comfort in denial, were not working. I left him alone and retraumatized.

When I returned for the afternoon session, he rightly condemned my conduct. He did not want to remember. All he wanted was to see his family. He described his life as one of degradation. My client's pain and the depths of his despair were overwhelming. I listened. I apologized. And I listened some more. Now, five years later, it is painful for me to look back at my notes from that meeting. I spent the remainder of our time together trying to instill some hope in my client. I spoke of his legal case that was finally moving forward and a transition in U.S. leadership that promised significant change. But I was wrong. The Obama administration would come to adopt the same legal positions as that of the Bush administration on issues critical to my client, reinforcing how little protection the law could provide him and how committed the law was to hiding the truth.

The first blow vitiated a legal win that was valued by my client. The summer before the January meeting, habeas courts ordered the government to provide at least 30 days notice to the court before transferring a prisoner out of GTMO. The notice order was initially sought by men who feared return to their home countries more than continued detention at GTMO. It was designed to provide these men with an opportunity to challenge transfers before they took place. Mr. al-Kazimi welcomed return to his home country; he feared a transfer that would plunge him back into imprisonment cloaked in secrecy more profound than he was experiencing at GTMO. He feared return to the Dark Prison.

The Bush administration had, of course, opposed issuance of the order, contending it was an inappropriate interference with the president's power and prerogative to determine when transfers and releases were appropriate. Soon after my January visit, the Obama administration embraced the same position and eventually prevailed on a higher court to throw out the order.

Once again, the rules changed. My efforts to convince the habeas judge to issue a notification order tailored to my client's history of torture and repeated relocations and legitimate fear of being spirited away to another prison were unsuccessful. The Obama administration's reaction was in lock step with that of the Bush administration. First, it sought to skirt the merits by invoking a procedural barrier. When that move did not bury the issue, the Obama administration claimed my client's fear of removal was "hypothetical" and "speculative" and had "no *present* likelihood of occurring." The characterization of my client's fear as "speculative" was particularly offensive. His fear was well grounded in light of his experience and the administration's limited assurance that there were no "present" plans to suddenly move him—which left plans for a subsequent move possible. The order was gone. The stability and predictability "the law" was designed to provide once again disappeared.

But when I arrived at GTMO a week after Obama's inauguration, all this was in the future. I did not anticipate the many ways in which the

Obama administration would continue on the same course as the Bush administration. Most disheartening to me and devastating to my client was the Obama administration's vehement stand against transparency. The Bush administration's heavy redactions of critical information that resulted in the Dark Pages would be surpassed by the Obama administration's terribly effective efforts to use law to hide the truth.

Upon my return from the wrenching January meeting, I demanded the records of secret detention and torture from the Obama administration, including video footage of my client I believed might exist. Obama's lawyers first responded by engaging in a pretense that the only relevant records were those involving U.S. custody, which meant when my client surfaced from the dark detention and became an "official" prisoner of the U.S. military—whatever came before was not deemed "U.S. custody." When I asked the habeas judge to order the administration to disclose records of detention that preceded military detention, Obama's lawyers would neither confirm nor deny such imprisonment and treatment had ever taken place and thus would neither confirm nor deny such records existed. Rather than reject the government's double speak and order it to reveal what had been done to my client, the judge created a legal fix that permitted Obama, like Bush, to keep the truth of war crimes covered up.

The judge avoided having to contend with the messiness and toxicity that records of torture would inject into the legal proceeding he was striving to keep focused and narrow. He simply decided that the records of secret imprisonment and abusive and inhumane treatment were not relevant because, in light of Obama's refusal to refute my client's facts of torture, he would, as a legal matter, deem the torture to have taken place. This legal fix appeared to serve everyone's interests. It certainly served the CIA's interest by keeping its conduct secret. It ostensibly served my client's interest by prohibiting the government from contesting the fact my client was tortured. But this was directly in conflict with my client's interests. He had an aching need for the U.S. to own up to what it had done to him. He was, counterintuitively, forgiving of the CIA's cruel trespasses on his health and dignity. What gnawed at him was the United

States' refusal to own up to what it had done. The Bush administration's contention, to this day, that it did not engage in torture tears at my client. The Obama administration is complicit in its silence and strenuous efforts to stave off investigation and disclosure of our country's crimes. Since he emerged from secret imprisonment into military custody, everyone—military interrogators, FBI interrogators, officers in charge, guards, and medical personnel—pretends it did not happen. It has exacerbated my client's trauma of torture to have it erased before his eyes.

This is the cruelty of the law—it is often not interested in what may matter most; relevancy looks only to what matters to the law. The law permitted the United States government to hide the shameful and criminal details of its unlawfulness. The government would not disclose its records because the records would confirm my client's memories and reveal more. For my client, the result of this legal wrangling left him stunned. It had the impact of Orwellian newspeak: if we do not speak of it, it did not happen. He could speak of it, but no one would listen—no one cared.

The fact is my client did not know all the facts of his treatment and torture. His ability to remember and recount was understandably compromised by the very treatment imposed on him. Cruel treatment, sleep deprivation, methods designed to cripple his mind, and use of unidentified drugs all impacted his memory. He knew the pain and damage it had caused him, but he did not know how even what may have been experienced by him as benign conduct was designed to undermine his will and cause him psychological damage.

I anticipated much better from the Obama administration since another executive order, issued just months after the inauguration, promised the administration would "operate with an unprecedented level of openness." But it got worse. Further litigation persuaded the judge that a narrow category of information from the period of Mr. al-Kazimi's secret imprisonment was "relevant"—his medical records—and should be provided to me. Rather than comply with the judge's order, Obama's lawyers filed a document with the judge that I have never been permitted to read, despite having the appropriate security clearance to do so.

From what I can piece together from the judge's subsequent decision, which was eventually made public in a heavily redacted form, it appears the Obama administration declared that our nation would be put at risk if my client's medical records were disclosed to me—just me, not the public—me, a licensed lawyer, law professor, and person deemed capable by the U.S. government to maintain the secrecy of classified and top secret government documents. Why, despite an elaborate system in place to facilitate habeas counsel access to classified information, was this specific and narrow set of information utterly off-limits?

And why were medical records—information about an individual's health and medical treatment—deemed "classified" in the first place? The president controls the definition and designation of classified information. Under current executive orders, classified information must implicate one of several national security–related topics, such as military plans, foreign government information, and intelligence activities, and its "unauthorized disclosure" could "reasonably be expected to cause *exceptionally grave damage or serious damage* to national security." Therefore, my client's medical records were deemed classified because apparently the "originating source" of the records determined that the contents placed our nation at risk.

What could be in those medical records such that disclosure, to a security–cleared lawyer, risks causing such harm to our country's security? It was chilling when Obama's lawyers told me the records would *never* be disclosed to me, and they never have been.

My client once told me that I love the law too much. He did not say it to criticize me, but to help me understand that he needed refuge from the law. The process of attempting to obtain, from "the law," some semblance of stability and reasonable prediction of the future was harming my client—serving only to compound his fear and disorientation. The law's promise to bring clarity, resolution, some semblance of predict ability, and accountability failed. Instead, my client feels a tremendous absence of law—for him, there is no law. His "legal status" makes little sense; he is ostensibly detainable until the end of hostilities, but hundreds of others have gone home despite the government's claim of continued hostilities. The Obama administration designated my client for prosecution, but no prosecutor has brought charges against him. Obama claims he intends to "close GTMO" before he leaves office, but his plan is to relocate GTMO to U.S. soil. He hopes to claim closure in hopes of burnishing his legacy, eliminating GTMO as a "recruiting tool" and reducing the astronomical cost of imprisonment at this offshore military base,* but Obama intends to continue imprisonment without trial indefinitely and dump the problem on the next administration just as Bush did to him. For my client, the "rule of law" permits the U.S. to hide its crimes and it permits the U.S. to take away liberty without trial for a wholly undefined length of time. There is, for my client, no law at GTMO—when he will be released, who will decide it, and under what criteria is utterly unknown.

Epilogue: My client remains imprisoned at GTMO. In 2011, Obama ordered an internal review of each prisoner at GTMO who had not yet been approved to leave and was not charged with a war crime in the military commission system. The Periodic Review Board, which is assigned this task, must determine whether contined imprisonment "is necessary to protect against a continuing threat to the security of the United States." The first hearing did not take place for two and a half years and, at the time of writing, only 18 of the approximately 60 men who are eligible have been reviewed. Mr. al-Kazimi has yet to be afforded a review. In 2013, Mr. al-Kazimi and most other prisoners were placed in solitary confinement to break a widespread hunger strike—an act of peaceful protest against being forgotten. He did not emerge from solitary until over a year later. At the end of 2014, Obama finally permitted the Senate Intelligence Committee to release a redacted executive summary of its torture report—the full report, numbering over 6,000 pages, remains secret. There is now a public document, other than my client's own sworn declaration, that confirms the CIA maintained secret

*Editor's note: Detentions at Guantánamo cost approximately $2.8 million per prisoner per year.

prisons under harsh conditions and engaged in brutal torture, and it includes my client as one of the "at least" 119 who were secretly imprisoned by the CIA. Sanad al-Kazimi's fate still remains wholly uncertain.

NOTES

1 The Constitution can be changed (amended), but this possibility was so remote I choose not to raise it.

2 Notably, Hamdan's conviction was later reversed by the U.S. Court of Appeals for the D.C. Circuit. By all reports, he lives a peaceful life in Yemen.

8

First, Do No Harm

ALKA PRADHAN

When I first hit "play" on the DVDs of Abu Wa'el Dhiab being force-fed at Guantánamo in June 2014, I was cringing in anticipation of what I was about to watch. It had taken several days of installing new software on the ancient computers at the Habeas Counsel Secure Facility (some of which use Windows 2000) and testing the 28 DVDs grudgingly sent over by the Department of Justice, to finally get to the point where they were ready for his lawyers to review. Even now, one minute into the first DVD, the software faltered and froze on an image, and I had to restart the computer and painstakingly set up the viewer all over again. Of course, I thought to myself, the government would make the videos as painful to play as possible.

The production of Dhiab's DVDs was the midpoint of a long year of constant litigation. In February 2014, the U.S. Court of Appeals for the D.C. Circuit ruled for the first time in *Aamer v. Obama* that Guantánamo Bay detainees could challenge the conditions of their confinement as part of their habeas corpus claims. It was a small, but important step forward for a group of individuals who had achieved very few legal successes. While they were no longer being held in the dog cages of early Guantánamo, some of the detainees had now been at Guantánamo for 12 years, and the slow trickle of transfers out of the prison had cut off their hope at the knees. There was distinct physical and emotional deterioration in my clients just between my visits in May and November. Litigation over their conditions of confinement (as opposed to its legality) was something new to keep us all going. Perhaps we would win, but more likely we would lose. At the very least, as my colleague Cori Crider said, we would make enough of a nuisance for the government that transfers might be seen as preferable to litigation.

Our legal team was a motley, efficient crew. From London, Cori directed our overall strategy and had the best knowledge of the clients. In Washington, I worked with Reprieve US board member Eric Lewis and his associate, Elizabeth Marvin; the three of us had the most constant access to the Secure Facility, from which a good portion of the litigation dealing with the classified videotapes had to be prepared and filed. And in San Francisco, Jon Eisenberg (with the help of his former colleague Lisa Jaskol) dashed off legal briefs right and left that contained as much passion as comprehensive analysis. Given our time zone span, Jon could complete a draft document during the evening in San Francisco, Cori could do a first edit in the morning in London, and Eric, Betsy, and I could finish and file by mid-morning the same day—within about 12 hours, without breaking a sweat, if we had to.

After *Aamer*, we moved forward with the force-feeding challenge of our client Abu Wa'el Dhiab, a 42-year-old Syrian who had been at Guantánamo since 2002. Dhiab had back problems that predated his imprisonment at Guantánamo; he had a wife and three children, one of whom died in his absence. The forcible cell extractions and other abuse at Guantánamo had left him in a wheelchair, although he could— and did—try to maneuver around using crutches when the pain wasn't too bad. Dhiab told us that the force-feedings were unbearable, that the medical staff were either untrained or deliberately aimed to cause pain during tube placement. He would often ask to drink Ensure, a liquid supplement, to avoid feedings but be refused just so that the medical staff could force-feed him, and even when he did eat parts of his meals or drink Ensure, the medical staff would insist on taking him for force-feedings anyway. Part of the problem was that the Joint Task Force Guantanamo (JTF-GTMO) commander, a man named Colonel John Bogdan who had no medical experience, was deciding when to force-feed detainees instead of leaving the decision to medical personnel. All of these feeding techniques were confirmed by the accounts of our other clients on hunger strike, men like Emad Hassan who, by 2014, had been on a continuous hunger strike for seven years. And then there were the forcible cell extraction (FCE) teams—a group of six guards kitted out in full riot gear with face guards and shields. The FCE teams at Guantánamo have a long, bloody history of detainee abuse dating back to the first barbed wire "dog cage" cells of Camp X-Ray. They had gouged out the eye of Omar Deghayes, a detainee who was later cleared by the U.S. government and released half-blind; they dragged my client Samir Moqbel around in the mud by a leash; and even a former Army specialist named Sean Baker suffered a traumatic brain injury during an FCE training session back in 2003 when his fellow guards believed that he was actually a detainee. It is not an exaggeration to say that nearly every detainee who has ever spent time at Guantánamo has a painful and degrading story about the FCE teams. Those stories are the reason that the Joint Task Force began videotaping each and every cell extraction. Those are the videos we would later find out about, the ones I and the rest of Dhiab's legal team spent days watching.

I've always wondered about those young, impressionable men and women who wear our country's uniform and are trained to perform such unnecessary violence. Every prison specialist I've spoken to in the year of Dhiab's litigation told me that forcible extractions are to be used only in the most urgent of cases, when the prisoner poses a real, cognizable threat to themselves or others, and even then only after negotiation and other tactics have failed. At Guantánamo there are few "negotiations." The guards are sent to Guantánamo for six-month periods of service (because longer than that would irreparably harm them) after being repeatedly told that the men they are guarding are the "worst of the worst." Even now, 13 years after the first interrogation commander at Guantánamo, Michael Dunlavey, went in a huff to Afghanistan to ask why Guantánamo was full of low-level fighters or straight civilians without useful intelligence, the myth persists. The guards are told what they need to be told to maintain the fiction that Guantánamo Bay is a national security lynchpin.

It's important to note that Dhiab and many of the other detainees on hunger strike did not—do not—want to die. They are not trying to kill themselves. These are men who have been locked away without charge or trial, some for more than a decade. What they can say publicly, with whom they can speak, for how long they may leave their cells each day, what they wear, when they bathe, what kind of razors they use—all is tightly controlled by the U.S. military. One of the only aspects of their lives over which the detainees have any control is whether they pick up the food off their trays and swallow it. My client Emad Hassan says that his hunger strike was motivated by Mohandas Gandhi and Martin Luther King—a peaceful protest against his continued detention at Guantánamo. The men all know that eventually they may have to be force-fed. All that Hassan and Dhiab and others are asking is for those feedings to be humane and medically sound.

According to Dhiab, even when he told the guards that he would come voluntarily to feedings, the FCE teams would be sent to his cell. He said that the six guards would announce themselves, tell him to get away from the door, and burst into the cell, slamming him against the floor with their shields. They would shackle his wrists and ankles, then carry him—injured back and all—out to the waiting stretcher or feeding chair. Dhiab described for us the pain in having one of his ribs broken by the teams once, and later, the daily agony as the teams would insist on crushing his injured back for every feeding. In July, after we'd seen the DVDs, we received word from another client that the FCE videotaping had suddenly been stopped, which frightened the detainees immensely. The one solace in being FCE'd was that at least there was some record of the prisoner's treatment and the constant pain. We also heard that Dhiab's wheelchair, which he used almost constantly by this point, had been taken away on orders from Colonel Bogdan.

This was astonishing to us. We had heard constantly from Dhiab himself and other detainees about the pain he suffered and his various back and kidney problems. "There is nothing wrong with his legs," said the Department of Justice multiple times over the next months. "He can walk." I wanted to ask them in open court if they'd ever had vicious kidney stones, a slipped or torn disc in their backs, or even just a violent upset stomach—and how much they felt like walking during any of those. But this wasn't about Dhiab being able to walk on his two legs, and we knew it. Not having his wheelchair meant that even if Dhiab was willing to go to his force-feedings, he couldn't physically do it. He would have to be FCE'd, and I truly believe that Bogdan relished the thought that the pain would be decisive.

How could I have any idea what Bogdan was thinking? Well, there was the fact that in the two years since he'd become commander of JTF-GTMO, the detainees had reported a surge in brutal treatment. Lawyers and observers had seen it firsthand as well. The Guantánamo presided over by Bogdan instituted degrading and intrusive genital searches of the detainees, even when coming back from attorney phone calls, as if I could have handed my client contraband over the phone! To the best of his ability, and to an extent that would have been met with outrage if it happened anywhere but Guantánamo, Bogdan interfered in attorney-client relationships and had finally admitted in February 2013 that the attorney-client meeting rooms at the base were bugged. His constant sweeping cell searches and the physical denigrations of the Koran on his orders had triggered the mass hunger strike during the summer of 2013. Most importantly, during the course of Dhiab's litigation, federal district judge Gladys Kessler had ordered Bogdan to answer written deposition questions.

Bogdan's answers gave fascinating, if troubling, insights into the man behind one of the worst commands in Guantánamo history. Responding to a question about the use of a painful five-point restraint chair for every hunger-striking detainee, Bogdan described how he'd made an exception for five detainees—Dhiab not included—and allowed them to sit in a comfortable armchair during force-feedings. The purpose of this exception, Bogdan said, was "to build a better rapport" between medical staff and the detainees, and "to incentivize these detainees to stop their fast." In short, Bogdan was willing to treat a small number of detainees humanely, but only if he believed that doing so would end their hunger strikes—the only means of peaceful protest available at Guantánamo Bay. Dhiab and our other clients daily voiced their willingness to be fed. They did not require the painful restraints at their wrists, ankles, waists, and head, particularly with Dhiab's continuing back and kidney problems. But they were also determined to maintain their hunger strikes (not eating solid food) as a means of protest, so Bogdan didn't see the point of treating them decently. They would be FCE'd, pain and all.

Dhiab's wheelchair was returned to him sometime in September by the senior medical officer, after Bogdan left Guantánamo. By that time, we'd just worked through yet another set of crises. In July 2014, Dhiab had told Cori during a phone call that one of the Navy medical officers at the base had refused to participate in the force-feedings of hunger-striking detainees. According to Dhiab, the nurse, an 18-year Navy veteran, called the feedings a "criminal" act and told Dhiab that he'd realized that the story he'd been told about force-feeding detainees humanely by the government was completely different from the reality he witnessed. According to medical ethical guidelines, the officer should have been allowed to withdraw from the feedings without penalty. But because every aspect of Guantánamo is so touchy for the Department of Defense, the officer's commander ordered the case brought before a Board of Inquiry, which could choose to retain the officer in service or discharge him either honorably or dishonorably. Because officers are not eligible for pensions until they complete 20 years of service, it is entirely possible that the officer's 18 years of dedicated—and principled—service to his country could now be thrown aside just to punish him for maintaining his medical obligation to do no harm. As I write this, the officer's case has not yet been decided, and a number of medical and legal organizations have spoken out on his behalf. In addition to my own vociferous defense of his actions in the press, I attended a superhero-themed Halloween party later in the fall dressed in my husband's old Navy uniform and wearing a Red Cross hat.

Further on the medical front, we had petitioned the court at the beginning of August to allow two independent doctors to evaluate Dhiab after it became clear that his condition had deteriorated drastically. Judge Kessler had ordered independent medical and psychiatric examinations, but it soon became obvious that we would have to negotiate over every single term of those examinations with the Department of Defense. We quickly engaged Dr. Sondra Crosby and Dr. Stephen Xenakis, both well-known medical experts who had worked previously with Guantánamo Bay detainees and understood the particular set of constraints and circumstances faced by both prison officials and the prisoners. A couple of weeks prior to their scheduled visits to Dhiab, I politely emailed the Justice Department to make a few routine requests for Dhiab's current medical records, access to his current medical caregivers, and the use of standard medical equipment, including a stethoscope and a reflex hammer. I also requested that the examinations take place at the Guantánamo medical facility, which has the standard medical lighting and patient benches. Finally, based on Drs. Crosby and Xenakis's previous experiences at the base, I requested that Dhiab be unshackled for at least the physical examination. Dr. Crosby pointed out that she could hardly be expected to assess Dhiab's ability to walk or move if he remained shackled to the floor. She'd previously been able to examine Abd Al-Rahim Al-Nashiri, one of the detainees facing trial by military commission for his alleged involvement in the 2000 attack on the USS *Cole*, without a shackle. It stood to reason that for Dhiab, a man long cleared for release and physically incapable of posing a threat to anyone, a shackle should not be imposed for a medical exam.

Reason has not traditionally been one of the government's strong suits regarding Guantánamo. In an increasingly tense series of emails, the DOJ (acting for the DOD) rejected nearly all of my requests outright, including the use of any medical equipment. When I explained that Dr. Crosby had previously had her personal equipment confiscated upon arrival at the base, there was no response. According to government figures, over $21 million was spent on the current Guantánamo

Bay medical and psychiatric facilities. But all of that money could not cure the pettiness of the government in prohibiting court-ordered doctors from temporary use of that expensive medical space or even what I assume—at that price tag—are state-of-the-art stethoscopes.

When it became clear that we were prepared to litigate, I received a flurry of concessions from the Justice Department. Happily, Drs. Crosby and Xenakis would not be forced to carry a set of scales to Guantánamo. The fancy medical facility had one that they could use. Also, the government would grudgingly allow the doctors to use a patient room in the hospital for 90 minutes, just enough time to complete Dhiab's physical exam. Guantánamo medical staff would not confer with the doctors, even though it is standard medical practice for consulting independent experts, but Crosby and Xenakis would be given Dhiab's current medical records to peruse. The shackle was to be left on.

The doctors' findings confirmed our understanding of Dhiab's situation. They were united in the opinion that he could not walk, although they could not pinpoint the reason due to a lack of necessary medical equipment, such as an MRI in that $21 million hospital. And both Crosby's and Xenakis's reports found that all of Dhiab's medical care, including his force-feedings, fell well below the standard of proper care and violated acceptable practices for the treatment of hunger strikers. A third doctor, Stephen Miles, who had extensive tube-feeding experience, closely analyzed Dhiab's medical records and concluded that Dhiab was being force-fed inappropriately, using the wrong metrics, and as a punitive measure. These findings were not surprising, but they were nonetheless alarming to hear from three experienced professionals.

Judge Kessler set the dates of October 6 and 7 for our merits hearing, which was quickly taking the shape of a full trial. We were asking for changes to be made to the force-feeding procedures, including an end to the unnecessary FCEs, removal of the five-point restraint chairs, and the force-feedings to be instituted only after a medical judgment, rather than the judgment of a military commander. To these ends, we had entered into evidence all of the force-feeding videos, Dhiab's medi-

cal records, the doctors' reports, the written deposition answers from
Bogdan and the two previous senior medical officers at Guantánamo,
the force-feeding protocols purportedly followed at Guantánamo, and
numerous declarations on behalf of Dhiab himself.

The week before the merits hearing was a roller coaster. The government had been angling to have the merits hearing held in secret, without
any press or public spectators. The government's tenuous argument was
that since some discussion of the classified videos would be necessary in
closed session, the entire two-day hearing should be closed. Of course,
it was understandable that the Justice Department had its knickers in
a collective twist over laying out the force-feeding regime for public
consumption. But the idea that two days of hearings should be entirely
closed—including the unclassified testimony of our three medical
experts—was ludicrous. This is an administration that President Obama
has called "the most transparent in history"! Judge Kessler dismissed
the Justice Department's plea with some well-chosen quotations from
the Supreme Court about the value of openness to our justice system. A
day later, an even more momentous decision was issued: Judge Kessler
ordered the force-feeding videos to be released.

In June, a group of 16 major media organizations had intervened in
Dhiab's case, calling for the release of the force-feeding videos on the
basis of the public right of access to judicial records under the First
Amendment. The government, as it has done with every attempt to declassify evidence regarding alleged wrongdoing in detention operations,
opposed the intervention and cited security issues. Judge Kessler's order
contained a few caveats to accommodate those concerns (for example,
the faces and any identifying details of servicemen and women were to
be obscured), and was accompanied by a lengthy, well-reasoned memo-
randum opinion. It is worth reproducing the central finding here:

> Even when the government's reasons for classification point to a substan-
> tial probability of harm, the court must assure itself that the justifications
> given are "rational and plausible." . . . In reviewing [those reasons], the

court finds—as it will now detail—that most of them are unacceptably vague, speculative, lack specificity or are just plain implausible.

Of course, one must learn to take the negative with the positive, and Guantánamo litigation resembles nothing so much as the myth of Sisyphus. The two-day merits hearing turned into three days, with three medical professionals who had either directly examined Dhiab or professionally analyzed his records providing live testimony before an open court—a victory in itself. In response, the Justice Department attorneys read monotonously from the Guantánamo Bay force-feeding protocols and highlighted passages from Dhiab's medical records on a projector. There were brief closed sessions in which the videos—still classified— were shown and discussed. In the end, Judge Kessler denied the relief we were seeking with regard to the specific force-feeding procedures. However, she noted the changes that the government had made during the pendency of the litigation, stating that

> [t]he Court feels constrained to make certain comments about the Government's treatment of Mr. Dhiab. It is very hard to understand why the Government refused to give Mr. Dhiab access to the wheelchair and/or crutches that he needed in order to walk to the room for enteral feedings. Had that simple step been taken, numerous painful and humiliating forced cell extractions could have been avoided. While the Government ultimately—but only a short time before the hearing—allowed Mr. Dhiab to use the wheelchair . . . common sense and compassion should have dictated a much earlier result. By the same token, the Government refused Mr. Dhiab's request to provide him with an additional mattress. What could be more reasonable than providing an additional mattress to a man with back pain so severe that he was given morphine to alleviate it?

Judge Kessler went on to say that "[i]t is hard for those of us in the Continental United States to fully understand [Dhiab's] situation and the atmosphere at Guantánamo Bay. He has been cleared for release since 2009 and one can only hope that that release will take place shortly."

In fact, on December 7, 2014 (exactly one month after Judge Kessler issued her opinion), Dhiab was transferred to Uruguay along with five other Guantánamo prisoners, and has begun the difficult road to recovery after nearly 13 years of painful and degrading abuse.

The groundbreaking litigation in his name continues, though. Shortly before the transfer, the Obama administration appealed Judge Kessler's order to publicly release the videos. That appeal is now before the D.C. Circuit, where we anticipate a lively debate about the benefits of correcting alleged wrongdoing instead of classifying potential evidence, and the meaning of transparency in a democratic society.

9

Nourishing Resistance

Tariq Ba Odah's Eight-Year Hunger Strike at Guantánamo Bay

OMAR FARAH

I was aware from the very beginning that the consequences would be bitter. Time has proven that I was right. Nevertheless, I made my decision to continue my hunger strike. Anyone enduring a similar experience will know how necessary it is to keep fighting, despite knowing you are in a losing battle. Why is that so? . . . Because it will prove to your captor that you are not small and he cannot tread on you as he pleases.
—Letter from Tariq Ba Odah, Oct. 4, 2013

Making Acquaintances

Tariq Ba Odah would be a slight man, even if he were willing to eat. His shoulders are barely wide enough to keep his orange prison uniform in place. His wrists are childlike and his hands delicate, veins visible all the way to the ends of his fingers. When his arm is straightened, he can almost touch the tip of his pinky to his thumb around his own bicep. The combination of his raised cheekbones and beard cast a shadow down the side of his face. His eyes and nose are naturally large, though they take on particular prominence now that his weight has fallen under 80 pounds. Tariq's curly black hair, which he keeps shoulder-length, does little to fill out his profile. The office chairs in the cells in Camp Echo, where Guantánamo prisoners and attorneys typically meet, appear to swallow Tariq up. Sores plague him. The pain in his stomach and back cause him to shift in place moment to moment. All of this gives Tariq the appearance of, as a fellow prisoner put it, a bird about to take flight. But Tariq has been caged at Guantánamo for nearly 13 years, despite being cleared for release by the nation's top national security agencies. He is 36 years old.

At the Guantánamo prison camps, Tariq is what is known as a "long-term" hunger striker. That euphemism becomes more absurd with each passing year. Tariq has not eaten—not voluntarily at least—since February 2007. As a result, he is force-fed, usually in the morning and again in the evening. Guards remove Tariq from his cell, often six at a time in full riot gear, strap him to a restraint chair, and medical staff force a liquid supplement through his nose and into his stomach. "Waterboarding," Tariq calls it, both for the obvious torture analogy and because, at times, it has caused him to urinate and vomit.

I traveled to Guantánamo to see Tariq in March 2015. I met with him again the following month. Tariq had recently passed the eighth anniversary of his hunger strike, but he was not in the mood to reflect: "I don't feel the days anymore." Tariq doesn't feel much of anything anymore. "My body gets so numb; no sensation," he said, rapping his knuckles on the arm of his chair to illustrate the point. Apparently, this is a symptom of starvation. And with military doctors saying Tariq is only 56% of his ideal body weight, there is no doubt he is starving. When Tariq lifted his prison smock, I had to look down. All I managed to write in my legal pad was "does not look like body of human; every bone visible." Imagine liberation photos of Holocaust survivors and you will have a sense of what I saw. Tariq sat back in his chair and said, "My life is not like it was. This is the hardest I have ever had it."

These last visits with Tariq were the most recent in a series of meetings that began five years ago. By the time Tariq and I first met face to face in 2010, I had already been his lawyer for two years. Agreeing to introduce himself to me in person was a decision Tariq weighed carefully. Guantánamo has taught him to be leery of leaving his cell. What follows is rarely pleasant—over the years, he has endured more humiliating in-

terrogations than he can remember; when the prison administration ro-
tates him to a new cellblock, typically it is to make his confinement more
isolative. Even visits to the prison clinic are coercive; Tariq complains of
an array of physical ailments, from a collapsing nostril to bloody stools,
but says simple medical assistance is withheld to compel him to abandon
his strike. Worse still, in recent years, the prison administration implemented pretextual searches of the prisoners' genital areas whenever they
enter or leave the cellblock. So it was understandable that Tariq consistently declined my meeting requests. Indeed, much of our initial contact
was through "refusal" notes—handwritten messages attorneys send to
persuade Guantánamo prisoners to attend a scheduled legal meeting.

Sending notes to Tariq became something of a ritual. Once in the
screening facility at Camp Echo, I came to expect the guard on duty to
tell me that my "detainee has refused." It happened each time I attempted
to meet Tariq. Although I assumed it was futile, I would send a note anyway. Rarely were they more than a few lines, containing only a greeting
and enough information to clearly identify myself. That precaution is
essential at Guantánamo. Among the more common complaints I hear
there is that guards withhold (or do not know themselves) the reason
for moving a prisoner. That a "meeting" has been scheduled offers little
comfort; historically, meetings were just as likely to be an interrogation
as a visit from an attorney or family telephone call. More than one client
has told me not to take a refusal personally: "I wasn't sure it was really
you," they tell me.

Whatever the practical obstacles, it must still seem odd to those un-
familiar with Guantánamo that someone enduring what amounts to an
indefinite sentence without ever being charged or tried would refuse the
assistance of counsel. But Tariq has seen well-meaning lawyers come
and go at Guantánamo for a decade, while little has changed for him. As
he observes, only the cells change, becoming rustier and more decrepit
by the year—a visual reminder of the time that has elapsed.

As the prison enters its 14th year of operation, all three branches of
the U.S. government must share blame for the Guantánamo impasse. Re-

cent transfers notwithstanding, the judiciary, Congress, and the White House together have made it wildly difficult for Tariq and the remaining Guantánamo prisoners to regain their freedom.

Form without Substance

In June 2008, shortly before I formally began representing Tariq, the Supreme Court decided *Boumediene v. Bush*, ruling that the Constitution guaranteed all Guantánamo prisoners a "meaningful opportunity" to challenge the legality of their detention in court. The promise of *Boumediene* was a chance to begin uncloaking one of the defining human rights violations of our time—a system of interminable detention punctuated by, among other horrors, solitary confinement, sexual humiliation, and the denigration of Islamic religious mores. Moreover, by virtue of our access to the prisoners and classified government documents, we knew firsthand what so many suspected, that the vast majority of men at Guantánamo were imprisoned on the basis of shoddy intelligence, false identifications, and compelled confessions. Lawyers for the men at Guantánamo could not help but be excited—and indignant. What else does one feel arguing, as I have for example, on behalf of a man whose detention is based on photographic identifications by just three other Guantánamo prisoners, two of whom say they were tortured, and the other the government itself diagnosed as mentally ill? Stories like this are legion among the Guantánamo habeas bar. If they seem apocryphal, it is only because the government has succeeded in keeping so much Guantánamo litigation shrouded in secrecy.

From behind closed doors, however, the lower courts performed their judicial role as fairly as could be expected in cases where the specter of 9/11 looms. In fact, the courts initially ruled in favor of Guantánamo prisoners, and against the government, with remarkable frequency. In the months following *Boumediene*, Guantánamo prisoners enjoyed a nearly 75% victory rate.[1]

Already by that time, Tariq had been on his current hunger strike for two years. Looking back, he adopted a purposeful indifference to the news swirling around the camps of habeas victories and losses. Though Tariq sympathized with fellow prisoners whose hopes were buoyed by the prospect of judicial relief, the disappointment that followed came as no surprise to him. With me, he has been less patient, at times chiding me for indulging the notion that a U.S. court might be of some assistance to him, a poor, Yemeni citizen accused of association with Al Qaeda and the Taliban. To make his point, Tariq has gestured to the lock on the cell door where we meet and said, "The men who brought me here on the first day, those are the only ones with the power to let me out when it's my last."

There is wisdom in Tariq's outlook. Even before the post-*Boumediene* celebration was over, the U.S. Court of Appeals for the D.C. Circuit began revealing its contempt for what the Supreme Court had done. And by 2011, just three years later, it had already rendered *meaningless* the high court's admonition that all prisoners be afforded a "meaningful opportunity" to challenge the legality of their detention. Prevailing in a Guantánamo habeas case is virtually impossible, no matter how vigorous the prisoner's defense or poorly sourced the inculpatory evidence. By now it is old news, but you can imagine Tariq's scorn at hearing, for example, that mere hearsay of a prisoner's travel along a well-worn route between Afghanistan and Pakistan can be persuasive evidence of his alleged association with Al Qaeda or the Taliban;[2] or that putting the government to the modest standard of "preponderance of the evidence," a standard used in ordinary civil cases, and not where individual liberty is at stake, spurred the appellate court to opine, unsolicited, whether the significantly lower "some evidence" standard would not be more appropriate.[3] What that would mean, of course, is that the government would win all of its Guantánamo cases before it ever entered the courtroom.

The D.C. Circuit tipped the scales still further though, ruling that the district courts sitting below it must *presume* that the government's

inculpatory evidence is accurate.[4] My Guantánamo clients see a method
to that madness: surely one way to cure "evidence" obtained during coercive interrogations in the dark, early days of Guantánamo is to simply
whitewash it by judicial fiat. For this reason, Judge Tatel's observation
that some colleagues on the D.C. Circuit were simply "calling the game
in the government's favor" was a refreshingly candid rebuke.[5]

For its part, the Supreme Court has refused to reenter the fray since
Boumediene, declining to hear the final appeals of Guantánamo prisoners who petition for redress. Setting aside the government's propensity
for mooting cases by transferring detainees when those cases seem not
to be going in its favor and some (cautious) optimism that a court might
find that the end of hostilities in Afghanistan erodes the legal basis on
which nearly all Guantánamo detentions rest, judicial avenues to achieve
the release of Tariq and other remaining Guantánamo prisoners are essentially closed.

House Rules: The Politics of Guantánamo

Tariq is as much a student of the legislative branch as he is of the judiciary. He understands well that, in many ways, Guantánamo is a symbol,
albeit one imbued with tremendous power in a U.S. political climate
where loudly proclaiming counterterrorism tropes, however cynical,
generates valuable political currency. When it comes to Guantánamo,
Tariq says the rhetoric on Capitol Hill always sounds the same. So he
did not raise an eyebrow when Congress began going out of its way to
express hostility toward plans to close Guantánamo through each annual
National Defense Authorization Act (NDAA).

As of fiscal year 2011, Congress began imposing onerous restrictions
on the use of Defense Department funds for the transfer of Guantánamo
prisoners off the island. The law initially prohibited transfers unless the
secretary of defense determined that a country set to receive a released
prisoner met certain rigid certification criteria. Among them, the receiving government had to agree to take action "to ensure" that the detainee

would not threaten the United States or its allies in the future.[6] Whatever might reasonably constitute a "threat," no state can guarantee that any future action will or will not occur. Undoubtedly that was the point: the law was drafted to discourage transfers and to keep the prison at Guantánamo open.

The two subsequent NDAAs renewed those restrictions. As a result, short of bold presidential action, Tariq and his fellow prisoners stood no chance of being released under the legislative framework extant at the time. Transfers ground almost to a halt between 2011, when Congress first turned to the NDAA to block Guantánamo's closure, and 2013. The 2014 and 2015 NDAA reauthorizations relaxed some preexisting restrictions, but GOP fearmongering following the *Charlie Hebdo* attack, including calls for a prohibition on all releases, illustrates just how perilous the legislative landscape is for Guantánamo prisoners. Tariq would be forgiven for mistaking today's arguments in favor of Guantánamo for the talking points parroted after the attempted underwear-bomber attack on Christmas Day 2010. That time around, President Obama's reflex was to summarily ban all transfers to Yemen, including of detainees whom his administration had cleared for release, because the attacker was linked to a Yemeni-based terrorist organization, Al Qaeda in the Arabian Peninsula (AQAP). Inflammatory rhetoric, so common to the discourse around U.S. national security, tends to have dire consequences for Guantánamo prisoners.

Congressional obstructionism is intensifying as President Obama's time in the White House draws to a close. My March 2015 trip coincided with Senator Tom Cotton's media tour, orchestrated to lend credit to his arguments for keeping the prison open—though one would have thought the freshman senator would have visited Guantánamo *before* his "rot in hell" stunt at the Senate Armed Services Committee hearing. My next visit followed the launch of Marco Rubio's presidential bid during which he, too, called for Guantánamo's expansion and farcically declared the six prisoners recently freed to Uruguay, each unanimously cleared by multiple national security agencies, "a danger . . . for our country and the world." Meanwhile, Senators Ayotte, McCain, and others are seizing on ISIL's bloodthirst to ram through legislation intended to halt all Guantánamo releases indefinitely. Yes, fearmongering around Guantánamo is old news, but the stakes remain high—higher now than ever. President Obama now says he failed to close Guantánamo only because of politics, rhetoric, and fear. It is a haunting admission considering the suffering Tariq so easily could have been spared.

Executive Inaction

Tariq reserves his harshest criticism for the president. To him, the Obama administration is consistent only in that it never does what it says it will. Upon taking office, President Obama vowed not only to close Guantánamo within a year, but also to ensure that living standards for the prisoners were compliant with the Geneva Conventions. For Tariq, however, 2009 is memorable only for a rapid deterioration in the conditions of his confinement.

During a meeting in March 2012, Tariq scoffed at praise President Obama receives for having abandoned the wanton cruelty now synonymous with Bush-era detention practices. Tariq had just finished recounting his experience being lifted from a restraint chair after a feeding session and then slammed to the floor with such force that his chin split. Discharged from the camp clinic and on his way back to his cell, a senior officer counseled Tariq that "all this could be avoided if you just ended your strike." Tariq favors humor whenever he tells similarly shocking accounts of his abuse. This time he quipped: "Did you vote for Obama? Personally, I miss Bush."

In some objectively measurable ways, Tariq's detention was more tolerable *before* President Obama took office. He says it was not until May 2009 that he was transferred to Guantánamo's notorious Camp 5, where prisoners are held in isolation cells. Almost without interruption, Tariq has been committed to solitary confinement ever since. "Days go by and I do not speak to a soul," Tariq said during a March 2012 meeting.

And the little recreation time he is allowed—sometimes just two hours per day—is often scheduled during hours not customarily devoted to physical fitness. "As I have already mentioned to you," Tariq wrote to me in a letter, "I've been spending 24 hours a day inside the cell for a long period of time, and that is due to the myriad problems I have been facing. The prison officials scheduled my two-hour recreational walk for three o'clock in the morning. The purpose of such scheduling is to increase the pressure on me. At that hour, I will still be on my own, even in the rec area." In response, Tariq has also gone on "no wash" protests, once refusing to leave his cell, shower, or cut his nails for four months. "I looked like I crawled out of a grave. Finally the military asked me to stop and gave me back my full rec privileges." The sad reality is that, whether alone or not, Tariq is often too weak to take advantage of the little sunlight he is permitted.

Like most at Guantánamo, Tariq is tormented by the rational fear that, after more than a decade, his cell may one day become his coffin. Nine Guantánamo prisoners have already met that fate.[7] The failing of the judiciary and Congress notwithstanding, the president alone has the power to avert such a disaster. From November 2014 through January 2015—in just three months—he freed 27 men. That was more than in the prior three years combined. [8] The White House wields remarkable power to effect transfers when it chooses to do so.

The White House, however, often demonstrates little interest in marshaling that power. From January 2011 through April 2012, not a single prisoner left Guantánamo alive—the longest period without a transfer since the prison first opened. President Obama has instead allowed opponents of Guantánamo's closure to dominate the discourse almost from the moment he took office. This is evident, for example, whenever I explain to audiences that Tariq was cleared for release by President Obama's Guantánamo Review Task Force approximately five years ago. Yet many are still unaware that this means every prominent national security agency in the U.S. government, including the Office of the Director of National Intelligence, the Joint Chiefs of Staff, and Departments of Defense, Homeland Security, Justice, and State agrees unanimously that Tariq ought to be freed. If the White House, rather than advocates for the prisoners, had made that point forcefully back in 2009 and 2010, perhaps Tariq's fate would have played out differently.

There is no shortage of blame to go around for Guantánamo's continued operation. In Tariq's view, the courts, lawmakers, and the president are all part of the same system that keeps him locked up and far from his family. I am hard-pressed to disagree. But, surely, as the person with ultimate power over Tariq's fate, President Obama bears unique responsibility for the fact that, as of this writing, Tariq remains in isolation at Guantánamo, having passed the eighth anniversary of his hunger strike, bracing himself for his next feeding session.

My Method, My Message, My Protest

My hunger strike has become my shield which . . . protect[s] me from the conspiracies and humiliation. . . . The hunger strike has nourished in me the sense of resistance and reminded me that the unjust cannot manipulate me as he pleases. He will not succeed in controlling me or controlling my destiny, for I am the one who controls it.
—Letter from Tariq Ba Odah, Oct. 4, 2013

Though Tariq does not despair, he is under no illusions about the Gordian knot ensnaring him at Guantánamo. No matter the occupant of the Oval Office, the partisan makeup of Congress, the base commander presiding, or the guards on duty, his detention is a cruel game the outcome of which is predetermined: the prisoners lose until someone more powerful spares them. In the interim, they pay a heavy price. As Tariq puts it: "Freedom should be much more precious for the human being than all the desires on earth." Detention, therefore, is brutal; indefinite detention, mercilessly so.

At Guantánamo, indefinite detention is compounded by the indignity inherent in a system that encourages prisoners' participation, only to mock them. For Tariq, why else create elaborate administrative and judicial processes—Combatant Status Review Tribunals (CSRTs), Administrative Review Boards (ARBs), Periodic Review Boards (PRBs), Guantanamo Review Task Force assessments, and habeas corpus hearings—that after 13 years still have so little to show for themselves? Tariq, like so many others at Guantánamo, sees it as little more than the elevation of process over justice. The purpose, Tariq says, is to pacify a prison population enduring unspeakable suffering. This is why he easily draws comparisons to the institution of slavery. "I was arrested on the second day of Eid Al-Fitr . . . ," he writes, "then sold into the United States' 21st century slavery market. As far as I am concerned, all of this pressure, humiliation, limitless injustice have been solely aimed at breaking me and breaking my brothers so that they could manipulate us . . . and plant in us despair and mentally enslave us just like they have physically enslaved those before us."

Redemption for Tariq is born of protest, one organized around the principle of nonparticipation. Tariq refused to submit to a CSRT—the sham tribunal established by the Bush administration to determine who, among the hundreds of men then at Guantánamo, were "enemy combatants." Tariq was similarly unwilling (and, in any event, physically unfit) to litigate his habeas petition. And as I recounted, from 2008 until 2010, he would not even sit down with his own lawyer. It goes without saying, however, that Tariq's refusal to eat is the most uncompromising form of resistance through non-participation. "I tell them again and again that I don't want any food from them . . . , I just don't want it. All I want is for them leave us alone, lingering in these cells. They want me to eat, but first I have to be subjected to humiliation. . . . The provocation is never-ending." Therefore, Tariq says his hunger strike will never end. "My method of delivering my message is through hunger strike. You can cut me to pieces, but I will not break it. I will stop on one of two conditions: I die, or I am freed and allowed to return to my family."

Tariq's discipline is humbling. His typical day is "split between praying, reading Qur'an, . . . and contemplating memories of the past." Sometimes he will practice walking in his cell for exercise, "three steps forward and three backwards." The monotony is interrupted only when guards arrive to force-feed him. Tariq views these as moments when his will is tested against the guards. Too often, discussion of force-feeding fails to go beyond the shocking physical details. That is understandable. According to Tariq, violently force-feeding prisoners has been the Department of Defense's preferred approach to breaking strikes. Tariq's descriptions of feeding sessions in 2006 and 2007 are grisly: "I was tortured with the restraining chair when they were filling my belly with two packs of Ensure. The doctors would introduce a 14 size tube with a metal end inside my nose to reach my stomach and sometimes my lungs and when they would take it out it would be filled with blood." Yet, for Tariq, hunger striking is an expression of his vitality. The physical pain, therefore, pales in comparison to the psychological trauma of having the very jailors responsible for his ordeal overbear his will in such an intimate way.

Though powerless to prevent feedings, Tariq nonetheless takes pride in his fortitude. He tells me he cannot help but laugh at the burly guards who periodically enter his cell. In just the moments its takes to shackle him for a move, Tariq says they grow claustrophobic. He teases them, "As strong as you are, you can't even handle a visit and yet I live here."

More importantly, Tariq believes he has accomplished a rare feat that, while a far cry from actual freedom, is profoundly liberating. As in any detention setting, much of the prison administration's control at Guantánamo comes from providing (and depriving) prisoners of "comfort items"—books, recreational time, communal living assignments, anything that makes imprisonment more tolerable. At times, the prison administration has observed few limits in what it is willing to take from prisoners. Tariq, for example, spent from 2004 through the middle of 2005 with nothing in his cell but a "paper-thin mattress, shorts and vest." Comfort items breed dependency, and in Tariq's experience, the very favor prisoners come to value most is the one they will be deprived of in order to break their will. As it is, Tariq has almost no privileges. The Department of Defense largely understands his protest as mere non-compliance. As a result, Tariq is punished essentially in perpetuity. His access to sunlight, human contact, books, and just about everything else is severely restricted.

Through his hunger strike, however, Tariq has removed the ultimate mechanism of leverage. In an environment as hostile as Guantánamo, for Tariq, even the primal drive to eat is a vulnerability to be conquered. He explained in a series of letters in 2013: "My body has become frail and weak, but spiritually I feel that I am a thousand times stronger than I was before. It has been seven years since I have tasted food." He wrote later that "even the pungent smell that used to stay on my fingers after eating" is a lost memory. "I have prevailed over man's innate weakness towards food and drink. I feel honored and proud because I sacrificed food and drink for the sake of my freedom. . . ." By his own definition, Tariq has prevailed, and yet that victory has surely taken its toll.

During one of our meetings in 2014, Tariq looked particularly weary. His physical deterioration is the predictable result of his protest, but it is no less unsettling. We talked for a little while about how he is holding up. I try not to dwell on the subject, however. Tariq chose this course with eyes open; it is arduous enough without worrisome questioning. In any case, he knows all too well how he has been transformed. Other than the occasional wry smile, his face recalls a death mask more than a man in his thirties. As Tariq writes, "One day, I looked at my face in the mirror and was shocked; I would say more saddened. I felt the mirror was looking at me [and] asking if that was really me. . . ." During this particular meeting, Tariq shared more than he usually does about how it feels to be bed-ridden in a filthy cell, carried away by force to be fed with tubes. He wondered openly how much more he will have to endure, but soon pivoted: "I am fine; deep inside, I feel fine. If I accepted all of this without protest, *that* would destroy me. . . ."

I had heard variations on that reassuring theme before and, yet, witnessing Tariq persevere through this advanced stage of his hunger strike,

I found myself fixating on his physical condition. His eyes were more sunken than usual, his hands shook more noticeably, and it seemed he could have slid his ankle out of the shackle attached to the floor if he had tried.

Homesick

After our meeting, back in the Guantánamo housing facility, I returned to some of Tariq's letters from spring 2013 to remind myself why Guantánamo provokes in him such fierce resistance. There are many clues in the way Tariq describes his life before Guantánamo:

> 1978 is my year of birth; but my real birth has not come yet. I have been waiting for it for 11 years. My place of birth is the Shabwah district of Yemen. I left Shabwah when I was one year old and spent my entire life in Jeddah, Saudi Arabia. I am the middle child. My mother and father were kind parents in a simple family untouched by typical familial problems. All that my father cared about was how to ensure happy and peaceful living for his family by providing us with education. Regarding my loving mother, she was and remains smiling all the time. I do not recall a day when she was harsh to me. We lived a wonderful family life, but all this changed since my capture . . .
>
> My 11 years of time spent in solitary confinement is trying to kill the 11 years of childhood I spent in Wadi Jamilah in Saudi Arabia. Now, I live on just the imagination of my wonderful childhood . . .
>
> At the moment when I am released, I would pray and kneel twice to Allah for the blessing of freedom, then go to my mother and hug her. As for my father, my chance to serve him is now gone because he passed away.

Tariq's suffering is as unnecessary as it is unforgivable. He was cleared for release approximately five years ago. No one disputes at this point whether he ought to be freed. And it is possible that those men Tariq describes, the ones who brought him to Guantánamo on the first day, will, at long last, come to release him. Perhaps even one day soon. In the meantime, Tariq has taken to scrawling the word "homesick" on the walls of his cell.

NOTES

1 Carol Rosenberg, *U.S. Has Now Lost 75% of Its Guantánamo Habeas Cases*, Miami Herald (July 8, 2010), http://www.mcclatchydc.com/2010/07/08/97211/federal-judge-order-release-of.html.

2 *Al Odah v. United States*, 611 F.3d 8, 14 (D.C. Cir. 2010).

3 See *Al-Adahi v. Obama*, 613 F.3d 1102, 1104 (D.C. Cir. 2010); *Esmail v. Obama*, 639 F.3d 1075, 1078 (D.C. Cir. 2011).

4 *Latif v. Obama*, 677 F.3d 1175, 1180–85 (D.C. Cir. 2011).

5 *Id.* at 1206 (Tatel, J., dissenting).

6 See National Defense Authorization Act for Fiscal Year 2012, Pub. L. No. 112–81, § 1028(b), 125 Stat. 1298 (2011).

7 Carol Rosenberg, *Dead Guantánamo Detainee Won, then Lost Court-Ordered Release*, Miami Herald (Sept. 11, 2012), http://www.miamiherald.com/news/nation-world/world/americas/guantanamo/article1942602.html.

8 Ken Gude, *Closing Gitmo: Obama Must Confront Congress*, Newsweek (Jan. 22, 2015), http://www.newsweek.com/closing-gitmo-obama-must-confront-congress-301286.

10

The "Taliban Five" and the Prisoner Exchange

FRANK GOLDSMITH

I was enjoying a peaceful Saturday afternoon at home on May 31, 2014, when my cell phone rang, showing a call from an unrecognized number. I decided to answer it. I am glad I did; it was from Ben Fox, an Associated Press reporter based in Florida with whom I had spoken over the years. Ben was in charge of the Caribbean desk for the A.P., which meant he covered the U.S. Naval Base in Guantánamo Bay, Cuba. I had always sought to cooperate with him, as I did with other good reporters, sharing whatever little information I was permitted to reveal about my representation of detainees at GTMO, as the base is informally known, and in return occasionally learning something from things the reporter had discovered.

"Your client is on a plane to Qatar as we speak," Ben said. Thus I learned that the man I had represented for the last seven years, Mullah Khairullah Said Wali Khairkhwa, had finally left the American prison after over a dozen years of captivity without charges. The government had not bothered to inform me or either of my co-counsel, Robert "Hoppy" Elliot and Griff Morgan, both from the same small law firm in Winston-Salem, North Carolina. Together we had collaborated in the representation of five detainees since 2007.

Khairkhwa's transfer to Qatar was instantly newsworthy. He was one of the "Taliban Five," all former top Taliban leaders held for a dozen years at Guantánamo, transferred to the custody of the government of Qatar for one year in exchange for the release by the Taliban of Sergeant Bowe Bergdahl. Our client was especially prominent. According to a *New York Times* article,

The most important figure is Khirullah Said Wali Khairkhwa, 47, a founding member of the Taliban and a confidant of Mullah Omar. He was the governor of Herat Province in western Afghanistan when the Taliban ruled, and is viewed by many officials in the Afghan government as a reasonable figure and possible interlocutor for future talks.

I was swamped with requests for media interviews, both print and broadcast, as reporters wanted to know more about my client, the conditions of the transfer, and my reaction to the prisoner swap.

Predictably, the politicians and pundits chimed in as well. In language reminiscent of the Bush administration's initial designation of all of the men imprisoned at Guantánamo Bay as the "worst of the worst," Sen. John McCain characterized the five men transferred as "the hardest of the hard-core," "the highest high-risk people," who are "possibly responsible for the deaths of thousands." They are "hardened terrorists who have the blood of Americans and countless Afghans on their hands," he said. Sen. Lindsey Graham called for a hearing, saying the prisoners "have American blood on their hands and surely as night follows day they will return to the fight." Fox News labeled the men "terror leaders," "a group of experienced jihadists" who had all served in various military and intelligence roles linked to Al Qaeda.

These hysterical statements were all wrong. They were nothing more than opportunistic hyperbole in the theater of partisan politics, part of the intractable posturing by Republicans determined to oppose the Obama administration at every step.

A more substantive objection was that the president's transfer of these detainees violated Section 1035 of the National Defense Authorization Act, which prohibits the Department of Defense from using appropriated funds to transfer any detainee unless the Secretary of Defense notifies certain congressional committees at least 30 days before the transfer.[1] President Obama did not give the notice; he said it was necessary to act swiftly because of reports of Sgt. Bergdahl's deteriorating health. Even some conservative commentators conceded that the congressional restriction on the executive branch's authority to trans-fer men whom it alone had decided to detain violated Article II of the Constitution, which enumerates the president's powers and makes him commander in chief of the nation's armed forces. The purported viola-tion of the restriction made for good political fodder, but it was hard for the Republican opposition to make the objection with a straight face, given their vigorous support for expanded executive power during the Bush regime.

But political theater aside, just who is Khairullah Khairkhwa?

There is no doubt that Mullah Khairkhwa was a high-ranking Tali-ban official. He never denied being a part of the administration of his country during the roughly five-year period that the Taliban formed the government of Afghanistan. At the time of the U.S. invasion of Afghani-stan in October 2001, he was serving as the governor of Herat Province, a large province in the west of Afghanistan, bordering Iran.

Khairkhwa rose to that position from humble beginnings. He was born in 1967 in a small village in the Arghestan district of Kandahar Province, in the ethnically Pashtun region of southern Afghanistan. His father was a farmer. After the Soviet Union invaded Afghanistan in 1980, Khairkhwa's family relocated to Quetta, Pakistan, a city some 70 miles from the Afghan border. He was educated in a madrassa, as was (and is) common for Pashtun boys.

In 1994, when the Soviets were finally expelled from Afghanistan, Khairkhwa returned to his country. He was introduced to some of the leadership of the Taliban, which had just begun its insurgency and had taken control of Kandahar Province. Khairkhwa was appointed the dis-trict administrator of Spin Boldak, one of the 14 districts in Kandahar Province closest to the Pakistani border. In his capacity as administrator, he treated people with respect; he proved to be a charismatic leader who could relate to people, even joking with them and making them laugh, according to those who knew him in this period. His skills as an effec-tive administrator caused him to be mentioned to Mullah Muhammad Omar, the one-eyed *mujahid* leader of the Taliban. The Taliban leadership appointed Khairkhwa to serve as a spokesman for the Taliban in the Pashto language, and he thereafter gave statements on behalf of the Taliban government to such international media outlets as the BBC and Voice of America. He was named as a member of the Shura, the governing council of the Taliban.[2] In 1996, when the Taliban took over Kabul, Khairkhwa was appointed its governor. Shortly thereafter, the acting minister of the interior, Qari Ahmadullah, was appointed as the head of Afghan intelligence, and Khairkhwa replaced him as acting minister of the interior. The Interior Ministry was responsible for the police force, which numbered about 7,000 officers for the entire country at that time, but because the Taliban were still fighting for control of the country, the Ministry of Defense, not the Ministry of Interior, took the lead in the actual conduct of military operations.

In October 1999, after the Taliban had secured control of most of the country, Mullah Omar appointed Khairkhwa as governor of Herat, a position he held until the collapse of the regime following the American invasion in 2001. When the bombs began falling on Herat, Khairkhwa fled to his home region of Arghestan in Kandahar. He was acquainted with Hamid Karzai, the newly installed president of the country, as they were both from the same general tribe, so he telephoned Karzai and asked if he had permission to remain at his home. Khairkhwa was given an appointment to meet with a Karzai emissary in a few days, but in the meantime he developed a medical problem requiring treatment that he could not obtain in Arghestan. So, leaving his family for what he believed would be a short trip to get medicine for his condition, he went to the nearby city of Chaman in Pakistan. He was invited for tea at the residence of Mullah Abdul Manan Niazi, who had also served as governor of Kabul and later as governor of Mazar-e-Sharif. Pakistani authorities raided the home looking for Niazi, who escaped. Khairkhwa did not try to flee; he remained in the home and was captured. He had his medication with him when he was arrested. He was turned over to the Americans, and in early 2002 he was transported, hooded and shackled, to the U.S. naval base at Guantánamo Bay.

I first met Khairkhwa in December 2008, shortly after we filed a habeas corpus petition on his behalf. He did not appear to be the sort of man who would joke and make people laugh. Wearing the customary dark full beard and dressed in a sage green jump suit, he sat at a table with his feet shackled to the floor of one of the small cubicles that served as interview rooms in Camp Echo. He had been sitting there for well over an hour before our arrival, and he was not pleased about the delay. We later learned that it was common practice to bring a detainee to the room at least an hour or two before the scheduled interview time and shackle him to the floor. Khairkhwa complained that due to an intestinal condition, he was required to use the bathroom frequently, and that it was unnecessarily cruel to leave him seated and shackled for so long. We agreed and passed along his complaint to the guard force, to no avail.

Khairkhwa warmed to us somewhat over time, but ours was never a relationship marked by close friendship. He was understandably mistrustful of lawyers and deeply skeptical about the American legal system. He predicted that when he left Guantánamo Bay, it would not be because of any court ruling, but rather through political negotiation. He was right.

Despite his well-placed cynicism, we made every effort to represent him vigorously. As we developed the case, we learned a great deal more about him than had appeared in the government's sweeping allegations that he was a close associate of Mullah Omar and was even connected with Al Qaeda, claims he vigorously disputed. The evidence we obtained painted a picture quite different from the government's accusations.

Although the government, in opposing Khairkhwa's release from Guantánamo, argued that he was a "hard-liner" among the Taliban (even though he was merely a political administrator, not a military commander), the unclassified evidence admitted at the habeas corpus hearing showed otherwise. We offered the live testimony of an Afghan witness, Hekmat Karzai (a cousin of the nation's president), a highly educated man who currently serves as director of the Centre for Conflict and Peace Studies (CAPS), an independent research institute in

Afghanistan founded in 2006 and dedicated to reducing the threat of political violence and to fostering an environment of peace and stability in that nation. CAPS has a main office in Kabul and a regional office in Kandahar, the area from which both Mullah Khairkhwa and Hekmat Karzai come.

Mr. Karzai is a scholar with a number of degrees, among them a bachelor of arts in political science from the University of Maryland and a master's degree in strategic studies from the American University. He served as an international fellow at the Edmund Walsh School of Foreign Service at Georgetown University, where he conducted research on terrorism, militant Islam, Afghan history, and Al Qaeda. He is also a former Afghan diplomat to the United States. His master's degree research focused on the Taliban and was published by the Kennedy School of Government at Harvard. Mr. Karzai is a senior fellow at the Joint Special Operations University, Special Operations Command, for the United States military forces, and he regularly briefs senior U.S. commanders in Afghanistan. He was born in Kandahar and is natively fluent in Pashto and Dari, as well as being fluent in English and Urdu. Karzai currently lives in Afghanistan and has known many of the senior Taliban leaders. He has researched the life and background of Khairullah Khairkhwa, including his role during the time the Taliban formed the government of that country.

To our surprise and delight, once we reached out to Mr. Karzai at the suggestion of an American professor, he volunteered to come to the United States at his expense to testify on behalf of our client. He did so because of his conviction that Khairkhwa was wrongly detained; that he was, in fact, known in Afghanistan as a moderate person with skills in mediating conflicts; and that he was a man who could be very useful to the Karzai government in reaching an accord with the Taliban insurgency. Mr. Karzai testified that from his research and knowledge, Mullah Khairkhwa received a religious education in Pakistan, and that upon his return to Afghanistan he rose in the ranks of the Taliban entirely as a civilian and never had any military role. Khairkhwa, said Karzai, is known for his moderate views and is held in respect by many people in Afghanistan.

At Khairkhwa's habeas hearing, we also presented expert testimony from Dr. Brian Williams, professor of Islamic history at the University of Massachusetts Dartmouth. Dr. Williams is a prolific author on the subject of war and terrorism in Central Eurasia and has testified as an expert witness in other Guantánamo proceedings. He also authored a book on the Afghan theater of operations for the U.S. Army, wrote the Joint Information Operations Warfare Command's field manual on Afghanistan, and has lectured on the Taliban and Afghanistan at the U.S. Special Operations Command, the CIA's Counter Terrorist Center, and various other high-level military and intelligence organizations. He is an expert on Afghan history and the emergence of the Taliban.

Dr. Williams refuted certain of the government's allegations against our client that were demonstrably historically inaccurate. For example, the government alleged that Khairkhwa was one of the commanders who led the conquest of a certain northern Afghan city by the Taliban in a certain year;[3] Dr. Williams, who had actually lived in the city in question, testified that no such conquest occurred in that year, and that Khairkhwa was never the commander of an assault in any year. (Williams named the commanders who led the eventual conquest of the city in a different year.) As Dr. Williams put it in his unclassified sworn declaration:

> I am familiar with all of the great Taliban commanders . . . but I have never come across a Mullah Khairkhwa. . . . I believe this lacuna is important. Simply put, had there been a Mullah Khairkhwa leading troops on the northern front from 1997 to 1998, one of these scholars or one of these opposing military commanders would have recorded his name somewhere.

As another example, the government alleged that Khairkhwa had somehow obtained intelligence regarding a planned American attack on Osama bin Laden at a specific training camp on a specific date in a specific year, and that his sharing of that intelligence had led to bin Laden's escape from the camp. But our unrebutted evidence showed that the camp in question had been destroyed by a cruise missile attack years earlier, under the Clinton administration, and Dr. Williams testified that there were no more attacks on the camp thereafter. The government's accusation was shown to be groundless.

In addition, we hired Zabihullah Noori, an experienced Afghan investigator fluent in Dari, Pashto, Urdu, and English, to interview people who had known Khairkhwa and his role in the Taliban administration. What we learned about our client was interesting. Noori managed to locate, interview, and provide declarations for two key witnesses: Mullah Abdul Salam Rocketi and Wakil Ahmad Motawakil.

Abdul Rocketi was a former military commander under the Taliban who served as a high-level commander in several provinces during the time of the American invasion. He initially fought against the Americans but later surrendered to them. Despite his military role in the Taliban, he was never imprisoned in Guantánamo but was allowed to go free. He ran unsuccessfully for the presidency in 2009, and today he serves in the Afghan parliament. He knew Khairkhwa from their service in the Taliban administration. He stated that Khairkhwa "was a civilian person, not a military commander. . . . He never had any military post and never undertook military command responsibilities." Rocketi added, "Mr. Khairkhwa was a scholar type of person. He was a man of service. He was a man of administration. He was a friendly person who wanted to behave with people in a lovely and friendly way. He wasn't interested in firing and shooting."

Wakil Motawakil was appointed as foreign minister of the Taliban government at the same time that Khairkhwa was appointed governor of Herat. Motawakil had been a close associate of Mullah Omar, having served as his advisor for political affairs. Following the American invasion, Motawakil was arrested, detained in Kandahar for four months, and then detained by the Americans in the prison at Bagram Airfield

Military Base for over a year. Thereafter he was allowed to live at home under house arrest for another year, after which he was released. For over ten years before giving his testimony, Mr. Motawakil had been living as a normal citizen of Afghanistan. In a declaration we submitted to the federal court, he stated that Khairkhwa "was not an officer, a military commander or a military person, and it is obvious. . . . He has always worked on the civil section. He was not a military man."

Mr. Noori also submitted his own declaration as a person who, living in Afghanistan and working as an investigator, had extensive knowledge of former Taliban leaders. He stated, "Mr. Khairkhwa has always been known as a moderate Taliban member by many Afghans. His reputation according to general consensus is that he was a pragmatic leader and was not an ideologue."

But perhaps the most persuasive proof that our client is not a violent, jihad-waging terrorist too dangerous to release, as charged by certain politicians and by the Obama administration's own Department of Justice, is how he is regarded by the current Afghan government itself. My colleague, Robert Elliot, decided to reach out to President Karzai and ask for his support in seeking Khairkhwa's return to Afghanistan to aid in negotiations between that government and the Taliban. He did that based on our client's representations that he would be known to President Karzai as a moderate member of the Taliban government during the time that it was in charge of the country, and that he could be effective in seeking a peaceful solution to the ongoing hostilities. Our letter was sent on November 19, 2010, and was translated and personally delivered to President Karzai's assistant by Zabihullah Noori. We obtained confirmation that the president had received the letter and had referred it to the High Peace Council, an arm of the Afghan government that had been established to, among other things, seek reconciliation with those Taliban members who were willing to work constructively for peace.

At first we heard nothing in response and were somewhat disheartened, though not surprised, given the enmity between the current government and its chief backer, the United States, and the Taliban insurgency. But in February 2011, we were delighted to receive a letter from Professor Burhanuddin Rabbani, himself a former president of Afghanistan then serving as chairman of the High Peace Council, calling for the release of Mullah Khairkhwa to live under government supervision in Kabul, because of the government's view that our client was a moderate member of the Taliban "who will positively contribute to the peace and reconciliation process in Afghanistan."[4]

President Karzai personally endorsed the proposal. When asked about the matter in a press conference, he said, "May God bring him. If Khairkhwa wants to make peace and play a good role in the peace process, . . . we can help him get his release." When a reporter pointed out that Khairkhwa was in Guantánamo, Karzai responded, "We will even bring him from there." Mullah Arsala Rahmani, himself a senator in the current government and a former Taliban minister, then serving as chairman of the High Peace Council's political prisoners committee, added that "Khairkhwa was an important man for the Taliban and his release would show the Americans are serious about negotiation. He is a good man and is well respected among the Taliban."

Of course, we immediately forwarded the letter and the report of President Karzai's endorsement of it to the U.S. Department of State and Department of Justice. We never received either an acknowledgement of the request or a reply of any kind, only silence. Reporters who became aware of the request sought the American government's reaction, but officials refused to comment.

And so we proceeded to challenge the legal basis for our client's detention under the uniquely narrow confines that govern habeas corpus litigation on behalf of Guantánamo detainees. As is the custom in these cases, the government called not a single live witness to prove that our client was a Taliban jihadist, or was linked to Al Qaeda, or was otherwise detainable under the law of war. The government did not need to. Under special rules tailored expressly for these cases:

- All hearsay is admissible; thus the government was permitted to "prove" that our client was a Taliban military commander in the late 1990s, *before* the American invasion—despite the lack of any evidence that he ever underwent any substantial military training—by citing newspaper comments by foreign reporters covering Taliban military campaigns from afar.
- Uncorroborated anonymous reports containing multiple levels of hearsay and that lack any of the indicia of reliability required by our own intelligence agencies are freely admitted and can be, standing alone, a sufficient basis to uphold the detention.
- Counsel are not permitted to share with our clients any classified information, and since all of the important disputed facts are classified, lawyers are severely hampered in preparing to meet the government's accusations.[5]
- The government may, with court approval, provide counsel with classified documents from which large portions have been redacted, despite the top secret security clearance held by the detainee's counsel; our motions seeking to know the basis on which the government contended that it could keep secret the information were denied.
- Proof by a mere preponderance of the evidence that the detainee was lawfully seized is sufficient to permit his imprisonment to continue indefinitely, perhaps for the rest of the detainee's life.
- Whether the detainee would pose a threat if released is irrelevant, as is evidence that the detainee is not an extremist but a moderate. There was not a shred of evidence that Khairkhwa had ever lifted a finger against an American or would ever do so if released, and none was required.

Perhaps the government conduct that has grated most on the habeas lawyers' sense of fairness is the insistence of the Obama administration, expressed in motions and briefs, that the government should be allowed to submit classified documentary evidence *ex parte* and *in camera* to the court, not merely for the court to determine whether redaction of certain material from the document was proper, but for the court to consider on the merits in deciding the outcome of the case. Such a secret procedure of adjudication outdoes even Kafka; not only may the accused not know the accusation, but neither may his lawyers, whom the government has otherwise deemed trustworthy to possess secret or top secret information. Some judges have granted such motions. The judge in Khairkhwa's case declined to rule on the issue, finding the remainder of the government's evidence sufficient.

Occasionally, and often as hyperbole, we are prone to label as "Kafkaesque" procedures we find unfair. But consider the eerie similarity between the following passage from Kafka's *Der Prozeß* (*The Trial*), published in 1925, and American justice in 2014 as administered to the men it has detained indefinitely without charges:

> K. must remember that the trial would not be public; certainly if the court deemed it necessary it could be made public, but there is no law that says it has to be. Naturally, therefore, the accused and his defense counsel do not have access even to the court records, and especially not to the indictment, and that means one does not know—or at least not precisely—what charges to meet in the first plea. . . . Conditions like this, of course, place the defense in a very unfavorable and difficult position. But that is what they intend. In fact, defense is not really allowed under the law, it's only tolerated, and there is even some dispute about whether the relevant parts of the law imply even that. So strictly speaking, there is no such thing as a counsel acknowledged by the court, and anyone who comes before this court as counsel is basically no more than a barrack room lawyer.

So in the end, given the low bar to sustain the government's right to detain, the judge determined that Mullah Khairkhwa, as a member of the Taliban "forces," had been properly detained, and that his moderate views and lack of dangerousness were irrelevant to the decision at hand. In an opinion filed on May 31, 2011, the judge denied the petition for writ of habeas corpus.

Of course, we were disappointed with the decision. We honestly believed we had won when we left the courtroom in Washington, D.C., after trying the case for the better part of a week. We appealed, knowing that an appeal was almost certainly futile, given the composition of the U.S. Court of Appeals for the D.C. Circuit at that time and its track record in other cases. Predictably, that court affirmed the denial of the writ on December 14, 2012, in a smugly written opinion cursorily dismissing Khairkhwa's concerns about the fairness and accuracy of the determination that he could be held in prison indefinitely without charges.[6]

But in the period between the denial of the habeas petition and the affirmance of that denial by the D.C. Circuit, rumors began to circulate in the press about preliminary talks between the Taliban and American officials. Early in 2012, the Taliban set up an office in Doha, Qatar. Marc Grossman, the Obama administration's special representative for Afghanistan and Pakistan, traveled to Doha for "a number of meetings" related to Afghanistan. There was talk by the Taliban representatives of the transfer of five particular Afghan detainees—our client included—from Guantánamo as a condition of negotiations, a condition downplayed, but not denied outright, by Mr. Grossman. Other Western and Afghan officials reportedly said that if any detainees were released, they would be transferred to house arrest in Qatar.

In fact, on February 29, 2012, as we were working on Khairkhwa's appeal in the Secure Facility just outside downtown Washington, I received a call on my cell phone from Jeh Johnson, then general counsel to the Department of Defense (now secretary of the Department of Homeland Security). Mr. Johnson asked if we could talk confidentially. I said we could. He said that the idea of a transfer of five men, including Khairkhwa, from Guantánamo to Qatar was being discussed, but that it was a very sensitive subject that had the potential to become controversial. Afghan officials were concerned that a transfer of one of their citizens to another country would violate their country's constitution. Getting the citizen's consent to such a transfer would solve that problem; hence the reason for his call. I assured Mr. Johnson that our client would consent, based on our conversations with him over the years. We discussed in general terms some of the other parameters of such a transfer—rigorous monitoring by the government of Qatar, financing by

Qatar of living quarters, family visits, and so forth—and we ended the conversation. And that was the last I ever heard from the United States government on the subject of my client's release from Guantánamo.

So it was to my surprise that on May 31, 2014—three years to the day from the denial of the writ of habeas corpus—I received the telephone call from reporter Ben Fox informing me that my client was on a plane to Qatar. The government had not breathed a word to any of the five men's lawyers that their clients were about to be released.

Predictably, there was an uproar about the release of five "terrorists" with American blood on their hands. Even respected think-tank commentators and reporters who should have known better swallowed whole the government's early characterizations of our client as a dangerous terrorist, just as they had accepted without question whatever the government had said about any detainee. Khairkhwa, they said was deemed likely to "return to the fight." "Deemed"—end of story. Deemed likely to return to a fight he was never in, and was never accused of being in: the fight against the United States and its allies post-9/11. None seemed willing to probe beneath the surface of the government's vilification of these five men to see if the accusations would withstand serious scrutiny.

To put the claims in context, it is helpful to recall that exactly such labels were carelessly applied to every one of the men who have been detained at Guantánamo Bay. Altogether, some 779 Muslim men from 43 different countries, of ages ranging from 13 to 90, were brought, hooded and shackled on clandestine flights, to GTMO, where they were be kept in isolation from family, friends, and—had the government had its way—from lawyers. Bush administration leaders claimed that they had been "picked up on the battlefield fighting American forces," were "the worst of the worst," "bomb-makers," "terrorists," "among the most dangerous, best-trained, vicious killers on the face of the earth," "associated with al-Qaeda."

Yet that administration, quietly and without court compulsion, released well over 500 of them, and the Obama administration, which in-

herited 242 detainees, has released others, bit by bit. A number of men
have died during their prolonged custody, some by their own hand. As
it turns out from the publically available facts, the overwhelming majority were not who the government claimed they were, according to a
study by Seton Hall University School of Law professor Mark Denbeaux.
United States forces captured only 5% of the detainees at Guantánamo.
Others were bought from tribesmen motivated by the large American
bounties. Eight-six percent were arrested by the Northern Alliance or
Pakistani authorities, having been captured for reasons that are, to say
the least, opaque. Some were seized from their homes, places of work,
or simply off the street, mostly in Pakistan, not Afghanistan, often based
upon anonymous allegations of a connection to Al Qaeda or the Taliban.
Most were never on a battlefield and have not been determined to have
committed any hostile act against the United States or its allies. The government officials and politicians simply misstated the facts.

In the cases of the Guantánamo detainees, we lawyers cannot discuss
all of the specific facts publicly, because we are required to trade our free
speech for access to the classified evidence necessary to represent our
clients. The government alone decides what to declassify and what to
continue to guard as a secret, and it is not surprising that it chooses to
declassify only the facts that support its case, facts seized upon by those
who, for whatever motivation, support the continued detention of these
men, without regard to "the rest of the story," as newsman Paul Harvey
used to say.

But it is telling that after over a dozen years of detention, the Government has managed to charge, try, and convict only a handful—
fewer than ten—of the 779 men it brought to the base, all, except one,
in military tribunals that have been criticized as fundamentally unfair
and one-sided.* This is not a record of ringing prosecutorial success. Of
the five men I represented, including Mullah Khairkhwa, none was ever

*Editor's note: One Guantánamo detainee, Ahmed Khalfan Ghailani, was transferred to the U.S.
District Court for the Southern District of New York, where he was convicted for his role in the
1998 bombings of U.S. embassies in Kenya and Tanzania and sentenced to life imprisonment. No
other Guantánamo detainee has been prosecuted in federal court.

charged with even the most minor infraction; they were simply held for years without charges until it pleased the government to send them back home. Where is the evidence that they are terrorists? Approximately half of the men still remaining at Guantánamo as of this writing have long been determined not to be a threat and have been approved for transfer; the only impediments to their release are political.

Of course, the other criticism of the transfer was that the price paid for the return of Sgt. Bowe Bergdahl was too high. Bergdahl was accused of being a deserter whose return was not worth the risk to the nation from the release of the five Taliban officials. From the comfort of their armchairs and news desks, some politicians and commentators assessed the quality of Bergdahl's service to the Army and found it wanting. Did he really get lost and then captured, or was he a soldier who deserted his post? Worse, did he intentionally cross over to join the enemy? Pontificating without benefit of knowledge of the facts, the critics second-guessed the administration's decision. The necessary implication of the partisan opposition to the exchange is that Bergdahl should have been left in Taliban custody, to suffer whatever fate his captors ultimately decided to impose.

I served on active duty during the Vietnam Era as a military lawyer in the Army's Judge Advocate General's Corps and handled many cases of desertion and absence without leave. Bergdhal has been charged with desertion and misbehavior before the enemy. The Uniform Code of Military Justice, a fair system of adjudication that governs courts-martial, will now determine his guilt or innocence. No one should evaluate a missing soldier's performance from afar, without knowledge of all of the facts, and conclude that we just leave him in the hands of the enemy. We should not leap to conclusions on the basis of media reports and judge Bergdahl in absentia, leaving him to the mercies of Taliban justice.

That kind of attitude is foreign to American military tradition and to the military traditions of many nations. I was first commissioned as an Infantry officer in 1967; I was taught, as I suspect all who served were, that one does not willingly leave comrades on the battlefield or in the hands of the enemy. Prisoner of war exchanges are now a routine part of every war, laudable progress from the days when prisoners were executed or enslaved. The Israelis, for example, have traded over a thousand Palestinian prisoners for the return of a single Israeli soldier. For them, such exchanges are almost routine, because of their belief in the ironclad principle that there exists a sacred bond of mutual loyalty between the nation and the citizen-soldier. The fundamental values of America's military have always been the same.

Moreover, President Obama gave up very little in approving the transfer of Khairkhwa and his colleagues. The war in Afghanistan is winding down, and soon it will end, as far as American involvement goes. Under firmly established principles of international law, uncharged prisoners of war such as these five men will have to be released. Based on these principles, John Bellinger, President George W. Bush's legal advisor to the State Department, has stated that "it is likely that the U.S. would be required, as a matter of international law, to release [these Taliban detainees] shortly after the end of 2014, when U.S. combat operations cease in Afghanistan. The Administration appears to have reached a defensible, hold-your-nose compromise by arranging, in exchange for the release of Sergeant Bergdahl, for the individuals to be held in Qatar for a year before they return to Afghanistan." Ben Wittes of the Brookings Institution put it this way: "We are, after all, winding down this conflict, and the authority to detain Taliban forces—as opposed to Al Qaeda forces—won't last that much longer than the end of combat. So what we may have traded here is one POW deserter (assuming that's what Bergdahl was, for a moment) in exchange for hastening the release of five Taliban by an indeterminate number of months."

Examination of the facts will puncture the hyperbole of those who claim to know all about Khairullah Khairkhwa and about the wisdom of exchanging him and his four colleagues for an American serviceman. Facts are inconvenient nuisances for partisan champions bent on securing political advantage.

دافغانستان اسلامی جمهوریت
دسولی عالی شورا
د ا، الئشا
High Peace Council
Detainee Affairs Committee

تاریخ ۷ ۱۱ / ۳۸۹

شماره (۸۹۵)

February 3, 2011

Mr. Robert M Elliot
426 Old Salem Road, Winston-Salem, NC 27101

Subject: <u>Khairullah Khairkhwa</u>

Dear Mr. Elliot,

I am writing in response to your request received through His Excellency the President's Office regarding Mr. Khairullah Khairkhwa's case.

After reviewing and discussing Mr. Khairullah Khairkhwa's case, the sub-committee for detainee affairs of the High Peace Council of Afghanistan, made the following recommendations:

- The High Peace Council is of the view that the release of Mr. Khairkhwa, th former governor of Herat Province who was a moderate official of the Taliban government, will positively contribute to the peace and reconciliation process in Afghanistan; and

- The High Peace Council supports the release of Mr. Khairullah Khairkhwa, from the Guantanamo Bay prison.

- After his release and transfer to the Afghan authorities, Mr. Khairkhwa and his family will live in Kabul under the supervision of government authorities

- The High Peace Council will provide any necessary support that can facilitate his release and safe transfer to Afghanistan

- The committee, therefore, recommends Mr. Khairkhwa's release

Through this letter, I would also like to assure you of the High Peace Council's support to you in defending Mr. Khairkhwa's case.

Should you require any further assistance from the High Peace Council, please do not hesitate to advise us.

Sincerely,

Professor Burhanuddin Rabbani,
Chairman, High Peace Council

High Peace Council, Joint Secretariat, Kabul Afghanistan

Letter from Afghan High Peace Council to counsel for Khairullah Khairkhwa supporting his release.

John Adams, the second president of our nation, was first a trial lawyer who knew the importance of focusing on the facts and the evidence, not on labels. In 1770, at the age of 34, he agreed to represent a British captain and eight of his soldiers who had, the previous night, opened fire on a crowd of protesting civilians, killing five of them, an event that became known to history as the Boston Massacre. In urging acquittal, he told the Boston jury this: "Facts are stubborn things, and whatever may be our wishes, our inclinations, or the dictums of our passions, they cannot alter the state of facts and evidence." That jury examined the facts, and it acquitted the British captain and six of his eight soldiers, convicting the other two only of manslaughter.

A similar respect for the facts would mitigate the partisan-driven calumny that characterizes public discourse over men such as Khairullah Khairkhwa. While no one can predict what a man unjustly imprisoned for over a dozen years without charges might do upon his release, there is no reason to believe that Mullah Khairkhwa will not return to his role as a respected, moderate mediator of conflicts upon his eventual repatriation to his country.

NOTES

1   Congress never imposed such a restriction on President Bush, who released over 500 Guantánamo detainees with no congressional involvement.

2   Actually, there were several such councils: a Supreme Shura that answered to Mullah Mohammad Omar *Akhund*, the spiritual leader of the Taliban and the self-proclaimed *Amir ul-Muminin* (Commander of the Faithful); a Military Shura; and the Kabul Shura, both of the latter being subordinate to the Supreme Shura. Some commentators tend to conflate these councils into one called simply "the Shura" or the "Supreme Shura." The evidence is unclear as to when Khairkhwa was made a member of a Shura, and there is conflicting information about which Shura it was, although no source says that it was the Military Shura. Mullah Khairkhwa was not captured because he was known as a Shura member; that fact is never mentioned in the unclassified accusations against him or in his interrogations in Afghanistan and Guantánamo.

3   The author cannot be more specific because it is unclear whether the government has elected to declassify for release to the public the details of the accusation.

4   A copy of the letter is appended. Tragically, Prof. Rabbani was assassinated in his home on September 20, 2011, his 71st birthday, by a suicide bomber posing as a

well-wisher who had hidden explosives in his turban. Also killed in the blast were four other members of the High Peace Council. Ironically, days earlier Rabbani had given a speech at a conference on "Islamic awakening" in Tehran in which he urged Muslim scholars to issue a fatwa banning the tactic of suicide bombings.

5 In another case, the Obama Justice Department even argued, unsuccessfully, that a detainee could not view his *own statements* if derived from a classified document.

6 As of this writing, the D.C. Circuit has yet to affirm a grant of the writ, and it has yet to reverse outright a lower court's denial of the writ. In open defiance of the Supreme Court's 2008 decision in *Boumediene v. Bush* granting detainees the right of habeas corpus and ordering meaningful judicial review of their detention, the Circuit has become a black hole from which no habeas applicant ever emerges successful.

11

Hamdan

The Legal Challenge to Military Commissions

JOSEPH MCMILLAN

The *Hamdan* litigation can be understood as two separate cases, both involving a Yemeni citizen named Salim Ahmed Hamdan. To understand *Hamdan II*, which was finally resolved during the Obama administration, one needs to understand the context created by *Hamdan I*, the landmark Supreme Court case decided in 2006.

Salim Hamdan served as a driver and auto mechanic for Osama bin Laden in Afghanistan from 1996 until the fall of 2001. In late November 2001, Hamdan was seized at a roadblock set up by anti-Taliban militia in a small town called Takh-te-Pul, about 20 miles south of Kandahar, as he returned from a trip to the Pakistan border where he had dropped off his wife (who was pregnant at the time) and his young daughter. He was evacuating his family and others from Kandahar as the military noose tightened around that city, the last major urban center under Taliban control following the introduction of U.S. troops into Afghanistan in October 2001. Upon capture, Hamdan was handed over to U.S. military personnel who were coordinating the efforts of the indigenous militia forces. He was interrogated for a week in Takh-te-Pul, and then transported to an undisclosed location (possibly the Panshir Valley) for further interrogation. In late December 2001, he was moved to the Bagram Airfield Military Base, where he was held as a "ghost detainee" (not identified to the International Committee of the Red Cross), and later to a military base in Kandahar. The interrogations, which included beatings and threats of torture and death, continued at all these locations. In late April 2002, he was transported to the Guantánamo Bay naval base in Cuba, where he would spend the next six and a half years.

For over a year after his arrival at Guantánamo, Hamdan was subjected to dozens of additional interrogation sessions, conducted using a variety of coercive techniques including blasting his cell with loud music, sleep deprivation, sexual humiliation, and (what he found most debilitating) prolonged periods of solitary confinement. In July 2003, following a final round of interrogation by a "clean team" who would provide testimony at trial, Hamdan was identified as a person whom the president had reason to believe was a member of Al Qaeda and had engaged in or conspired to commit acts of terrorism. He was among the first group of detainees slated to be tried by a military commission that would be convened under the terms of a military order issued by President Bush on November 13, 2001.

Hamdan I

Hamdan v. Rumsfeld ("Hamdan I") was the case litigated in U.S. federal courts challenging the legality of the military order and the system of military commissions it established. The case came to us at the Seattle office of Perkins Coie in February 2004, when the detailed military defense counsel, Lt. Commander Charles Swift, and a Georgetown law professor who was assisting Charlie, Neal Katyal, asked us to associate with them to file a petition for a writ of habeas corpus on Hamdan's behalf. Neal and Charlie were looking for a venue in the U.S. Court of Appeals for the Ninth Circuit because there was a circuit split over whether federal district courts had jurisdiction to consider habeas petitions filed by Guantánamo detainees. The Ninth Circuit, in *Gherebi v. Bush*, had ruled that jurisdiction existed.

I got involved immediately after the first substantive communication with Neal and Charlie, when my partner Harry Schneider told me he had just completed an initial telephone conference with them. I immediately urged that we take the case. That afternoon, Harry and I met with two associates in our office, Charles Sipos and David East, both of whom had already agreed to work on this pro bono effort. (David had taken the initial call to the firm from Neal, who had been one of his former professors at Georgetown School of Law). We got to work immediately, focusing initially on procedural issues around filing materials in conformity with the Classified Information Procedures Act (CIPA), Charlie's status as "next friend" for Salim (the representative for purposes of a habeas action, where the prisoner cannot act himself), jurisdiction, and whether venue in a federal court in Seattle could be proper.

We also began educating ourselves on military commissions, which none of us at Perkins Coie had ever heard of before. For good reason: the last time military commissions had been used by the United States was in the World War II era. They had not been used in Korea, Vietnam, the first Iraq war, or any other U.S. military operation since the 1940s. When we got involved, Salim had not even been charged with a particular crime. When Charlie asked the Convening Authority what the charge was, he was told it would be whatever he succeeding in having his client plead guilty to. In February 2004, Charlie wrote to the Convening Authority, invoking the speedy trial rule under Uniform Code of Military Justice (UCMJ) Article 810. He received a written response telling him that the UCMJ did not apply. The government was already on record in saying that neither the Constitution nor the Geneva Conventions applied at Guantánamo. Thus, it was the government's position, essentially, that *no law applied*, apart from whatever further orders the executive might promulgate to guide the workings of the military commission. Charlie was also told that his access to Salim was contingent on his making progress in negotiating a guilty plea.

By mid-March 2004, Neal forwarded to us for review a draft petition for a writ of habeas corpus for Salim. What most struck me about this initial draft was its limited request for relief based on two arguments that, while certainly part of our case, I thought failed to come to grips with the main issue, i.e., the legality of the use of military commissions in the alleged "Global War on Terror." The two issues raised by the draft were (1) a speedy trial demand based on Article 810 of the UCMJ, and (2) relief from solitary confinement (which the government referred to as "pre-commission segregation") while awaiting trial based on Article 103 of the UCMJ and/or Common Article 3 of the Third Geneva Convention.

By this time, I had learned enough to know that military commissions were originally created as battlefield courts dispensing summary (and usually severe) justice in locales where civilian courts could not operate. They were courts of necessity established to fill gaps in the jurisdiction of courts-martial, designed to operate only in war zones or areas of occupation. Accordingly, I felt that the initial draft petition was far too modest in that it failed to challenge the fundamental premises of the commissions or of the president's action in unilaterally establishing them. The relief requested by the draft could be granted in its entirety without halting Salim's military commission trial, without inhibiting the president's future use of these antiquated military tribunals, without even giving Salim the opportunity to challenge his indefinite detention and regain his liberty.

It was my view that if we were going to question the president on a matter of national security, then we should make it a meaningful challenge, one that would put a significant dent in the aggressive program of unilateral executive action unconstrained by law that was animating so much of the administration's conduct. There was also the legal imperative that in habeas jurisprudence a petitioner is barred from filing a second or successive habeas petition. In other words, this thing could not be done in a piecemeal fashion, as courts generally will not entertain a request for further relief in a follow-up habeas petition. Any relief we wanted for our client had to be sought in the initial petition, which might be the only one that Salim would have the right to file, assuming he was even able to file one at all since the entire question of federal court jurisdiction over habeas petitions from Guantánamo detainees was still unresolved at that point.

Accordingly, I felt that the draft petition needed to be reworked to present a far more thoroughgoing challenge to the legality of the military order and the military commission system it created. Among other things, the military order proclaimed that the United States was involved in a global war on terror, dramatically expanding the scope of Congress's Authorization for Use of Military Force (AUMF), passed days after the 9/11 attacks. It stated that individuals detained in that "war" would have no recourse to civilian courts, whether domestic or international, and would instead by tried by military commissions.

Military commissions are relics of a bygone era that are antithetical to the principles of civilian rule and adjudication by an independent judiciary. They could only be justified by the logistical realities of the period in which they emerged (the 18th and 19th centuries), where in theaters of war or zones of occupation civilian courts were unable to function. They were composed of a panel of military officers untrained in the law, and they typically focused on simple factual determinations on or near a battlefield. In the post-9/11 era, however, there was no need for the United States to employ these *ad hoc* tribunals to dispense rough justice on or near a battlefield. Indeed, we were not proposing to do so. Instead, the United States was transporting men and boys halfway around the world to the Guantánamo Bay naval base, detaining and interrogating them for years before deciding whether criminal prosecution was warranted. There was absolutely no exigency that justified stripping these individuals of the rights of a civilian trial or of a court-martial (which, since the enactment of the UCMJ in 1950, had evolved to provide similar if not greater procedural protections for the accused than regular civilian courts). Indeed, under the law of war, which the administration itself relied on in maintaining that the president was authorized to establish military commissions, any person seized in a war zone claiming the protections of the Geneva Convention (as Salim was) could only be tried "by the same courts according to the same procedure" as the military personnel of the detaining power. This meant that Salim (who at that time was entitled to presumptive POW status under Article 5 of the Third Geneva Convention) had a right to be tried in a court-martial, not in some jury-rigged *ad hoc* tribunal for which rules and procedures had not even been established.

In March 2004, I presented these views to Charles Sipos and David East in a meeting among the three of us in my office, and they readily agreed that we should be more ambitious in our objectives in this case. Neal and Charlie were also receptive to our suggestion that the scope of the legal challenge be significantly expanded. Over the next couple of weeks Neal, Harry, and I rewrote the petition to include an array of more fundamental legal claims, including constitutional challenges to the president's authority to create military commissions, equal protection claims, and challenges to the subject matter and personal jurisdiction of the commission based on the UCMJ and international law. In early April 2004, we filed the petition in the United States District Court for the Western District of Washington, sitting in Seattle.

The government immediately moved to hold the case in abeyance pending the Supreme Court's decision in *Rasul v. Bush*, which raised the question whether federal courts had any jurisdiction over Guantánamo at all. At a hearing on the motion in early May, district court Judge Robert Lasnik offered a few trenchant observations:

[T]he fact that we're in federal court talking about these things I hope sends the message to the Executive Branch that part of what makes this country so great is not just that we have the most military power, or the most wealth, but we have a system in the federal courts where the most vulnerable and the most powerless still can get into the courthouse and have their cases heard to some degree. . . . [W]hat separates this country from other very powerful, very rich, and very militarily strong countries [is] to have an independent judiciary that can make decisions that are respected by the Executive Branch and the Congressional Branch, even when they strongly disagree with it.

Ironically, of course, the executive branch in this case was determined to do everything in its power to *prevent* exactly what Judge Lasnik was honoring with these remarks. Over the course of next two years, the government employed every possible device and advanced every conceivable argument to deny Salim a hearing in federal court and avoid a ruling on his case. The government's next move, after the *Rasul* decision clarified that jurisdiction existed, was to get the decision out of Judge Lasnik's hands, as the tenor of his comments from the bench clearly did not conform to the executive's view of the deference it was owed. Conveniently for the government, a Ninth Circuit ruling in *Gherebi* led Judge Lasnik to conclude that he was required to transfer the case to the D.C. District Court in Washington, D.C., a change of venue that occurred in August 2004.

Over the next two years, Neal Katyal, Charles Sipos, and I were primarily responsible for briefing the legal issues (though others contributed, particularly with research), first to the district court, then to the U.S. Court of Appeals for the D.C. Circuit, and finally to the Supreme Court of the United States.[1] Meanwhile, Lt. Commander Swift was focused on matters before the original military commission (before proceedings there were halted), and was chiefly responsible for communications with our client since he was best positioned to gain physical access to Salim at the Guantánamo Bay naval base.

Hamdan I was a long shot. I knew that from the beginning, but I believed deeply in what we were doing and in the positions we were advancing. I had enough experience at that point in my career to know that litigation is usually more akin to a marathon than to a sprint, and the path to a final result is almost never direct. This certainly proved true in *Hamdan*. First, following a hearing at the D.C. district court in which Neal, Charlie, and I all presented parts of our argument, Judge Robertson granted the writ in November 2004, stopping Hamdan's first military commission in its tracks. A pretrial hearing at Guantánamo was abruptly adjourned in midsession on the day the writ issued. Next, a unanimous panel of the D.C. Circuit reversed on all counts in July 2005. Five days later, one of the judges on the panel, John Roberts, was nominated for a position on the Supreme Court by President Bush. Then the Supreme Court granted certiorari in November 2005, after declining to act on our petition for review at weekly conferences throughout October. Congress then passed the Detainee Treatment Act (DTA) in December 2005, which purported to strip the federal courts (including the Supreme Court) of jurisdiction. That in itself constituted a remarkable event from a separation of powers perspective, as never before had Congress attempted to strip the Supreme Court of jurisdiction over a case which it had already determined was worthy of its review.

Fortunately for Salim, the Supreme Court was not impressed. The government moved to dismiss based on the DTA, we opposed (arguing that the jurisdictional strip did not apply retroactively and was in any event an unconstitutional suspension of the Great Writ), and the Supreme Court responded by simply giving each side an additional 15 minutes of argument to address the issue. The jurisdictional provision in the DTA was the last and most formidable of numerous technical and procedural bars that the government invoked to try to avoid a ruling on the merits. Ultimately, the Supreme Court accepted our position that the DTA did not apply retroactively. At the oral argument in March 2006, Neal did an excellent job in moving through the troublesome jurisdictional and abstention issue to effectively engage with the merits.[2]

Hamdan I culminated in the Supreme Court's June 2006 decision striking down the president's unilateral scheme of military commissions. The Court ruled that the military order was not a lawful exercise of executive power. Rather, whatever power the president had to convene commissions was constrained by the UCMJ and by the laws of war (a subset of international law). In ignoring those constraints, the president had violated separation of powers principles, the UCMJ, and the Geneva Conventions. A plurality (though not a majority) of the Supreme Court further explained that the single charge sworn out against Salim, conspiracy, is not a war crime, and therefore the military commission lacked subject matter jurisdiction. Of particular significance was the Court's ruling that Hamdan was protected by Common Article 3 of the Geneva Conventions, which the U.S. violated by attempting to try him in a court that was not "regularly constituted." As Justice Kennedy pointed out in his concurring opinion (providing the crucial fifth vote in a 5–3 decision, as Justice Roberts recused), the regularly constituted military court in the United States is a court-martial, not a newly minted military commission whose rules were still being written and revised as the *Hamdan* case proceeded. Overall, Justice Stevens's closing line in his opinion for the Court summed up the matter nicely: "in undertaking to try Hamdan and subject him to criminal punishment, the Executive is bound to comply with the rule of law that prevails in this jurisdiction." Standing alone it is a modest enough statement, and should be entirely uncontroversial, but in the context of 2006, it was a pointed rejection of the aggressive assertions of executive prerogative that were being advanced in the Global War on Terror. As former Acting Solicitor General of the United States Walter Dellinger put it, "*Hamdan* is simply the most important decision on executive power and the rule of law ever. Ever." Whether that assessment is true or not, it is clear that the significance of the case extended well beyond Salim's unique situation.

The holding that Common Article 3 applied to detained Al Qaeda operatives, and that even an accused terrorist like Hamdan had standing to seek relief for its violation, seems to have caught our senior national security officials completely off guard. Indeed, under applicable U.S. law at that time (the War Crimes Act), *any* violation of Common Article 3 was a war crime. Even more troubling for an administration that had authorized waterboarding, wall slamming, close confinement (i.e., cramming people into small boxes), sleep deprivation, sexual humiliation, stress positions, and other so-called "enhanced interrogation techniques," Common Article 3 also prohibited "cruel treatment and torture" and "outrages upon personal dignity, in particular humiliating and degrading treatment." To the great shame of the United States, such conduct was at the heart of the brutal interrogation regime put in place by the Bush administration, with approval from the highest levels of our national security leadership. The claim that such conduct was "legal" was based on the infamous "Torture Memos" from the Justice Department's Office of Legal Counsel, one of which expressly stated that Common Article 3 did not apply in the war against Al Qaeda. Now the Supreme Court had spoken on the issue, holding that Common Article 3 *did* apply.

The Bush administration mobilized immediately to address the fall-out from the *Hamdan* decision. The result was the Military Commissions Act of 2006 (MCA), introduced in September and hastily enacted by Congress in October 2006, without the benefit of public hearings. The act revived the military commission system, providing the legislative support that had been lacking from the president's initial scheme. Like the DTA, it again attempted to strip the federal courts of jurisdiction over habeas petitions from Guantánamo detainees. (Later, in its 2008 *Boumediene v. Bush* decision, the Supreme Court struck down this provision as an unconstitutional suspension of the Great Writ.) Also included in the legislation was a section amending the War Crimes Act, which (if legal) would have the effect of retroactively exculpating anyone who had violated Common Article 3 by attempting to try Hamdan in an irregular court, or who had engaged in torture or inhumane conduct in the "enhanced interrogation" programs. The validity of this remarkable provision has not been tested, primarily because President Obama, upon assuming office in January 2009, made a truly lamentable policy decision that those responsible for such conduct, including torture, would not be held accountable for their acts. That decision gravely undermines the moral standing of the United States to challenge human rights abuses abroad and weakens our ability to protect our own citizens (including our men and women in the armed forces) who might be subjected to such abuse in the future.

Hamdan II

The MCA's passage set the stage for *Hamdan II*, which became the second war crimes case initiated by the United States against Salim in April

2007, when new charges were sworn out against him. The case proceeded under the name *United States v. Hamdan*. Salim's victory at the Supreme Court in June 2006 (*Hamdan I*) had not resulted in his release. On the contrary, he was still being held at Guantánamo as an enemy combatant, although (for a few months at least) not as an accused war criminal. Now Salim was once again charged with "conspiracy" (despite the plurality holding in *Hamdan I* that conspiracy is not a war crime), again moved into solitary confinement, and again slated for trial by a military commission at Guantánamo, this time a commission convened under the new MCA. Hamdan and a young Canadian, Omar Khadr, were the first referrals by the Convening Authority under the new system.

By this time, the legal team defending Salim had changed somewhat. Neal had let us know after the Supreme Court decision that he could no longer continue, at least at the all-consuming level of activity he had previously devoted to the case. (He did consult with us periodically, however.) At Perkins Coie, we were pressing forward with the habeas case, which continued to challenge the legality of Salim's detention and seek his release from Guantánamo. In addition, following the passage of the MCA, we expected new criminal charges. For his part, Charlie Swift had been passed over for promotion for a second time in 2006, so under the Navy's "up-or-out" system, he would have to retire from the JAG Corps in the spring of 2007. Upon learning of the new charges against Salim, however, he decided to continue, like us at Perkins Coie, as civilian defense counsel, a role that was permitted under the MCA and the Rules for Military Commissions, newly promulgated in January 2007. We also gained two valuable new team members: the newly detailed military defense counsel, Lt. Commander Brian Mizer, a brilliant young Navy JAG lawyer, and Andrea Prasow, a talented and dedicated civilian attorney who had joined the Office of the Chief Defense Counsel.

It was only after we signed on as civilian defense counsel for the military commission trial that we at Perkins Coie (Harry Schneider, Charles Sipos, and I) were able to get orders allowing us to travel to Guantánamo to visit our client. The logistics of the situation were awful, a completely artificial situation created by the government, which was determined to hold the detainees offshore in order to argue that they had no rights under U.S. law, except those conferred by the MCA. Getting security clearances created the initial delays. Then, for Harry, Charles, and myself, it took two full days of travel to get to the base (one day to get to the East coast from Seattle; another day to get to Guantánamo on either a military flight or one of the few small commercial carriers allowed to land at the airfield). In general, communications with Salim were possible only in face-to-face conversations at the prison camps, scheduled through the staff judge advocate's (SJA's) office at JTF-GTMO. Meeting times were restricted, notes were subject to review and even seizure by camp personnel, and the process of preparing and transporting the detainee to the meetings could be (depending on location) sufficiently onerous for the client that he would not even want to meet with counsel.

My first trip to the base was in April 2007. I traveled with Charlie Swift, our translator, Prof. Charles ("Chuck") Schmitz of Towson State University, and our paralegal, an enlisted Air Force specialist, Kim Lindee. As I previously described in *The Guantánamo Lawyers*,[3] Salim's condition was not good. By that time, the months of solitary confinement that had resumed in late 2006 had taken a heavy toll on his ability to control his emotions and to concentrate on the pressing matters that we hoped to discuss. He was angry and desperate, overwhelmed by the apparent hopelessness of his situation. He had, after all, won his case at the Supreme Court. But he remained trapped in the same nightmare— facing war crimes charges before a military commission—only worse, as he now endured the crushing isolation in a newly constructed supermax prison. His life was a windowless 6' x 12' room for 23 hours a day, with no access to natural light or air, and no human contact. The conditions were absolutely debilitating.

The charges preferred against Salim were (1) conspiracy, and (2) material support for terrorism. They were based primarily on the fact that Salim admitted that he served as Osama bin Laden's driver, and was generally armed as he traveled about Afghanistan. Indeed, a videotape showing Salim carrying a weapon in bin Laden's presence, dating from January 2000 (over a year and a half before the 9/11 attacks), was probably the government's strongest piece of evidence in the case. In other words, the government's case was built on mere proximity, and on an inference that ran essentially as follows: anyone who was that close to bin Laden must have been a trusted associate who was involved in his crimes. While the first half of that proposition may be reasonable (i.e., Hamdan was trusted by bin Laden), the second half does not necessarily follow. Instead, the government would have to prove beyond a reasonable doubt that Hamdan entered into an agreement to commit the alleged crimes (which were the embassy bombings in East Africa in 1998, the attack on the USS *Cole* in 2000, and the 9/11 attacks), and that he knowingly provided material support for acts of terrorism or to a terrorist organization.

From the spring of 2007 until July 2008 when the military commission trial started, the majority of my time as a lawyer was devoted to this case. Charles, Harry, and I traveled to Guantánamo on numerous occasions to meet with Salim and to argue pretrial motions. There were, as there had been in *Hamdan I*, numerous ups and downs along the way. In June 2007, for example, the military judge granted our motion to dismiss based on our argument that the government had never established that Hamdan was an *unlawful* enemy combatant (a jurisdictional prerequisite for the military commission under the MCA). Instead, the government was relying entirely on a finding by a Combatant Status Review Tribunal that Hamdan was an enemy combatant, without the necessary component of *unlawful* combatancy.

As we expected, the dismissal in June 2007 was not the end. Instead, in September 2007 the Court of Military Commission Review (a military commission appeals court newly created by the MCA) reversed the decision and returned the case to the trial judge for an evidentiary hearing at Guantánamo on whether Salim was an unlawful combatant. In November 2007, shortly before the three-day hearing, the government showed us its evidence against Salim at a secure facility in Washington, D.C. The evidence included a videotape of the initial interrogation at Takh-te-Pul, as well as photographs of the contents of the vehicle in which Salim was traveling when he was captured. Along with the January 2000 videotape showing Salim in bin Laden's presence, these materials would be the primary evidence against Salim at both the jurisdictional hearing on unlawful combatancy and at the trial the following summer. Among the items in the vehicle heading back to Kandahar were two SA-7 surface-to-air missile components.

In December 2007, our team headed to Guantánamo for the evidentiary hearing, which we knew would be a dress rehearsal for the trial. Our team was now comprised of Harry Schneider, me, Lt. Commander Mizer, Andrea Prasow, Charlie Swift, and our translator, Chuck Schmitz. We lost Charles Sipos in the summer of 2007, as he began a one-year clerkship with Judge Betty Fletcher of the Ninth Circuit. As it turned out, however, Charles would return to the team after the military commission trial, in time to play a key role in the appeal of Salim's conviction for "material support for terrorism."

I have already described some of the events leading up to the trial in *The Guantánamo Lawyers*, so I will not repeat them here. Suffice it to say that there was a tremendous amount of work undertaken to prepare Salim's defense, including a trip to Yemen by Brian and Andrea in early 2008 to interview potential witnesses, and numerous defense motions and hearings at the Guantánamo Bay naval base. The motions challenged many aspects of the government's case, including the charges (neither of which are war crimes), its flawed theory on when the war began (according to the government, it was underway in February 1996, the approximate date of Salim's first trip to Afghanistan), the failure to provide us with adequate discovery (the major battle here involved our attempt to obtain evidence from the high-value detainees held at the base, whom the government alleged were Salim's co-conspirators), efforts to exclude evidence that the government obtained through coercive interrogation techniques (partially successful, in keeping out statements from Salim's period of detention at Bagram), and an array of constitutional and statutory challenges to the commission system itself. In general, the briefing was handled by me, Lt. Commander Mizer, and Andrea Prasow, though several young lawyers at Perkins Coie also made important contributions, notably Rebecca Engrav (for example, on the effort to gain discovery from the high-value detainees) and Eric Merrifield (on the effort to exclude evidence obtained through coercion). Throughout this period, and for the entire month that we spent on the base for trial in July–August 2008, we were assisted by our paralegal, Trisha Marino, who worked seamlessly with Kim Lindee, the paralegal at the Office of the Chief Defense Counsel, to ensure that we were always squared away on the documents and infrastructure essential to execution of our strategy.

After the Supreme Court ruled in June 2008 in *Boumediene* that the MCA's provision stripping federal courts of habeas corpus jurisdiction violated the Constitution's Suspension Clause, we immediately moved for reconsideration of the many motions denied by the military judge on the grounds advanced by the government, i.e., its contention that the Constitution did not apply at Guantánamo. We were also able to obtain Neal's assistance again, briefly, in connection with a motion for a preliminary injunction that he and I quickly drafted and filed with the D.C. District Court. Judge Robertson set oral argument on the motion for Thursday, July 17, just four days before the trial at Guantánamo was set to begin (Monday, July 21). During that week before trial, however, I was already at Guantánamo for hearings on the motions for reconsideration, as well as dealing with a thousand other details of pretrial preparation (including reviewing thousands of pages of documents that the government provided in last-minute discovery). I argued two of our motions on Monday, and then traveled from Guantánamo to Washington, D.C., to split the argument on the preliminary injunction with Neal before Judge Robertson. Judge Robertson declined to issue the requested injunction, ruling that the trial should go forward and that Hamdan's legal challenges to the commission be addressed on appeal. I flew back to the base on Saturday, on the same plane carrying the military commission members, most of the government's witnesses, and a small army of other personnel associated with the trial. On Monday, the first U.S. military commission trial since the World War II era would begin.

One of the most important moments of a jury trial occurs at the very outset—jury selection. And this trial was no different, except our task was to select commission members, who would serve as the jury in this case. Charlie Swift and I had previously developed a juror questionnaire, which the military judge agreed could be distributed to the panel members. Voir dire and selection of the commission members came off well from our perspective. One panel member was removed for cause, and we exercised our peremptory challenges in a way that I think helped ensure a fair outcome. Ultimately, six high-ranking military officers, from all branches of the military, were selected as the commission members, with one alternate.

Harry gave the opening for our side, emphasizing that Salim merely worked as a driver for a monthly salary. Lt. Commander Stone opened for the prosecution, painting a portrait of Salim as a dedicated Al Qaeda terrorist. The government then called a long list of witnesses from the FBI and other agencies who had participated in the numerous interrogations of Salim from the date of his capture (November 2001) up through mid-2003. As noted above, the government's evidence showed that Salim was one of bin Laden's drivers and had been captured with missile components and other Al Qaeda–related material in the car he was driving towards Kandahar (including, for example, a hand-held radio and a set of "brevity cards," containing various codes for radio communications). Harry conducted most of the cross-examinations, though Brian, Charlie, and I each cross-examined certain witnesses as well. The cross brought out a number of significant points, including that Salim had not, at the time of his capture, acted in a manner characteristic of a diehard militant and had cooperated with his captors in significant respects.

In my cross of one FBI witness, my primary objective was to display a written record of the interrogation that stated that Salim had never pledged "bayat" to Osama bin Laden. Despite vigorous objections from the prosecution, I was finally permitted to display the record to the commission members. Bayat—a pledge of loyalty—was a key concept in the case, because it was the basis for the prosecution's contention that Salim had entered into a conspiracy with bin Laden and committed himself to his agenda. I was pleased to see that, despite my lack of direct questioning about bayat, the highly perceptive commission members nevertheless took note of the entry recording that Salim had *not* pledged bayat. That became apparent when, immediately following my cross of the FBI agent, the first written question was submitted by the commission members. The question: "What is bayat?"

The government also showed the videotaped interrogation of Salim from Takh-te-Pul, as well as a multipart video called *The Al Qaeda Plan*, compiled by the government's "expert," Evan Kohlmann, from opensource, online content (mostly propaganda clips about Al Qaeda from various internet postings). We were disappointed by the military judge's decision to admit that completely unauthenticated, hearsay material, particularly as none of it depicted or even mentioned Salim Hamdan. Subsequently, the military judge also admitted the testimony of agent Robert McFadden (despite the program of sleep deprivation imposed on Salim coinciding with his interrogation), who testified that Salim had admitted to pledging bayat. Harry's cross of McFadden, combined with the contrary interrogation record mentioned above, seems to have created doubt about this point, as the verdict would later reflect.

For the defense case, I conducted the direct examination of our two expert witnesses. The first of these, a law professor and former JAG Corps officer on law of war matters, Geoffrey Corn, testified by video hookup from the U.S. Embassy in Madrid. Professor Corn's testimony related to a jurisdictional point we hoped to establish concerning the onset of U.S. involvement in the armed conflict in Afghanistan. He testified that, based on rules of engagement provided to U.S. military personnel at the time, U.S. involvement in the armed conflict commenced in early October 2001. This was significant because the military judge

had declined to rule as a matter of law on when the relevant armed conflict began (and hence when events would fall within the jurisdiction of
a law-of-war military commission), and instead held that such a deter
mination would be for the commission members to decide. We believed
this ruling was erroneous (as the evidence regarding the date on which
the war started consisted of undisputed fact), but we were compelled by
the court's ruling to address the issue at trial.

Our second expert was professor Brian Williams, who testified by
video hookup from the U.S. air base in Incirlik, Turkey. Professor Wil
liams is an expert on militant jihadist groups within the Islamic world,
and he provided important context on Al Qaeda's activity in Afghanistan
in the years prior to the 9/11 attacks. He pointed out, for example, that
Al Qaeda was allied with the Taliban in its ongoing conflict against the
Northern Alliance for control of Afghanistan, and that the camps which
the government routinely characterizes as "terrorist training camps"
were in reality primarily devoted to training combatants for operations
in that conventional war, not for "outside operations" (i.e., terrorist attacks against the United States or its allies). The implication, of course,
is that the possession of weapons by individuals such as Salim in that
environment was by no means evidence that they were intended for use
in terrorist attacks.

Lt. Commander Brian Mizer then examined two witnesses in a session that, due to the government's invocation of a national security
privilege, was closed to the public. Until that material is declassified (an
event unlikely to happen anytime soon), we are unable to describe that
testimony. The defense closed its case by offering into evidence written
answers we had received from certain of the alleged "high-value detainees" present at Guantánamo, including Khalid Shaikh Mohammad and
Walid bin Attash. The government had vigorously opposed our request
for access to these alleged co-conspirators, despite the fact that, based
on the government's own allegations, they would obviously be witnesses
with highly relevant knowledge. After protracted motion practice and
oral argument, the military judge compromised by allowing us to submit

written questions to these witnesses. The answers that came back were redacted by U.S. security personnel, but they still clearly showed that Salim had no foreknowledge of, or role in, any of the attacks to which the government was trying to connect him. The military judge allowed these answers to be provided to the commission members over the objection of the government.

Capt. John Murphy gave the closing argument for the government, characterizing the testimony heard from the witnesses as evidence that Salim was a hardened Al Qaeda terrorist and the "last line of defense" for Osama bin Laden. Brian and I split the closing argument for the defense. Brian did an outstanding job of carefully reviewing the oral testimony and reminding the members that the issue was Salim's conduct, not the crimes of others. For my part, I reviewed in detail the written answers from the high-value detainees and focused on the jury instructions that set forth the elements that needed to be proved. As I stepped back from the podium at the close of my remarks, I glanced down the table at Salim. He smiled at me, flashed two thumbs up, and quietly whispered (in English), "Thank you." I think he understood that all of us were giving our best efforts in his defense.

Following the closing arguments, and undoubtedly prompted by my remarks during closing, the government moved for changes to the jury instructions. This was an extraordinary request, given that the military judge had already approved the instructions and read them to the members. I had, of course, relied heavily on those instructions (which I had largely drafted), building my closing around the government's failure to prove the elements of the offenses charged. The government's belated objection related to whether it was a war crime for an individual out of uniform (such as Salim) to direct fire at uniformed enemy soldiers on the battlefield. The government argued that such an act constituted "murder in violation of the law of war" (or attempted murder in violation of the law of war). This was highly significant for the conspiracy charge (though I suspect that most members of the press corps covering the trial did not recognize this), because that charge (to state it in its complete form) alleged "conspiracy to attack civilians or civilian objects," engage in "terrorism," or "commit murder in violation of the law of war."

From the government's perspective, the presence of the shoulder-fired SA-7 surface-to-air missiles in the car was evidence that Salim conspired to commit murder in violation of the law of war, as he or his confederates could be expected to direct those weapons against U.S. airmen. But I had argued to the contrary in the closing, relying on the definitions of "protected persons," "terrorism," and "murder in violation of the law of war" in the instructions. Based on those definitions, I explained to the commission members that directing missile fire at helicopter gunships or other military aircraft in a war zone is *not* a war crime, even if the shooter is not in uniform (i.e., it is *not* murder or attempted murder in violation of the law of war, as alleged in the conspiracy charge). The fact that the shooter may be an "unlawful" combatant (because out of uniform) would merely strip him of his "combatant immunity"; in itself, it did not make him a war criminal for engaging in combat. Without combatant immunity, the shooter could be subject to prosecution under applicable *domestic law*, but not under *the law of war*. The law of war would certainly prohibit a shooter from directing fire at civilians or other noncombatants (including wounded or captured soldiers), but not for directing fire at enemy soldiers engaged in combat in a war zone. I explained that there was no evidence that the missiles in the car were intended for attacks on civilians or noncombatants (i.e., for acts of terrorism). Rather, the logical implication was that they were intended for use in the defense of Kandahar against advancing anti-Taliban forces. Again, based on the verdict, I think the commission members understood the distinction.

We debated this issue in a protracted oral argument before the military judge on two separate days while the jury was deliberating. I argued for the defense that the instructions as submitted were correct, and that any change at this point (after closing argument) would constitute a mistrial. The prosecution argued that the instructions should be modified and the members informed that, under the MCA, unlawful belligerency (e.g., engaging in combat while out of uniform) is a war crime in itself, with the clear implication that Salim's mere possession of the missiles could be deemed evidence of conspiracy to commit one of the charged offenses (in particular, murder in violation of the law of war). In the end, the military judge denied the government's motion and declined to modify the instructions, a decision that I think helped secure the acquittal on the conspiracy charge.

After about six and half hours of deliberations spread out over several days, the commission returned a verdict of not guilty of conspiracy, but guilty of providing material support for terrorism (based on providing driving and bodyguard services to bin Laden). Salim was extremely upset, knowing that the sentence for any conviction could be very lengthy. Indeed, while the MCA did not prescribe a range, we understood that the sentence could be decades or even life in prison.

Following the verdict, the sentencing phase of the trial began. The government sought leave to introduce evidence from individuals who were present at Ground Zero on 9/11, but the military judge ruled that, in light of the acquittal on the conspiracy charge, it would not be appropriate to hear evidence at sentencing linking Salim to the 9/11 attack. Nevertheless, in a statement to the commission members, the government asked that Salim be sentenced to life in prison, or not less than 30 years. For the defense, we called Dr. Emily Keram, a psychiatrist who had spent almost 100 hours interviewing Salim to assess his mental condition. Dr. Keram testified concerning Salim's upbringing, experiences, and psychological profile, and offered her opinion that he was not ideologically committed to jihad (far from it) and was unlikely to represent a threat of violence in the future. In reality, his family was the overwhelming focus of his life, and all he wanted was to return to his wife and children in Yemen. Dr. Keram's testimony was hugely significant in humanizing Salim for the commission. Salim also read a prepared statement to the commission members, apologizing for any conduct on his part that could have indirectly contributed to bin Laden's awful crimes.

He admitted that he had respected and admired bin Laden, and was flat-tered by the respect he received in return, but he now recognized that bin Laden's conduct was wrong.

While deliberating, the commission members sent a question to the military judge asking whether Salim would be given credit for time served. The military judge ruled that he would be given credit for approximately 61.5 months. A short time later, the commission returned a sentence of 66 months. That was a moment of high drama in the courtroom. Salim at first did not seem to understand its import (and it may have been that the simultaneous translation was not being communicated correctly). I was sitting next to him at counsel table, and quickly wrote out on a pad of paper: "66 months—61.5 months credit = 4.5 months remaining." I handed it to Salim and Chuck, and Chuck whispered the message to Salim. It took a minute or two, but the message seemed to slowly sink in as the final moments of the proceeding played out, with the judge thanking and dismissing the commission members. By the time Salim was led from the courtroom, after the commission members and military judge had retired, he was smiling broadly, and he turned and waved to all those remaining in the room: "Bye, bye, every-body," he said in perfect English. It seemed that everyone in the room, aside from those at the prosecution table, was quite pleased at the result.

There remained a huge question, of course, of whether the government would actually release Salim after the four and one-half months of additional time was served. Indeed, a Department of Defense spokes-man had stated in the immediate aftermath of the trial that Salim could continue to be held as an enemy combatant even after he served his sentence for material support for terrorism. I anticipated that this would be the next round in this unending contest. Then, in late November 2008, we got a call from the Convening Authority telling us that Salim was being transferred from Guantánamo to Yemen to serve out the remainder of his sentence. We had one last opportunity to speak with him, by means of a hastily arranged teleconference. It was a memorable call. We spoke for about an hour. Our message to Salim was simple: be cooperative, but don't sign anything that we haven't seen, and don't do anything that could put this possible development at risk. We later learned that within hours of our call, Salim was the sole passenger on a military flight heading for Yemen.

When he arrived in Yemen, Salim was held for several additional weeks by the local authorities, but then in early January 2009, released to his family. A month or so later, to my considerable surprise, I got a call from Salim at my office in Seattle. He sent an email as well, in Arabic. The gist of his message was, "when I last saw you at Guantánamo, you said you'd come see me again, but you never did." That was Salim's way of inviting to us to come see him. Harry and I did not need much prompting, despite the fact that the situation in Yemen was quite unsettled, to say the least. He was still our client, and even though the Convening Authority had not yet reviewed the record of trial and approved the sentence, I was planning to appeal the conviction on the material support for terrorism (MST) conviction. Harry was on board with that, but we needed Salim's approval to continue that effort, and a trip to Yemen would give us the chance to fully explain the legal situation and get that approval.

Like conspiracy, MST is not a war crime, and therefore the military commission did not have jurisdiction over that charge. This time, however, we would not be taking on the executive branch alone. Rather, our appeal would have to take on the authority of Congress as well, which had identified MST as a war crime in the 2006 MCA, and given jurisdiction to a military commission to try that offense.

But the appeal would not be ripe until the Convening Authority reviewed the record and approved the sentence, which did not occur until July 2009. In April 2009, therefore, as we waited for the Convening Authority to act, we took advantage of the delay to accept Salim's invitation and visit him in Yemen. Harry, Brian, Chuck, and I met in Dubai and then caught a connecting flight to Sana'a. As we stepped out of the airport (where heavily armed security forces were much in evidence) onto the sidewalk facing a large parking lot, two little girls came running up to us. The younger of the two reached out and took my hand, looking up at me, giggling and exchanging glances with her sister. It was Salim's youngest daughter, whom I immediately recognized from photographs we had gathered for use during the sentencing phase of the trial. From across the parking lot Salim was approaching, wearing his finest traditional robes, with the Yemeni janbiya (a curved, ceremonial dagger) prominently displayed at his waist. It was a wonderful greeting, and the beginning of several excellent days visiting with Salim and his family in the heart of that ancient city. As Salim drove us to our hotel, I produced two silver-and-turquoise bracelets for the girls, gifts from my own daughter, Michelle, who had written a short note to Salim's girls and enclosed a photograph of herself in the package containing the bracelets. Chuck translated the message to the girls into Arabic as Salim expertly navigated the vehicle through the crowded streets. The girls stared at the photograph for a long time, spoke to one another about it, pointing out little details of the image to one another, and then carefully wrapped it in paper and placed it with the bracelets in a small purse that one of them was carrying. It was, I think, a message from a different world, and to my mind, it somehow captured the exotic quality of the entire experience for all of us, an experience that was finally moving from a grim past into a hopeful future.

As we dined with Salim on our first night in Sana'a (on an excellent meal of fish, vegetables, flat bread, and tea in a very simple restaurant off of a busy street), we asked Salim what he thought when he was put aboard that military flight leaving Guantánamo. He said he expected it was another trick, that he would be flown around for hours and returned to Guantánamo. He didn't really believe he was home until his wife and mother-in-law came to visit him at the prison where he was held in Sana'a before his release. When he first saw them, they were dressed in the traditional black abaya, with their faces veiled. He only knew who they were when they spoke. That's when he realized he was

home. I asked him when he first trusted us. He smiled and said, "Now."
Over the course of our discussions about many things over the following
days, Salim agreed that we should pursue the appeal to try to clear his
name of the MST conviction.

By that time, the spring of 2009, the Obama administration was in
office, and it was my hope and expectation (based on his statements
about civil liberties during the campaign) that military commissions
would again fall into the obscurity they so richly deserved. I was deeply
disappointed, therefore, when in the summer of 2009 I learned that the
administration was supporting a revised Military Commissions Act,
which was eventually enacted by Congress in October 2009 (the 2009
MCA). The new act fixed some of the most glaring problems with the
2006 MCA (for example excluding evidence obtained through torture
or coercion, and allowing the accused to see the evidence introduced
against him), but others remained, including the admissibility of hearsay under lax standards, and the stifling role of the national security
privilege. In Salim's trial, for example, the government successfully invoked the national security privilege to prevent Harry from asking a
question about the 9/11 Commission Report, a national best-seller.

The most significant failure of the 2009 MCA, however, is that (like
its predecessor) it discards the hallowed traditions of civilian rule and
an independent judiciary, traditions that are fundamental to our form
of government and to the rule of law. It confers jurisdiction on military
tribunals for the trial of noncombatants, which is a grave encroach-
ment on the jurisdiction of civilian courts. Under the act's terms, military commissions may try "unprivileged enemy combatants," where
that term is defined to include (among others) anyone who is not a
privileged combatant, but who has nevertheless "purposefully and
materially supported hostilities against the United States or its coalition partners." That definition broadly extends commission jurisdiction over civilians who may have supported war efforts by working
in supply industries or in transportation or other ancillary services.
Under international law, such individuals cannot be deemed "combat-

ants" and cannot be stripped of their rights to a civilian trial. No U.S. law should depart from these principles to authorize such a dangerous expedient.

The act, like its predecessor, also offends equal protection principles by applying only to noncitizens, not to U.S. citizens. While citizenship is certainly a relevant status for the availability of certain benefits, there is no basis for denying noncitizens the same procedural protections afforded to citizens in a criminal trial, where their life or liberty is at stake. A trial is supposed to be a truth-seeking mechanism, but the stripped down version of procedural rights authorized by the MCA (of both 2006 and 2009) tilts the field in favor of convictions at the expense of truth and fairness.

In many ways, the appeal of Salim's MST conviction could be deemed a separate, third phase of this marathon case. It ran from July 2009, when the Convening Authority finally approved the sentence (which by then had been fully served), until January 2013, when the period for the government to seek Supreme Court review of the D.C. Circuit's decision to vacate Salim's MST conviction finally expired. As always in this case, there were many twists and turns over the course of those three and a half years before we reached a final resolution.

Once again, the personnel working on the case changed. The appeal was largely handled by me, Charles Sipos (who had returned from his clerkship), and a new team member from the Office of the Chief Defense Counsel, the civilian attorney Adam Thurschwell.

The first issue we advanced on the appeal, which I took responsibility for briefing, was that MST is not a recognized war crime. Rather, it is a vague, ill-defined offense (almost a blank check for prosecutors) set forth in the U.S. criminal code. It was originally added to the domestic criminal code in the mid-1990s, and it has been amended many times, in several cases following court challenges to its vague terms. Despite the fact that no other country, international tribunal, or treaty on law of war issues had ever identified MST as a war crime, Congress incorporated this offense into the 2006 MCA as one of the offenses triable by military commission (and it remained in the 2009 MCA, although Salim's case was governed by the earlier statute).

This argument proceeded on several levels. First, we argued that in defining MST as a crime "traditionally . . . triable" by a law of war commission, Congress not only ignored historical reality, but also overstepped the limited grant of power conferred by the Define and Punish Clause of the U.S. Constitution (pursuant to which Congress has the power to "define and punish . . . Offenses against *the Law of Nations*"). We further argued that, even if Congress were deemed to have acted within the scope of the Define and Punish Clause by "defining" a nascent offense that (theoretically) could be in the process of gaining recognition as international law evolves, Salim's conviction was the result of an *ex post facto* prosecution prohibited by both the U.S. Constitution and international law. This is because the purported war crime of which he stood convicted had only been defined for the first time in the 2006 MCA, almost five years *after* he was seized by coalition forces in Afghanistan.

Moreover, we argued that the *ex post facto* principle could not be avoided by pointing to the domestic crime of MST identified in the U.S. criminal code, as Salim was prosecuted for an MCA-based offense that retroactively criminalized a broader range of conduct than that proscribed by the domestic statute at the time of his capture. More fundamentally, we explained, granting a law of war commission (an Article I court) jurisdiction over a purely *domestic* crime would violate Article III of the Constitution, which vests the judicial power of the United States in federal courts whose independence is protected by structural safeguards absent from the scheme established by the MCA.

The second major issue we advanced, which Charles generally took responsibility for briefing, was that Salim's trial by military commission violated equal protection guarantees. Specifically, the MCA provided Salim fewer substantive rights and procedural protections than would be afforded to a similarly situated U.S. citizen facing the same charges. Such discrimination against noncitizens violates the Equal Protection

Clause of the U.S. Constitution, as well as equal protection principles enshrined in international law.

The court that would initially hear Salim's appeal was also a new creation of the MCA, the Court of Military Commission Review (CMCR). Under the statute, it would consist of an undetermined number of appellate military judges. At the time we began working on Salim's appeal, however, no judges had yet been appointed to this court.

Our appellate brief was submitted to the CMCR in October 2009. The government opposed, arguing that deference was due to Congress's determination that MST is a war crime and that, in any event, conduct similar to that offense had been punished by military commissions in the past. The bulk of the government's evidence for this latter point consisted of the same Civil War–era commission records that the Supreme Court plurality had reviewed, and rejected, in *Hamdan I*. Those commissions, the Court explained, were not pure law-of-war military commissions. Rather, they were exercising the jurisdiction of both law-of-war and occupation courts, so their rulings did not provide precedent for the law-of-war commission at issue in this case.

In January 2010, I argued the appeal to a three-judge panel of the CMCR, sitting in Washington, D.C. Army Col. Francis Gilligan argued for the government. Then we waited. And waited. And waited. Months went by with no ruling. Finally, in September 2010, we received an order stating that the court, on its own motion, had decided to consider the case *en banc* (i.e., by all the judges on the court), and that additional judges who had been appointed *after* the January 2010 argument would now participate in deciding the appeal. In addition, we learned that several of the newly appointed judges were actually no longer appellate military judges, as required by the MCA. The whole thing had an air of irregularity about it, which was, unfortunately, a pattern throughout the entire case. We promptly moved to disqualify the two new judges who were ineligible to serve under the statute. The grounds for doing so seemed irrefutable, but no decision was forthcoming for the rest of 2010. Finally, in January 2011, a year after the briefing on the appeal had been submitted and oral argument heard, we received another order. This one informed us that the two judges we had challenged recused themselves from the case and, for that reason, our motion to disqualify was denied as moot.

A month later, in February 2011, the court ordered the parties to submit additional briefing and present additional argument on two separate issues: (1) did a "joint criminal enterprise" theory of liability impact whether the *charged* conduct constituted an offense triable by military commission; and (2) was the offense of "aiding the enemy" limited to those who betrayed an allegiance or duty to a sovereign nation?

So, once again, we were presented with a highly irregular development. The appellate court, on its own initiative, had not only altered the personnel who would rule on the appeal, *post hoc*, but they were now also introducing new issues and, indeed, apparently considering an entirely separate charge (aiding the enemy). From our perspective, it seemed that the court was actively searching for a theory by which it could uphold the MST conviction.

Regardless of our suspicions, of course, we complied with the order. We briefed the two issues, and in March 2011, I returned to Washington, D.C., to argue before the CMCR again, this time with the court sitting *en banc*. Col. Gilligan again argued for the government.

In late June 2011, the CMCR ruled, issuing an 86-page opinion rejecting our arguments and affirming the MST conviction. Most of the opinion was devoted to the issue of whether MST could be deemed a war crime. The court reviewed in detail the posture and record of the *Hamdan* case, the language and congressional intent evident in the MCA, international conventions regarding terrorist-related conduct, and military commission rulings from earlier periods in American history. It discussed "aiding the enemy" as a form of conduct similar to that with which Salim was charged. At the end of that lengthy survey, the court concluded that deference to Congress was required. Accordingly, it upheld the congressional determination that MST is a war crime. "Congress did not create a new offense," said the court. Instead, MST "was an existing law of war offense since at least 1996." On equal protection, the court agreed with the military judge's ruling that those rights did not extend to Guantánamo detainees. In short, Salim had no right to the same trial procedures as a U.S. citizen facing criminal prosecution.

The decision, while disappointing, was not unexpected. We thus moved forward to the next step, which would take us back to an Article III civilian court, the D.C. Circuit Court of Appeals. Our briefing to the D.C. Circuit largely tracked the arguments we advanced before the CMCR, slightly modified to address what we regarded as the major errors in the CMCR's opinion. In preparing the section on equal protection, Charles was assisted by another talented young lawyer in our office, Angie Jones. Adam Thurschwell and I focused on the lengthier sections devoted to MST—first, whether it was a war crime, and second, whether the prosecution violated the Ex Post Facto Clause. We received excellent contributions for those sections of the briefing from Rebecca Engrav and Abha Khanna, also from the Seattle office of Perkins Coie. Throughout this phase as well, our paralegal Trish Marino played a key supporting role.

Our opening brief was submitted in November 2011, the government's opposition in January 2012, and our reply in March 2012. In early May 2012, I once again traveled to Washington, D.C., to deliver the oral argument. Our three-judge panel included some of the court's most conservative members, so I expected to be closely questioned from the bench. I welcomed that prospect, however, as a conversation with the panel members would help me address their concerns. Justice Department attorney John De Pue argued for the government.

Perhaps the most interesting new issue in the case at this point was the extraordinary position advanced by the government, for the first time ever, that the content of the law of war is not limited to offenses recognized by the international community. Rather, it argued, the law of war also encompasses a uniquely "American common law of war," which, it maintained, criminalizes the kind of peripheral role that Salim was alleged to have played in this case. This was an entirely novel, unprecedented, and unsupported position, one we thought was directly refuted by many Supreme Court decisions that have consistently characterized the law of war as a subset of international law. We interpreted this as a tacit recognition that the historical evidence advanced by the government (and accepted by the CMCR) to establish MST as a preexisting offense was, in the end, unpersuasive. Also of note was the government's contention that the Define and Punish Clause was not the only source of Congress's power to prosecute MST as a war crime. Instead, it argued, that power derived from the whole array of general war powers conferred by Article I (the power to raise and support armies and to make rules for the regulation of land and naval forces, for example). Here again, we saw this as a transparent attempt to shift attention away from the key limiting language of the Define and Punish Clause, which focused on defining and punishing "Offenses against the Law of Nations." The government was doing everything possible to take the international community out of the equation.

Judge Kavanaugh was the most active questioner on the panel, and he signaled that his main concern was whether MST was an offense under the law of war at the time of the alleged conduct (1996 through November 2001). I readily agreed that he had identified the key issue, and urged that, because MST was not such an offense at the relevant time, the case against Salim was an *ex post facto* prosecution. My colloquy with Judge Kavanaugh also touched on whether Congress had the unilateral authority to identify MST as a war crime going forward. While we did not agree on that issue, that would not change the outcome of the case.

In October 2012, the D.C. Circuit issued its decision. First, the court said, the case was not moot, as Supreme Court precedent instructs that a direct appeal of a criminal conviction is not mooted by a defendant's release from custody. Second, the court interpreted the MCA in a manner that avoided a serious *ex post facto* issue, holding that Congress did not intend to authorize a retroactive prosecution for MST, which was not a war crime prior to the passage of the MCA in 2006. Third, the court said that under the U.S. statute that *did* authorize military commissions at the time of the relevant conduct, UCMJ Article 821, the war crimes that could be prosecuted were limited to *international* law of war offenses, and did not include the purported "American common law of war" offense that the government identified. The upshot was that the military commission had no authority to try Salim for MST, and his conviction was, accordingly, vacated.

Victory. For the moment, at least. But it would certainly be appealed, I thought, because, along with conspiracy, MST is the prosecution's favorite charge. It is a prosecutorial blank check that virtually dispenses with the need to prove actual criminal acts. All a prosecutor need do, essentially, is show that the accused affiliated in some sense with Al Qaeda (or other terrorist) personnel, and then argue that such affiliation was the provision of material support (if nothing else, "providing personnel; to wit, himself," in the language of the *Hamdan II* charge sheet). Under the applicable rules, the government had until mid-January 2013 to seek further review, either from the D.C. Circuit sitting *en banc*, or from the U.S. Supreme Court. To my surprise, it let that deadline pass without filing a petition for further review. And so the victory for Salim, and to some extent for the integrity of international law, stands.

NOTES

1 Journalists writing about the case have said some odd things about *Hamdan I*, which is not surprising given that most of them have never spoken (at least substantively) with those of us at Perkins Coie who were deeply involved. For example, Jess Bravin, in his 2013 book *The Terror Courts: Rough Justice at Guantánamo Bay* (which has many virtues, including an excellent chapter on the military order), writes that "[h]undreds of lawyers, professors, consultants, and students attracted by a historic cause had joined Hamdan's defense team, taking small roles and large, as the case evolved into a constitutional showdown between executive power and individual rights" (Bravin at 289). While correctly assessing the significance of the issues presented, that remark is flatly wrong in its description of "Hamdan's defense team." The "team" in *Hamdan I*—a case that involved almost pure legal issues and was therefore primarily an exercise in legal research and briefing—was largely Katyal, Sipos, and myself. We were the ones writing the briefs and making the key decisions about the arguments and authority to put forward. At the Supreme Court stage, Kevin Russell (from what was then the law firm of Goldstein & Howe) also assisted with the briefing. Bravin's remark about "hundreds" of defense team members is probably a reference to the fact that Neal would often delegate research projects to law students and research assistants at schools

with which he was associated, while Kevin enlisted the assistance of students at a Supreme Court clinic that he was teaching. What this meant for us at Perkins Coie (having responsibility for finalizing and filing most of the briefs) was that integrating this often disjointed material of varying quality and diverse format into a unified, coherent brief was challenging, to say the least. Neal's style (which we attributed to his academic position at the time) was to include all possible arguments. Hence his insistence, to cite a single example, that we include a Thirteenth Amendment "slavery" claim in the original petition. I generally resisted that approach, and tried to cut out what I regarded as obscure and often irrelevant authority wherever possible. A common dynamic was that we at Perkins Coie (Charles and I) would have one version of a brief in progress, while Neal would have another version going at the same time. Drafts being exchanged would often contain huge swaths of "redlined" edits—typically me cutting material from Neal's version, and Neal putting it back in. Neal was generally more gracious and more politic—he would just demote any of my text with which he disagreed into a footnote, rather than delete it entirely. Ultimately, compromise versions would be filed, usually a product of sheer exhaustion and the arrival of the filing deadline. *Hamdan I* also involved a handful of oral arguments, and Charlie Swift played a role in these, at least at the district court level and in the court of appeals. But from my perspective, oral argument played a far less significant role than the briefing in determining the outcome. Journalists often portray oral arguments as highly significant and dwell on them at length in their reporting. But in most cases that reflects a misunderstanding of how the process actually works. Rhetorical flourishes may make good newspaper copy, but federal judges are more impressed by reasoned arguments about legal precedent, clearly set forth in well-crafted briefs.

2 Through the many rounds of briefing in the case, a rough division of labor emerged: Neal generally tackled the abstention (and later the nonretroactivity of the DTA) issues, Charles focused on the failure of commission procedures to conform to UCMJ protections in violation of UCMJ Article 836, and I focused on the violations and enforceability of the Geneva Conventions (as major codifications of the laws of war), and their incorporation into the UCMJ provision that recognized commission jurisdiction, Article 821. That provision implicitly denied the executive the power to convene a military commission that disregarded these fundamental protections of international law. In addition, Neal and I both spent a great deal of time honing our argument that the one charge eventually preferred against Salim, "conspiracy," is not a war crime. Rather, it is an inchoate offense recognized in Anglo-American jurisprudence, but generally not recognized by the international community. For example, it is not identified as a war crime in any of the treaties governing the law of war, and was rejected by the International Military Tribunal at Nuremberg.

3 See *The Guantánamo Lawyers: Inside a Prison outside the Law* (New York: New York University Press, 2009), 179–83.

12

A Tale of Two Detainees

DAVID FRAKT

On November 3, 2008, I sat silently at the counsel table while the military commission located at Guantánamo Bay, Cuba, announced the sentence against Ali Hamza al Bahlul. Mr. al Bahlul, the Yemeni detainee whom I had been ordered to represent against his will, was seated as far as he could get away from me at the opposite end of the long table. Not surprisingly, given that I had put on no defense, he was given the maximum permissible sentence: life imprisonment. Ordinarily in a military tribunal, counsel and the accused stand for the verdict—out of respect to the court—but we remained seated. Mr. al Bahlul was boycotting the proceedings, refusing to recognize the legitimacy of the military commissions, and I joined his boycott, both in deference to my client's wishes and in protest of the commission's refusal to honor Mr. al Bahlul's request to represent himself, which had placed me in this awkward position. After the sentence was announced, Mr. al Bahlul was taken away in shackles and moved to a different wing of the prison complex where he remains to this day; convicted prisoners were not permitted to be housed with ordinary detainees. It was the last time I ever saw him.

There were few spectators in attendance that day. The entire press corps, save one lone pool reporter from the Associated Press, had decamped to the mainland to cover the historic presidential election that was to take place the following day. Although the trial of Mr. al Bahlul was only the second military commission trial of the Bush administration, and the first to produce a significant sentence (there had been one plea bargain resulting in a nine-month sentence and one litigated trial resulting in a five-month sentence after accounting for time served), this historic event passed with barely a notice, buried in the back pages of the newspapers, if they bothered to cover the story at all. And so the era of the Bush military commissions went out not with a bang, but with a whimper, overshadowed by the immensity of the impending election of our first African American president.

The following night, I watched the election returns from the lobby of the Guantánamo naval base's visiting officer quarters with a great sense of excitement and satisfaction, confident that this historic election signaled the end of the disastrous military commission experiment, as presidential candidate Barack Obama had made plain his intent to scrap the military commissions. Accordingly, for many of the defense counsel assigned to represent detainees facing trial by military commission, the primary strategy had been delay, in hopes of fending off a trial in a system heavily slanted in favor of the prosecution until the next administration could come in and put a stop to the whole embarrassing enterprise. Although the election came too late to help Mr. al Bahlul, I was optimistic that it portended good things for my other client, Mohammed Jawad, who, along with Canadian Omar Khadr, was one of two detainees captured as children who were facing military commission charges. The decision by the Bush administration to make the United States the first country in modern history to try alleged child soldiers for war crimes was highly controversial, and much criticized by the international human rights community. It seemed inconceivable to me that President Barack Obama would permit these cases to continue. My faith in the new president, however, turned out to be misplaced.

By way of background, I had arrived at the Office of Military Commissions in late April 2008, and was immediately appointed defense counsel for both Mr. al Bahlul and Mr. Jawad, who were both arraigned in separate hearings on May 7, 2008. Although both detainees initially resisted my help, and Mr. al Bahlul ultimately rejected me completely, Mr. Jawad gradually accepted me as his attorney. Over the summer and fall of 2008, through numerous visits and multiple pretrial hearings, we developed a strong rapport. Mr. Jawad even granted me permission to file a habeas corpus petition on his behalf.

Mr. Jawad's case was factually quite simple. He was accused of throwing a hand grenade at a U.S. military vehicle in Kabul that had injured two U.S. soldiers and their Afghan interpreter. There was only one charge: "attempted murder in violation of the law of war." Unlike every other detainee to have been charged in the military commissions, he was not charged with terrorism, or material support for terrorism, or conspiracy, nor was he alleged to be a member of Al Qaeda or the Taliban. Because of the relative simplicity of the charge, the case was moving forward to trial rapidly. At the time Mr. al Bahlul's trial concluded, Mr. Jawad was next on the docket. His trial was scheduled to begin January 5, 2009, and last two weeks—the last two weeks of the Bush presidency.

Although the trial date was fast approaching, by November 2008, the case against Mr. Jawad had already begun to unravel. In September, the lead prosecutor, Army Reserve Lieutenant Colonel Darrel Vandeveld, had courageously resigned, asserting that he could no longer ethically continue to prosecute the case. The military commission judge, Army Colonel Stephen Henley, had rejected the government's theory of the case, ruling that Mr. Jawad's mere status as an alleged "unlawful enemy combatant" was insufficient to prove that his claimed belligerent act violated the law of war. Perhaps more importantly, Judge Henley had suppressed the prosecution's primary evidence in the case, two purported confessions, on the basis that these self-incriminating statements were the product of torture. Recognizing that they had no hope of gaining a conviction without at least one confession (there was scant evidence corroborating the confessions), on November 24, 2008, the government filed a notice of an appeal to the Court of Military Commission Review (CMCR), a new military appeals court created by the Military Commissions Act of 2006, seeking to have one of the suppression orders reversed. Pending the outcome of the appeal, the trial was indefinitely postponed.

I argued the appeal on January 13, 2009. Lacking its own courtroom, the CMCR borrowed the U.S. Court of Appeals for the Federal Circuit for the occasion. The issue before the appellate panel was whether a statement made to U.S. authorities could properly be considered the product of torture if it was a result of torture by Afghan authorities earlier that same day. The trial judge had held that because there was no break in circumstances, the torture by the Afghan authorities that had yielded the first "confession" also tainted Mr. Jawad's statement a few hours later. Although the judge had followed well-settled principles of constitutional law in reaching his ruling, the government argued that those precedents did not apply in military commissions. Rather, the government argued, a statement could be the product of torture only if it was elicited directly during a torture session. The court did not seem to find the government's logic persuasive. At the conclusion of the oral argument, I felt confident that the court would uphold the suppression ruling. I was never to find out if I was right.

The same day as the oral argument, I, together with the ACLU, filed an amended habeas corpus petition in the U.S. District Court for the District of Columbia on Mr. Jawad's behalf. After Mr. Jawad had authorized me to file the petition, I learned that the Center for Constitutional Rights had already filed a petition on his behalf some years earlier as part of a group of Afghan petitioners, based on permission from a member of Mr. Jawad's family. The petition had languished for years while the federal courts grappled with the issue of whether detainees had the right to seek habeas corpus (and whether Congress had the power to revoke this right). Although the Supreme Court had ruled that detainees did have habeas corpus rights under the U.S. Constitution in *Boumediene v. Bush* in June 2008, there was a huge backlog of habeas petitions in D.C. District Court. Those detainees facing trial by military commission, like Mr. Jawad, were at the back of the line, as the District Court had refused to intervene where there were ongoing military commission proceedings. Although we knew that Mr. Jawad's habeas case would continue to be stayed so long as he was facing criminal charges, in anticipation that the military commission charges would be dismissed if there were a favorable ruling on the CMCR appeal, we wanted to be ready to move forward quickly on the habeas corpus case whenever the District Court was ready to take it up. The habeas petition would challenge the government's authority to hold Mr. Jawad even in the absence of any pending charges in a military commission. In support of the amended habeas petition, we included an extraordinary sworn declaration by Mr. Jawad's erstwhile prosecutor, Lt. Col. Vandeveld.[1] The Vandeveld Declaration offered his opinion that there was insufficient evidence to convict Mohammed Jawad, confirmed that Mr. Jawad had been abused in U.S. custody, and concluded that Mr. Jawad posed no threat to the United States if released. It also contained a stinging indictment of the entire military commissions experiment.

The next week was an eventful one. On January 20, 2009, President Obama was inaugurated. I woke up early and braved the bitter cold and teeming crowds to attend this historic event in person. I particularly wanted to hear what he was going to say about Guantánamo. A few weeks earlier, in December, I had been invited to the Pentagon by members of President Obama's transition team. Mr. Jeh C. Johnson, shortly to be named Defense Department general counsel, was leading the transition team's review of legal issues facing the Defense Department. Mr. Johnson had sought my advice on how the military commissions already in progress could be stopped, and I had offered my thoughts on the matter. This gave me great hope that the president would announce an immediate end to the military commissions. Although he did not address Guantánamo directly, there was one line in the inaugural address that seemed to be a veiled reference to Guantánamo and the military commissions: "we reject as false the choice between our safety and our ideals."

Later that day, Secretary of Defense Gates directed the chief prosecutor of the military commissions to "cease swearing charges, to seek continuances for 120 days in any cases that have already been referred to military commissions, and to petition the Court of Military Commission review to hold in abeyance any pending appeals for 120 days" in order "to provide the Administration sufficient time to conduct a review of detainees currently held at Guantánamo, to evaluate the cases of detainees not approved for release or transfer to determine whether prosecution may be warranted for any offenses these detainees may have committed, and to determine which forum best suits any future prosecution." On January 22, 2009, President Obama signed Executive Order 13492, directing a review of all detainees at Guantánamo and ordering the secretary of defense to "ensure that during the pendency of the Review . . . all proceedings pending in the United States Court of Military Commission Review, are halted." The following day, the government sought a stay from the CMCR in Mr. Jawad's case, asking the court to withhold ruling on the interlocutory appeal. Over my strenuous objection, the court granted the request.

Sometimes when one door closes, another opens. Although I was disappointed not to get a prompt ruling on the merits of the appeal (the CMCR's rules required them to issue a ruling within 30 days), my co-counsel[2] and I realized that the suspension of military commission proceedings might create an opportunity in federal court. We filed a motion seeking to compel the government to respond to our habeas corpus petition on the merits. We argued that since the military commission proceedings had been suspended, there was no longer any basis for postponing the habeas corpus petition. Shortly thereafter, we had a stroke of good fortune. Mr. Jawad's habeas petition was transferred to District Judge Ellen Segal Huvelle, a no-nonsense judge who had little patience for the government's dilatory tactics in the habeas cases. On April 22, 2009, she ordered the government to respond on the merits to Jawad's petition.

The issue in a habeas corpus case is whether there is a lawful basis to detain. For Guantánamo detainees, the government had to prove that the detainee was an alien unlawful enemy combatant, which could be proven by involvement with Al Qaeda or through direct participation in a hostile act against the United States. In its response to Mr. Jawad's habeas petition, the government's asserted basis for his detention was exactly the same as the basis for the criminal charges against him—his alleged involvement in the hand grenade attack that injured the two U.S. soldiers. As supporting evidence for the lawfulness of detention, the Justice Department offered the very same statements from Mr. Jawad that had been suppressed by Judge Henley in the military commission case, claiming that the suppression rulings by the military commission did not bind the district court.

Judge Huvelle was not impressed. At a July hearing, in a scolding that made headlines in the *New York Times*, she described the case as "an outrage" that was "riddled with holes" and accused the government of "dragging this out for no good reason." She ordered a suppression hearing to determine the admissibility of the statements. Shortly before the hearing, the Justice Department made an abrupt about-face. It not only dropped its reliance on Mr. Jawad's statements, but also conceded that all of the statements he had made in detention were the product of torture and agreed that our motion to suppress should be granted. When the Justice Department claimed that it had additional evidence to support Mr. Jawad's detention, Judge Huvelle called its bluff. She set the case for an expedited merits hearing in early August and told the government lawyers to "bring me a witness." Once again, the government capitulated. Shortly before the hearing, the Justice Department informed the court that the government had decided to "no longer treat Mr. Jawad as detainable" and conceded that the writ of habeas corpus should be granted.

On July 30, 2009, Judge Huvelle held the final hearing in the case. The government submitted a proposed order of release within three weeks of the hearing, to enable the Justice Department to comply with a blatantly unconstitutional statute recently enacted by Congress that required advance notice before transferring any detainee from Guantánamo. I requested that the court make one amendment to the proposed release order. I asked that the government be ordered to treat Mr. Jawad humanely until he was released. Incredibly, the government lawyers objected. Judge Huvelle settled on some compromise language, ordering that "petitioner Jawad shall be treated humanely consistent with respondents' legitimate security and operational concerns."

The following day, in response to my demand, the Convening Authority for the military commissions dismissed the charges against Mr. Jawad, thereby mooting the government's appeal, which was also dismissed. Three weeks later, Mr. Jawad was flown back to Afghanistan by military transport, where, through the timely intervention of my military co-counsel, Major Eric Montalvo (USMC, ret.), he was released to his family.

While the Justice Department's reversal on Mr. Jawad's petition and his unconditional release was a positive outcome to his case, regrettably, it did not signal a broader change in administration policies toward Guantánamo detainees. Rather, the Justice Department's change of heart seems to have been driven by the torrent of negative publicity generated by Mr. Jawad's case, which a *New York Times* editorial referred to as "emblematic of everything that is wrong with Guantánamo." The Obama administration did nothing to assist in Mr. Jawad's reintegration to civilian life; no compensation, transitional assistance, or social services were provided. In fact, the government refused my request to have a member of the defense team present for his repatriation, forcing me to raise funds from human rights NGOs and private donors to pay for Major Montalvo's trip. As for other detainees, the administration continued to vigorously oppose virtually all habeas corpus petitions, even in several cases where the administration's own Guantanamo Review Task Force had cleared the detainee for release.

President Obama has tried, to no avail, to shut down Guantánamo. But he made no effort to fulfill his campaign pledge to shut down the military commissions, choosing instead to try to reform them. Shockingly, President Obama did not even abandon his predecessor's effort to convict child soldiers in the military commissions, allowing the prosecution to press on with charges against Canadian Omar Khadr (under the same status-based war crime theory rejected by Judge Henley in Mr.

Jawad's case) until Mr. Khadr finally agreed to plead guilty in 2010. The legitimacy of Mr. Khadr's conviction, like every other conviction obtained in the military commissions to date, is in grave doubt, for at least some of the charges to which he pled guilty have since been found to have been improperly before the court. Only two men have been convicted in a military commission trial, Salim Hamdan and Ali Hamza al Bahlul.* When the appeals of Mr. Hamdan and Mr. al Bahlul finally reached the U.S. Court of Appeals for the D.C. Circuit, the court vacated both of their convictions because the crimes for which they were convicted (material support, conspiracy, and solicitation) were not recognized offenses under the law of war at the time of the conduct in question. By the time the court ruled on Mr. Hamdan's case, he had long since been released, and the government did not appeal the ruling. But in Mr. al Bahlul's case, the government appealed the ruling to the full D.C. Circuit. In this appeal, the Justice Department argued that I had waived the right to appeal Mr. al Bahlul's convictions by failing to object at trial and, therefore, that the convictions must be reviewed under a "plain error" standard. Under this standard, the legal error must be so obvious that the trial court should have acted on its own even without a defense objection. Applying this extraordinarily pro-government standard, the court nevertheless vacated the material support and solicitation convictions, finding that it was so clear that these offenses were not war crimes that the trial judge should have dismissed the charges on his own motion. The court remanded the case to the original three-judge panel for additional consideration of the validity of the conspiracy conviction.

On June 12, 2015, the three-judge panel finally issued its ruling, and it was a stinging defeat for the U.S. government. In a 2–1 opinion, the majority held that conspiracy was not a recognized crime under the international law of war, but rather was a domestic crime. As such, the U.S. Constitution did not permit the offense to be tried in a military

*Editor's note: Salim Hamdan's case is discussed in depth in Joseph McMillan's "Hamdan: The Legal Challenge to Military Commissions," chapter 11 in this volume.

commission, but rather only in an Article III (federal) court. The court vacated the sole remaining conviction of Mr. al Bahlul, which also happens to be the last remaining conviction from a Bush-era military commission.[3] Once again the government appealed to the full D.C. Circuit, which agreed to hear the case. Oral arguments were held on December 1, 2015. If history is any guide, it will be several months before the full court issues its ruling, at which point the losing side will likely appeal to the Supreme Court, potentially delaying a final decision in the case for many more months. If Mr. al Bahlul ultimately prevails, he could be charged with some other offense or, more likely, moved back into indefinite detention, along with several dozen other detainees determined to be unprosecutable, but too dangerous to release. Meanwhile, Mr. al Bahlul, one of the first men brought to Guantánamo, approaches his 14th anniversary of detention on the island prison, with no clear end in sight.

NOTES

1 This powerful statement, which has come to be known as the "Vandeveld Declaration," was one of the most extraordinary documents to come out of the entire war on terror, and is featured in the forthcoming documentary *Reckoning with Torture*. More info at reckoningwithtorture.org.

2 Jonathan Hafetz of the ACLU National Security Project and Art Spitzer of the ACLU of the Nation's Capital.

3 The only other person to be convicted of a crime by military commission during President Bush's tenure in office was Australian David Hicks. Mr. Hicks's conviction for material support for terrorism, resulting from a guilty plea in 2007, was vacated by the CMCR in 2015, after the D.C. Circuit ruled that this offense was not a war crime under international law and, therefore, could not be tried by military commission for conduct that predated the 2006 Military Commissions Act.

13

More Kafka than Kafka

JASON WRIGHT[1]

"Guantánamo Isn't a Place, It's a Concept"

I first traveled to Guantánamo Bay in September 2011 at the start of my sixth year as an Army judge advocate. I had spent the previous two years defending soldiers accused of felonies and misdemeanors in Germany before military courts. These two short years—in the Army's eyes—made me a suitable candidate to represent detainees in these untried and troubled military commissions. I would soon learn that experience counts for little in this botched experiment at justice.

When I first stepped off the plane in Guantánamo, the military commissions were on a hiatus. Even though I was assigned to two cases, *U.S. v. Khalid Shaikh Mohammad,* and *U.S. v. Obaidullah,* nothing was happening. Mr. Mohammad had been captured in 2003 on suspicion he had served as Osama bin Laden's chief planner for the attacks on September 11, 2001. While Mr. Mohammad had been categorized as perhaps the highest of the "high-level detainees" by the U.S. government, Obaidullah occupied the other end of the spectrum—a so-called "low-level detainee" captured in Afghanistan in 2002 on a paid informant's claim that there were landmines buried near his family's property.

As of August 2011, President Obama and Congress had been embroiled in a very long staring contest. Immediately after assuming the presidency, Obama had shut down *U.S. v. Mohammad* "Round 1" and had the case dismissed because he wanted to fulfill his pledge in 2009 to close Guantánamo Bay within one year. Although more than one year had passed, the president still wanted to have the 9/11 case tried in federal court in the United States.

Obaidullah, and other "law of war" detainees arrested in Afghanistan and elsewhere, faced far more uncertainty. In 2008, the government drafted a charge sheet against Obaidullah for conspiracy and material support for terrorism, but later withdrew the charges in June 2011 without explanation. There had been no allegation in these documents that Obaidullah had ever harmed anyone, and no judicial process loomed on the horizon.

In early 2011, Attorney General Holder announced that Mr. Mohammad would at some point face a trial by military commission for complicity in the attacks on September 11, 2001. Nearly ten years later, Mr. Mohammad and his defense team had received no indication as to when the government would reinstitute a charge sheet. Nonetheless, it was apparent that the Department of Defense was gearing up for *U.S. v. Mohammad* "Round 2"—despite Obama and Holder's sentiments that the military commissions were untested, untried, and unfair.

Enter me, the Army captain with two years of criminal defense experience who gets assigned to defend a so-called high-value detainee in what the FBI has described as "the largest criminal investigation in the history of the United States." During my first trip to the island penal colony, I quickly learned two things:

(1) There is no "usual" in Guantánamo, and
(2) Experience doesn't matter when the other side gets to make up the rules.

Access to Counsel: "Yes, Captain Wright, Peanut Butter Is Classified"

The U.S. government has silenced torture victims. To my knowledge, there is no country in the world, aside from the United States, where a government has declared that every word, every utterance, and every breath of a prisoner is classified. For Obaidullah, an Afghan villager indefinitely imprisoned for more than 12 years without trial, the U.S.

government requires both his habeas corpus and military defense counsel to hold security clearances at the "Secret" level. From the start, this requirement to obtain a security clearance eliminates Obaidullah's pool of available attorneys to those U.S. citizens who are eligible to obtain one. For Mr. Mohammad, as with the other so-called "high-value detainees," the U.S. government will not allow an attorney to meet with him unless the attorney possesses a "Top Secret" security clearance.

The U.S. government has a troubled history of denying access to these prisoners. Take Mr. Mohammad, for example. According to declassified U.S. government documents, Mr. Mohammad was arrested in Pakistan in March 2003. Yet, despite his requests for an attorney—from his initial arrest and interrogation through so-called FBI "clean team" interviews at Guantánamo Bay—he was not provided access to an attorney until some five years later in 2008. And when such access was finally granted, it was subject to a regime of "presumptive classification."

I had never heard of "presumptive classification" before, but I soon learned about it at a briefing after receiving my "fully adjudicated" Top Secret security clearance. I learned in the fall of 2011 that every word that passed from Mr. Mohammad's lips was "presumptively classified" at the Top Secret level. Apparently, Mr. Mohammad possessed powers akin to Magneto from the X-Men—his mere utterances would expose the United States government and its citizens to "exceptionally grave danger." It was for this reason that lawyers and their staff had to possess Top Secret security clearances and had to handle his words and writings as if they were classified. Of course, there were always exceptions! This rule appeared to apply only to his lawyers; I later learned from the government prosecutors that Mr. Mohammad and the other so-called high value detainees were routinely exposed to personnel from Joint Task Force Guantanamo (JTF-GTMO) who did not possess such clearances, such as guards, drivers, escorts, and medical personnel.

Nonetheless, I was truly stupefied about this "presumptive classification" regime that seemed to apply only to the lawyers. During my Top Secret clearance in-brief (a prerequisite before I could meet with Mr.

Mohammad), I needed some clarification: "So, hypothetically, if Mr. Mohammad said: 'I like peanut butter,' would this statement be classified as Top Secret"? The answer from my briefer from the intelligence community: "Yes."

The defense repeatedly challenged the presumptive classification regime in *U.S . v. Mohammad* "Round 2," and, as a result, the military judge later invalidated the government's "presumptive classification" constraint as being contrary to law and policy. However, any evidence regarding Mr. Mohammad's torture by the U.S. government while being held in black sites remains classified. The government claims that exposing this information would injure the United States. In reality, exposing this information would confirm instances of U.S. atrocities committed during the "War on Terrorism."

Aside from silencing torture victims in violation of the right to complain under the Convention Against Torture, an international treaty signed by more than 150 nations, the U.S. government logistically restricts access to counsel through a conflicting web of SOPs (standard operating procedures) that change with each new rotation of guards, approximately every six to nine months. The rule to silence, however, remains etched in stone. While the Justice Department's Bureau of Prisons allows convicted prisoners in Supermax facilities to call their lawyers and their family members on the telephone, JTF-GTMO prohibits this. Defense counsel must travel to Guantánamo Bay and spend about a week there just to be able to speak to their clients, even if for only one two-hour meeting. And only recently did defense counsel win the right before the military commissions to write their clients with assurances that their communications would not be intercepted and read by JTF-GTMO.

Governmental Interference with the Right to Counsel

Virginians who, like me, grew up in the state's public school system with its proud traditions and contributions to this nation's founding, took as their birthright the tradition of colonial struggle against the tyranny of the Crown. The freedom to speak, this thing called "due process," and the right to a fair trial were not just ideas, but were ethos. You didn't memorize the Bill of Rights, you breathed it.

I never would have believed 30 years later that I would witness my own government's tyranny: Torture. Indefinite detention. Complicity in war crimes. Denying access to counsel. Destroying evidence. Withholding evidence. Intimidating lawyers. Spying on lawyers. Destroying careers. Lying to the American public. The list continues, and the lack of universal public outrage and condemnation in the U.S. speaks not to the gravity of the offenses, but to our collective cognitive dissonance.

When two facts, beliefs, or emotions are mutually inconsistent, our minds must find a way to release this dissonance. Like the smoker who knows that smoking causes cancer, it is easy to rationalize that *it's not that bad* or *it's a light, filtered cigarette.* If we, collectively as Americans, believe that we are the "beacon of hope for the world" and the "champions of human rights," how can we reconcile the injustices and abuses our government has committed against Guantánamo prisoners? We can't.

It's not apathy. It's not a lack of compassion. It's that we simply cannot pay attention and bear witness to ourselves. It's just too difficult to reconcile our own beliefs about ourselves (i.e., we are the beacon of hope) with what has been done for our "freedom" (i.e., the injustices and abuse of prisoners). We just can't reconcile it—and this fits the classic definition of cognitive dissonance. It is for this reason that Guantánamo is ignored. The best way to release the conflict in your mind is to ignore it, to put your head in the sand because that is the easiest thing to do.

The defense bar at Guantánamo is legally and ethically obligated to confront this dissonance and to bear witness—to tell the full story of what happened to these men and to bring the light of truth to this dark period in American history. This is precisely what makes us such a great country—this ethos to bear witness even unto ourselves.

Congress empowered the defense bar to represent zealously the interests of the accused, to hold the government to its burden of proof, and to ensure that the process is fair. Yet, despite this constitutional and congressional mandate, the government, through negligence or intentional design, has acted to impede defense efforts at every turn.

Seizing Attorney-Client Materials. With the 9/11 case, for instance, JTF-GTMO, in advance of the prosecution's second indictment of the 9/11 defendants before military commission "Round 2" in 2012, seized, reviewed, and copied privileged attorney-client communications properly stored within the cells of the prisoners during a three-day period in October 2011 without consulting with their lawyers or obtaining a court order. Two months later, the JTF camp commander issued an order directing that he wanted his staff, comprised of law enforcement and intelligence personnel, to review every written correspondence between attorney and client. Because attorneys are legally and ethically barred from disclosing client confidences, the attorneys could not abide by this order and, as a result, were unable to communicate in writing with their clients for nearly two years until the military judge overruled the camp commander in the fall of 2013. From December 2011 through November 2013, defense attorneys were unable to share the most basic written materials with their clients—from the charge sheets to the written rules of evidence and procedure.

Spying on Attorneys? During pretrial hearings in the 9/11 case in January 2013, an intelligence agency intervened in the military commission proceeding at Guantánamo and severed the audio feed to the public. The commissions have a 40-second audio delay. This means that everything a courtroom actor says is delayed by 40 seconds before the observers in the gallery, who sit behind a soundproof and bulletproof wall, hear those words. The observers at the remote viewing sites in the U.S. also hear the court discussions 40 seconds later. These 40 seconds allow for the court security officer, who is seated to the right of the judge, to review what is being said before the public hears it. If the security officer believes that either the judge or the counsel has said something that is classified, he has the obligation to sever the audio feed to protect the classified information. When the audio feed is severed, the security officer pushes a red light that we have all nicknamed the "hockey light" based on its resemblance to the red light that flashes when a hockey puck makes its way into the net.

On this day in January, David Nevin, lead counsel for Mr. Mohammad, was at the podium speaking to the military judge. In the middle of a sentence, some trigger-happy member of the intelligence community perceived that that Mr. Nevin had just said something classified (which he had not), and severed the audio feed *unbeknownst to the judge or to the court security officer*. In other words, the judge had no idea that the intelligence community had control over his courtroom. This was clearly no puck in the net for the military commissions. This matter remains in active litigation as the defense is still trying to seek permission from the military judge to discover the facts as to who and which agencies had (or have) control over the courtroom, but for the time being, the military judge ordered that only he and his staff have the authority to sever the audio feed.

It gets weirder. Around the same time, defense counsel started to become increasingly alarmed that the private conversations they had been having with their clients in the Guantánamo meeting rooms for a period of years have been monitored. While the defense attorneys were told that their meetings were monitored by video (for force protection purposes), they were told JTF-GTMO "never listened" and did not "have the ability to listen." Around the same time as the infamous hockey light incident in January 2013, my team had a shocking revelation from above—literally, from above.

Looking up into the ceiling one day during a client meeting, the circular smoke detector caught our eye. Standing on a chair to get a closer look, the dime-sized black "test" button in the smoke detector's center looked oddly fuzzy.

"It's a mic!" Yes, what appeared to be a smoke detector was, in fact, a listening device. The military judge subsequently ordered that these listening devices be removed from the meeting rooms, but to this day, the U.S. government has never explained fully the various stories and inconsistencies provided to the military judge and defense counsel concerning the capability for audio monitoring and recording. For instance, the camp commander testified that he did not know that the capability existed, yet two months earlier he signed a work order to authorize the repair of broken lines for the system. The defense teams are still trying to obtain further information from the U.S. government concerning the scope of the monitoring and the interference with the attorney-client relationship.

Compromising Defense IT Systems. Defense attorneys must treat all client confidences and case-related materials as privileged, and prevent people from outside the attorney-client privilege from gaining access to then. For this reason, defense attorneys assigned to the federal defender services who represent indigent defendants in federal court have an IT system and computer system that is completely separate from the judiciary and from the prosecutors at the Department of Justice. Not so in the military commissions. From December 2012 through the summer of 2013, the defense teams—the military's version of public defenders—discovered that people outside of their respective defense teams had access to their confidential files and their emails. IT personnel at the Pentagon during this period inadvertently destroyed approximately seven gigabytes of data, turned over approximately 500,000 defense emails to the prosecution, and caused defense emails to vanish into the far reaches of cyberspace. The situation was so bad that for nearly six months, the top defense lawyer, the chief defense counsel, who provides ethical and supervisory guidance, directed all members of her office *not* to use their work emails or network drives to transmit or store *any* confidential materials.

In order to try to get the job done, many of us were relegated to filing motions and corresponding with our fellow defense team members using our personal email accounts at local coffee shops—whether in Virginia near our stateside offices or at the coffee shop next to the jerk shack in Guantánamo. To this day, we are still experiencing complications with the lack of a stand-alone IT system.

Forced Resignation of Defense Counsel. Military attorneys representing Guantánamo Bay prisoners have suffered adverse career consequences. Several have been "passed over" for promotion after completing their duty requirements in Guantánamo Bay, and, most recently, I was forced by the U.S. Army to sever my attorney-client relationship with Mr. Mohammad and to resign from the Army.

I have been representing Mr. Mohammad since September 2011, and have appeared on his behalf as one of his detailed military defense counsel since the arraignment in May 2012 and throughout the pretrial progression of the case (approximately ten hearings). I have traveled extensively to meet with witnesses, and have been working nearly full time on the case (aside from my obligations to Obaidullah) for nearly three years. I have spent nearly 250 days in Guantánamo during this period.

In August 2013, the U.S. Army promoted me to the rank of major. Typically, upon promotion to major, U.S. Army judge advocates are compelled to attend a year-long education course administered by the Army to obtain an advanced degree in military law. Selected officers, however, may request to defer this course for operational or personal reasons. There is no limit to the number of deferrals a newly promoted major may request; and, accordingly, I was granted a deferral from attending the 2013–2014 course due to my representation of the lead defendant in the 9/11 case. In January 2014, I was once again notified that I had been selected to attend the 2014–2015 course and, once again, I requested a deferral. This time, however, the U.S. Army denied my deferral request without explanation. The top lawyer in the Army, the judge advocate general, declined to provide a reason to the military commission and to me, and instead informed her subordinates that I could not continue to work on the case on a part-time basis while taking the course and that I could not be reassigned to the case after completing the course.

On February 26, 2014, I was issued orders to report to the school from August 2014 through May 2015. Under Army regulation, this forced a decision on my part. I had two choices: (1) go to the school as directed and continue my Army career, thereby "voluntarily" severing the attorney client relationship; or (2) resign.

Because I have a legal and ethical obligation to represent the best interest of my client—be it a capitally charged client or a private facing an AWOL—I had to choose the option that extended the attorney-client relationship the furthest. Resignations take approximately six months to take effect in the Army, which would permit me to continue representing Mr. Mohammad throughout two additional hearing sessions in June and August of 2014. Attending the course, on the other hand, would require me to move and leave the case in June 2014. For these reasons, I was obligated by the Rules of Professional Responsibility governing lawyers to choose that option that best served the interests of my client and preserved my representation the longest. Paradoxically, this required my resignation.

To this day, neither the U.S. Army nor the judge advocate general has provided a reason for removing me from the active representation of a capitally-charged client. Yet they continue to allow the chief prosecutor, an Army JAG too, to stay on the case, in his own words, "as long as it takes."

FBI Attempts to Infiltrate the 9/11 Defense Teams. The 9/11 defense teams learned in mid-April 2014 that the FBI approached a member of the defense team for Ramzi Bin al Shibh. Agents accosted him on a Sunday as he returned home from church with his children and asked him about activities on both Mr. Bin al Shibh's team and Mr. Mohammad's team. They convinced him to sign an agreement where he agreed to develop a confidential relationship with the FBI and to not disclose the contents of his discussions with the FBI to anyone. This matter is now in active litigation, and has caused a near-complete stop in the case until further information is provided to all of the parties.

The prosecution claims it was unaware of this happening, even though one of its active trial counsel was also dual-hatted as the chief of staff to the deputy director of the FBI. It was ostensibly for this reason that the 9/11 prosecutors had to step aside on this issue and request that a special trial counsel represent the interests of the government in this litigation.

In the meantime, the judge ordered that additional attorneys be appointed to assist Mr. Bin al Shibh to advise him on whether a conflict of interest exists between him and their current defense team in light of the apparent investigation into the defense attorneys. This, like all things in Guantánamo, will take some time to work through. Although the Pentagon recently assigned new military attorney to advise Mr. Bin al Shibh on the conflict issue, just imagine the job announcement:

> Brand new U.S. court system outside of the reach of the U.S. Constitution and in a foreign country seeks a qualified U.S. citizen to advise a client on a conflict of interest that may or may not be based on any facts that may or may not be provided to the attorney or to the client. Must be able to obtain a Top Secret security clearance, be willing to have his or her confidential letters read, conversations recorded, work-product lost, and future career prospects diminished. Foreign travel required. Preferential treatment will be provided to those applicants who agree that peanut butter could be classified.

Although this advertisement will never make it to the job boards, the investigation and litigation into this matter tied up the military commissions for the duration of 2014 and occupied much of the docket through 2015. Yet one thing has remained clear, first through a government-directed leak to the *Washington Post* and later in a brief filed by the government: the defense teams did nothing wrong. According to some reports, the government has subsequently been reviewing whether its own field agents acted improperly by trying to recruit, as a confidential informant, a member of the 9/11 defense team.

This falls short. There needs to be a broader policy review of all of these interferences with the right to counsel—from the "smoke detectors" to the FBI infiltration. Guantánamo isn't a place, it's a concept. Government lawlessness comes to mind.

The Design of the Not-So-Reformed "Military Commissions"

The degree of "reform" to the military commissions system ushered in by Congress in 2009 in the "reformed" Military Commissions Act, which modified the 2006 Military Commissions Act, is a subject of intense academic and legal debate. To offer a perspective from the inside, as an attorney who has practiced in this system for three years, this is what I can offer: I often feel that Congress set a narrative stage drawn from one of four books. Sometimes the story line is based on a single one, and other times it unifies all four simultaneously: *Catch-22*, *1984*, *anything* by Kafka, and one of the great works of American literature, *A Confederacy of Dunces*.

Many have said that the law for military commissions is designed for secret show trials that operate to secure convictions while concealing any wrongs committed by the U.S. government in pursuit of the War on Terrorism. I agree. But don't just take my word for it, take the government's word. The U.S. government has maintained that it has the authority to continue to imprison Guantánamo Bay prisoners *indefinitely* even if they were to be found not guilty of the charges against them. When the outcome of a trial doesn't mean anything, that's called a show trial.

In light of this overarching defect of the military commissions system, the rest of the significant due process problems pale in comparison. Yet they do bear mentioning. While the list is long, here are just a few of the design flaws. There is no statutory right to a speedy trial. There is no grand jury requirement or equivalent process (called an Article 32 hearing for courts-martial) for securing the right to indictment and presentment. The freedom from unreasonable searches and seizures is limited as evidence obtained without a search warrant or other lawful authorization may be admitted. Hearsay evidence is admissible. The defense is not entitled to "equal" access to witnesses and evidence as per court-martial practice, but only "reasonable" access. The courts-martial pretrial practice that allows for the dismissal of charges or other sentencing relief for unlawful pretrial punishment is not included in the Military

Commissions Act. The trial judiciary is a component of the executive branch and, as such, does not function independently consistent with the requirements for federal trials under Article III of the Constitution.

Mentioned above are just some of the flaws in the statutory design of the military commissions. These flaws continue to be tested in *U.S. v. Mohammad* "Round 2," which began with the arraignment of the 9/11 prisoners in May 2012. From May 2012 through the end of 2015, there have been 17 pretrial hearings (each lasting about a week), yet there is no trial date in sight. It took the U.S. government more than nine years to initiate these proceedings against Mr. Mohammad and his co-defendants.

The first three years the government had the case, it horrendously abused Mr. Mohammad by subjecting him to 183 mock executions on the waterboard. For the next several years, the government continued to deny Mr. Mohammad access to a lawyer even while imprisoned in Guantánamo Bay. Since arraignment in May 2012, the overwhelming majority of the delays in the process have concerned the government's various interferences with the right to counsel under the Sixth Amendment: seizing privileged attorney-client correspondence, blocking the right to communicate privately in writing, shutting down the audio system in the courtroom, disguising listening devices in the attorney-client meeting rooms, corrupting electronic data, removing defense attorneys, spying on attorneys, and intimidating defense attorneys with a faux criminal investigation.

Some days it's Kafka, and other days it's *A Confederacy of Dunces*.

NOTES

1 The views of Jason D. Wright are his own and were made in his official capacity as a defense attorney representing detainees before the U.S. Military Commissions under the authority provided by the Regulation for Trial by Military Commissions, paragraph 9 -7 (2011). Mr. Wright does not represent the views of the Department of Defense or the Department of the Army.

14

Storytelling #Guantanamo

ALIYA HANA HUSSAIN

For my so-called millennial generation, Barack Obama symbolized everything we wanted in an America we hoped was possible. On the bulletin board above my office computer, there's an image of him—the ad, torn out of the *New York Times*, was placed by the American Civil Liberties Union (ACLU) the week after he won the election in 2008. In it, the ACLU urged the new president to fulfill his campaign promises and restore America's moral leadership in the world by closing Guantánamo on his first day of office. I worked at the ACLU when the ad came out and it is a bit of swag, a piece of history, that traveled the 40 blocks or so uptown with me to my current job at the Center for Constitutional Rights (CCR). Quoting the audacious candidate, it reads: "As President, I will close Guantánamo, reject the Military Commissions Act and adhere to the Geneva Conventions." It is now creased, and the crisp black and white has faded—a striking reminder of the many years that have passed since these promises were made. I truly believed his presidency had the power to change the world for the better. Didn't we all?

Next to this piece of iconography is a photograph of me demonstrating outside of the White House for the first time with my CCR colleagues and hundreds of other activists to demand the closure of Guantánamo. It was the tenth anniversary of the prison's opening—a rainy and cold January 11, but I stood there defiantly, a budding activist, as much for myself as for the man whose face adorned the sign I carried. In January 2015, Guantánamo turned 13.

Also scattered across my board are photographs of some of the men that CCR represents. Though he was only 15 or 16 years old, Fahd Ghazy already looked like a young man in his portrait, which was taken before he was captured, over a decade ago. It is only a paper copy, but the blue in his scarf, echoed in the blue background, is nevertheless piercing. It stands in stark contrast to the white shirt he now wears and the sterile cell in which we meet in Guantánamo's Camp Echo. Another picture, this one of Tariq Ba Odah, is a worn copy of an image taken by the Red Cross in the prison.* His hair is long, parted in the middle, with curls cascading down each side of his neck. Tariq's smile, which lights up the room, is surely meant for his family in Saudi Arabia, where the original photo traveled thousands of miles to reach them. He looks so handsome. When I see his face, I forget momentarily the physical toll that more than eight years of hunger striking has taken on his body.

The faces of these men are jarring against the backdrop of my freedom, commemorated by letter-pressed birthday cards, photographs from family celebrations, and souvenirs that I have collected during my travel over the years. Our clients' stories—and how they have become part of my own story—reinforce the need to make connections between experiences, people, and places that most would deem different worlds.

* * *

I was 26 years old when I started working at CCR. I joined the Guantánamo Global Justice Initiative as a legal worker in October 2010, shortly after a steady stream of transfers of clients who were either repatriated or resettled in third countries in Europe. In my job interview, there was talk of how the prison's closure was imminent and how, after years of leading the fight against unjust detentions at Guantánamo, CCR would soon be redirecting its focus on other human rights and national security issues. Guantánamo would finally be closed.

So close, yet so far.

---

*Editor's note: Tariq Ba Odah's story is described in detail in Omar Farah's "Nourishing Resistance: Tariq Ba Odah's Eight-Year Hunger Strike at Guantánamo Bay," chapter 9 in this volume.

Just over a year later, with my newly minted security clearance, I made my first trip to Cuba in 2012. I had no idea what to expect. Sure, I knew about the prison. The liberal, social justice narratives were deeply ingrained in my mind: a legal black hole where torture and other heinous crimes took place; an internment camp where Muslim men from dozens of countries all over the world were brought—most without rhyme or reason—because of a landscape of fear, hate, and war; a place shrouded in layers of secrecy and propaganda that prevented the public from knowing exactly what happened in the island prison and who the men detained there really were. I was familiar with our clients' cases too: where they were from, their ages, why the government alleged they should be there at all, and also what kind of books they liked to read and what food they requested. But still, I didn't really *know* what it would be like once I got there or how to prepare myself for feelings I couldn't predict.

Like most of my peers, to me, a trip to the Caribbean meant spring break, margaritas, and days on the beach. I had never visited a prison before, and my first trip would be to the controversial offshore military detention facility coined "the gulag of our times" by Amnesty International. I had trouble reconciling my life as a twentysomething Brooklynite with the fact that I possessed a high level national security clearance and was about to set foot somewhere most people in the world would never be permitted to go. In a sea of mostly corporate pro bono habeas attorneys, I was an exception—a young Pakistani American Muslim woman with a pierced nose and left-leaning politics. Not only was I *not* a lawyer, I was the same age or younger than the men with whom I would be meeting. I could barely string together a full sentence in Urdu or Arabic, even though I looked like I should be able to. What would it feel like to be in a situation where my words could only be understood once they were morphed into something entirely foreign to my own ears—maybe shortened, maybe polished—by the translator sitting next to us? Our clients and I shared Islam as a faith, but there was no way of predicting what that would mean in practical terms. Having straddled two cultures my entire life, figuring out the "appropriate" way of presenting myself was often a struggle. Should I cover my head, make eye contact? Could I shake their hand or would it be better to wait to see whether they gestured first as I did with some family members? Would our similar roots and the color of our skin make it easier or harder for us to relate to one another?

What I discovered during my first visit would forever change me: the men I met were more like me than they were different. Over the years, I have made nearly ten trips to the prison to meet with clients. I have spent hours sitting across the table from young men who have been detained without charge for over 13 years. In fact, many of them were cleared for release by the U.S. government long ago. There's no doubt in my mind that if the public could sit across from Fahd, Tariq, Ghaleb, and Mohammed as I have, and hear the compassion in their voices, learn about their families, and see how they struggle every day to prevent the prison from claiming them, others would be closer to understanding the human cost of Guantánamo as acutely as my colleagues and I do.

But that's the thing—the government doesn't want anyone to see our clients' humanity. Since the prison opened in 2002, the U.S. has blocked the public, the media, even the United Nations from having access to the men there. The complex classification regime that regulates court filings and attorney-client communication severely restricts—and, consequently, shapes—the narratives that advocates can share. Photographs of some detainees are available online, but even those are usually mugshots taken by the prison authorities, which are then linked to documents detailing the government's allegations of their supposed wrongdoings. On the rare occasion when video footage from inside the camps is available for primetime public consumption, prisoners' faces are blocked from view, their voices are muffled or silenced completely, and their brown bodies, if you can see them at all, are interchangeable. So it's all too easy for the uninformed to conclude they must be there for a reason. Why else would they be banished, living in a cage? It is the dehumanization and isolation of the men at Guantánamo above all that allows for the continued operation of the prison after all of these years. As a result, surfacing Guantánamo's human stories is the most subversive way to dismantle these dominant narratives. Yet it continues to be one of our biggest challenges.

As I became more involved with CCR's advocacy work, it was clear that my colleagues and I had a responsibility not only to bring attention to our clients' stories of injustice, but also to help construct a new narrative, one that would reach people on a profoundly personal level, including a new generation that has grown up in a world where Guantánamo has always existed and for whom endless warfare is the new normal. At CCR, my job is to tell stories that will make Guantánamo personal for others too. More than six years after President Obama promised and failed to close the prison, the ongoing injustice had to be understood as more than just an intellectual or legal supposition. It had to be felt, *and felt deeply*, in order to move people to act.

* * *

I remember attending a dinner party in Brooklyn shortly after returning from one of my trips a few years ago. "Aliya just got back from Guantánamo," my friend interjected loudly across the dining room table. Exposed and a little unsure how the subject of Guantánamo would go over as dinner conversation, I shared some of what I'd learned from my visit, at least what I could speak about publicly: of the hip hop music our clients preferred, the comedies that made them laugh, their ruminations on the writings of Martin Luther King Jr., and the beautiful art they painted over the years as they waited for their release. I described the process of handpicking books at Barnes & Noble and visiting specialty stores to buy my favorite Pakistani sweets to bring down to the base for our meetings. "Can you believe they've been there for over a decade? That means more than a third of their lives." The group listened closely. Their curiosity was obvious, but they struggled to make sense of what that meant. "But what's worse is that they are our age," I told them. In that moment, before they turned back to their wine and talk of the newest must-see exhibit in town, I could feel the gap between "us" and "them" grow slightly smaller.

For me, the formula for reaching people at a party or while you have their captive attention at an event seemed easy enough. The challenge would be to make these narratives live beyond that moment. In this age of clickable Facebook content and Twitter's 140 characters or less, it was imperative that we figure out how to transform the same stories that engaged my peers that night at dinner into a stripped-down but powerful essence, transferable at any place and any time.

Though prisoners' stories have always been central to the creative lawyering and advocacy efforts of Guantánamo lawyers, the promise of this emerging strategy became particularly pronounced in 2013 when the detainees engaged in a mass hunger strike. In the two years leading up to the hunger strike, detainee transfers were at a standstill. The courts, Congress, and the administration had abandoned the men at Guantánamo. Those of us working tirelessly on the prisoners' behalf had few avenues left to explore. We were at a loss about how to make people care on a large enough scale to effect real change. Remarkably, it was the men themselves who succeeded where we were failing. They exemplified a central tenet underlying CCR's philosophy: those most directly impacted by injustice are the best positioned to demand social change. By taking matters into their own hands and putting their bodies on the line as a form of protest, they refocused the world's attention on Guantánamo. And as their lawyers and advocates we had an obligation to bring their stories—their pleas—out of the prison in order to keep the spotlight on their courageous protest and the pressure on the administration to resume transfers.

Their collective protest generated heightened urgency. The outpouring of harrowing stories from the prison forced the media to take interest in Guantánamo again. CCR, in turn, took a new direction in its public advocacy, using a storytelling and storysharing approach through online platforms. As events unfolded quickly, we relied on social media to help us carry our clients' messages of resistance and amplify it to ensure it could not be ignored. This form of storytelling relied on surfacing universal themes that would move even those least engaged with these issues, and finding a way to confront the passage of time and explain in concrete terms the devastating psychological impact of over a decade of indefinite detention. Of course identifying the right strategy is one thing; implementing it is another matter altogether.

Traveling to the base during the hunger strike was one of the most difficult things I have ever had to do and certainly the most trying visit I have had to make. The men I had seen just five months earlier looked like shells of themselves; their weight had dramatically dropped. The human suffering was staggering, making it all the more remarkable that the men persevered in the face of such cruelty and injustice. Their spirits endured, and many felt empowered that their actions were effecting change. I found that their stories were now as much about the future as about the years they had lost—they spoke to the life that could be possible whenever their nightmare was over.

Social media allowed us to get our clients' stories out in as close to real time as possible. On May 1, 2013, shortly after we wrapped up a long and challenging day in the camps, my colleague and I posted this entry to CCR's Facebook page:

> Today CCR's legal team met with our client, Fahd Ghazy, and celebrated his 29th birthday in a cell in Camp Echo. Fahd was sent to Guantánamo as a juvenile at age 17, and has spent more than one third of his life in the prison. Fahd, who has never been charged with a crime and was cleared under President Bush in 2007, is now on his third month of a hunger strike. Fahd has said, "All I hope for upon release is to meet my wife and daughter, my mother and brothers, and to live an independent life with them. To complete my studies and get a decent job." Fahd's daughter, Hafsa, will celebrate her 12th birthday later this Spring.

The Twitter version was similarly direct: "This is our client Fahd Ghazy. He's been at #Guantanamo since he was 17. Yday he turned 29. Never been charged." Accompanying both of these posts was the same striking photograph of Fahd that is on the bulletin board in my office.

Fahd's 29th birthday message and his story—albeit the abridged version—was our most widely viewed and shared Guantánamo social media post to date. Perhaps it was the rank injustice of his prolonged imprisonment despite having been cleared for release for years that incensed people; maybe it was confronting a human face that compelled people to share. I'd like to believe it's that learning of his story appeals to our common humanity.

I was given the peculiar task of articulating Facebook and Twitter advocacy to men who have not had access to the Internet for more than a decade, if ever. "We want to get people talking about you and your story in an effort to have them so moved that they take action—tell their friends about the injustice you and others face in the prison, or maybe even write to President Obama urging him to release you and the other brothers," we wrote to our clients. Enclosed was also a glossary of the newest digital vocabulary: "likes" meant someone read the post and wanted to show their support; "sharing" went a step further and enabled people to pass on the message to their networks because they thought it was important enough to do so; and while a statement could be powerful on its own, adding a "hashtag (#)" inserted it into a worldwide conversation in which anyone could take part. "It's easy for us to post stories to remind the public about your situation while we're sitting at our desk. In a way, it's like we're spreading your words to tens of thousands of people just by clicking a button."

During the hunger strike, social media helped propel prisoners' stories into the mainstream. When Samir Moqbel, a Guantánamo client of a London-based organization called Reprieve, entered that global conversation, the impact was enormous. He penned an op-ed featured in the *New York Times* from his cell. "I just hope that because of the pain we are suffering, the eyes of the world will once again look to Guantánamo before it is too late," it concludes. In the comment section there is a simple note from Minneapolis, in which a young man named William tells the young man from Yemen whom he has never met: "You are in my prayers." Moqbel's op-ed was one of the top e-mailed stories on the *Times* that week. His story traveled the world instantaneously.

A few months later, Yaasin Bey, formerly known as Mos Def, made a video in which he was painfully force-fed according to Guantánamo's standard operating procedures. The *Guardian* headline read: "In an instant, he was no longer Mos Def—rapper and Hollywood star—but a powerless prisoner, experiencing what hunger strikers in Guantánamo Bay endure daily." Over six million people have viewed that video. Those millions may have been drawn to the clip by Mos Def's celebrity. But because he dared to put himself in another's shoes, they left knowing of the torturous and humiliating process of force-feeding that happens every day to men like CCR client Tariq Ba Odah.

The impact of social media on the perception of the Guantánamo hunger strike cannot be overstated. Not only did strangers all over the world show solidarity with men they didn't know, but the President of the United States finally came out from hiding to confront his failure to bring an end to the injustice there. "Imagine a future—10 years from now, or 20 years from now—when the United States of America is still holding people who have been charged with no crime on a piece of land that is not a part of our country," President Obama said in his May 2013 speech at the National Defense University. "Is this who we are?"

* * *

Fahd made a similar charge during a meeting once: "This life will be over one day in 20 or 30 years. Everyone must decide where they want to place themselves in this history whenever it is complete." In trying to answer that question, I have learned that there is wisdom in trying to put yourself in someone else's story, breaking down the walls that divide us, real or imagined, and moving toward a place of empathy and encouraging others to do the same.

In November 2013, two of my colleagues travelled to Yemen to meet with Fahd's family. Accompanied by a film crew, they sought to create a portrait of the life that awaits his return. Our goals of the project were simple: to show the rarely seen story of Guantánamo, one that reveals the impact of indefinite detention on both the prisoners and their families, and ask people to share it through social media and screenings. "Waiting for Fahd: One Family's Hope for Life beyond Guantánamo" launched in December 2014, and the response has been overwhelming. Within two months, tens of thousands of people had viewed the film, and it had been tweeted to over a million people.

Accompanying the short film was a powerful personal appeal from Fahd to viewers. "Here, at Guantánamo, I am never heard. I am only ignored. In 13 years of imprisonment without charge, I've never been able to tell anyone who I really am," Fahd wrote. "I am not ISN 026. That is the government's number. My name is Fahd Abdullah Ahmed Ghazy. I am a human being—a man—who is loved and who loves." His appeal was published on Huffington Post and within days it had been translated into five other languages for readers from Brazil to Korea—and shared by thousands all over the world.

We could track the success and reach of Fahd's story in views, Facebook likes and shares, and tweets, but it wasn't until just a few weeks after the launch that I was able to truly grasp its impact on others. Witness Against Torture, a grassroots ally in the fight to close Guantánamo, had their annual convening in Washington, D.C., that would culminate with dozens of groups gathering for the 13th anniversary of Guantánamo's opening on January 11, 2002. Activists from all over the country gathered in a church to watch the film. They reflected as a community on what Fahd's story meant to them by remembering the people in their own lives whom they love and recalling instances of separation and reunion with them. A friend wrote about the process of sharing those personal stories: "We brought our families and friends into our circle. We also brought the men in Guantánamo into the circle, knowing they have loved ones that they dearly miss and hope they will soon be reunited with. We understood the importance of seeing the prisoners in all of their humanity, not just as numbers in a prison."

The night before I caught a train to D.C. to join them in marking another shameful year of Guantánamo, I came across a short video of some of those same activists outside the White House earlier that week reading excerpts of Fahd's appeal. Next to them was a large banner with a painting of the same portrait of him that hangs on the wall in CCR's office. I was overcome with emotion as I watched. Fahd's words had reached them hundreds of miles away, and now they were amplifying his voice so others could hear him. It is the kind of success you cannot measure, to see with your own eyes a story start to become part of someone else's and the distance between each of us diminish.

"Now that you have heard my story and seen my dreams, you cannot turn away," Fahd concluded his appeal. "You are excused only when you do not know. But now that you know, you cannot turn away. Be a voice for the voiceless—for another human being who is suffering."

* * *

Not a single day goes by that I don't think about those who remain detained. The men that I have met and their stories have become part of my life, interspersed like the objects on the corkboard above my desk. In the digital age, wherein so much of our lives are captured in different places online, I cherish having this collection of memorabilia surround my desk. Without needing any words, they tell the story of my own coming of age—the challenges and heartache, the growth and joy, are palpable.

A watercolor that our client Djamel Ameziane painted during his 11-year detention at Guantánamo also hangs up on the board.* It is a boat out at sea weathering a storm, but you can see in it glimmers of sunlight breaking through the clouds. It was a long and difficult road for him to get where he is now, but Djamel is finally free and slowly rebuilding his life. Tucked in with that and the other images pinned to the wall is something that I cut out of a French magazine years ago in part because

*Editor's note: Djamel Ameziane's story is recounted in J. Well Dixon's "President Obama's Failure to Transfer Detainees from Guantánamo," chapter 3 in this volume.

I knew it would never get through the Guantánamo censors and into the detainee library, and in part because I wanted to hold on to it. The picture is of an art installation—lining a long hall are painted cutouts of prisoners in orange jumpsuits, their faces covered with hoods, kneeling on the ground with their hands tied in front of them. Resting on their chests are signs of "HOPE." Despite all its best efforts, one thing Guantánamo cannot destroy is my hope for just endings.

ABOUT THE CONTRIBUTORS

J. Wells Dixon is Senior Staff Attorney at the Center for Constitutional Rights.

Omar Farah is Staff Attorney at the Center for Constitutional Rights.

Mark Fleming is Partner at WilmerHale in Boston.

David Frakt is a criminal defense attorney and legal scholar, and a Lieutenant Colonel in the U.S. Air Force JAG Corps Reserve.

Frank Goldsmith is at the Goldsmith, Goldsmith & Dews Law Firm in Marion, North Carolina.

Jonathan Hafetz is Associate Professor of Law at Seton Hall University School of Law.

Aliya Hana Hussain is Advocacy Program Manager at the Center for Constitutional Rights.

Gary A. Isaac is Counsel at Mayer Brown LLP in Chicago.

Shayana Kadidal is Senior Staff Attorney at the Center for Constitutional Rights.

Pardiss Kebriaei is Senior Staff Attorney at the Center for Constitutional Rights.

Joseph McMillan is Partner at Perkins Coie in Seattle.

Alka Pradhan is Human Rights Counsel at the Guantánamo Bay Military Commissions, and was formerly U.S. Counsel for Reprieve.

Martha Rayner is Clinical Associate Professor of Law at Fordham University School of Law.

Sabin Willett is Partner at Morgan Lewis in Boston.

Jason Wright is at the Wright Law Firm in New York and a Professor of Practice at Washington & Lee University School of Law.

INDEX